Software Process Improvment: Concepts and Practices

Table of Contents

Preface

Software process improvement has become highly visible over the past several years. Because this topic can only be effectively addressed by blending people, process and technology issues, it has provided a rich field for both conceptual and practical research in industry and academe. Industry practitioners are searching for better models of quality software development. Academic researchers are initiating rigorous streams of process-related field research. The Software Engineering Institute (SEI) at Carnegie Mellon University, as it continues to develop and integrate maturity models and frameworks, has established strong linkages with both industry and academe to complement their respective activities in this area.

The topic of software process improvement is also finding its way more strongly into university curriculums. For example, the American University Computer Science and Information Systems graduate curriculum now includes electives on Software Process Improvement and Personal Software Process. These courses provide the foundation for a new graduate certificate program focused in this area.

The chapters in this book constitute additional evidence of the importance of this topic. The chapters reflect different aspects and views of the topics that are indicative of the wide range of thought and research currently underway in this area.

As an emerging technology, the effectiveness and potential impact of process improvement efforts have been debated, but not fully tested or validated. At the very core of this technological evolution is the idea that the quality of a software product is highly dependent on the quality of the process used for its development. Branching from this central idea are three categories of innovations: process models, modeling techniques, and the novel concept of process maturity assessment. In "Software Process Modeling", Rick Gibson examines the current state of the practice regarding software process models, modeling techniques, and assessments. Particular attention is directed at the most recent process improvement initiative, Humphrey's Personal Software Process.

Peter D.C. Bennetts, A. Trevor Wood-Harper and Stella Mills argue that only a systems-based approach to information systems development (ISD) and software process improvement (SPI) are likely to cover all the recognised issues. In their chapter, "The Soft System Methodology as a Framework for Software Process Improvement" they examine reports in the literature concerning problems associated with ISD and implementation. The characteristics of these problems are identified.

Process improvement efforts are becoming pervasive within IS organizations as they attempt to meet the growing challenges of today's complex and dynamic environment. A popular framework often used in these efforts is the Capability Maturity Model (CMM) developed by the Software Engineering Institute. The model focuses specifically on software process improvement, neglecting the other functions of IS. Russell Purvis, Jose Santiago and V. Sambamurthy's chapter, "An Analysis of Excluded IS Processes in the Capability Maturity Model and Their Potential Impact" assesses which IS functions are excluded by the CMM by comparing it to a earlier, more comprehensive model, the Information Systems Management Architecture developed by IBM. The comparison of models is followed by a discussion of the potential ramifications of a model with such a narrow focus.

An organization is comprised of strategic and operational management systems, both of which are essential in maintaining maturity, profitability, and competitiveness. A strategic management system defines the industries and specific markets in which the organization competes. An operational management system makes explicit the goals, the processes, and the feedback mechanisms on how to attain the desired competitive position. Each of these management components plays a role in the long-term success of an organization. What is missing is a link between the strategy formulation and the implementation of an operational management system? This question is address in "Linking Strategies and Operation Goals" by Shirley Becker and Mitchell Bostelman. The chapter describes the dimensions of strategic management in order to develop a foundation upon which an organization establishes it operational goals. The chapter discusses the use of a structured goal setting approach in order to identify a comprehensive set of goals and metrics to support strategic management. Then, the chapter is concluded with future research opportunities in strategic management and operational implementation.

In "Software Development and Organizational Viability: An Account of the Impact of Organizational Issues upon Quality", P. Kawalek and D.G. Wastell detail the impact of organizational issues upon software development. The Viable System Model (VSM), which has been developed from cybernetic theory, is discussed. The chapter describes the VSM and presents two case studies of its application.

The Software Engineering Institute (SEI) is a federally funded research and development center established in 1984 by the U.S. Department of Defense with a broad charter to address the transition of software engineering technology—the actual adoption of improved software engineering practices. The SEI's existence is, in a sense, the result of the "software crisis" —software projects that are chronically late, over budget, with less functionality than desired, and of dubious quality. Mark C. Paulk in "Using the Software CMM with Small Projects and Small Organizations" discusses SEI's model that depicts the activities of an improvement program.

In "IS Change Agents in Software Process Improvement" Eugene McGuire and Kim Randall examine the complex organizational and software development environment in which IS professionals commonly function today. Skills and competencies appropriate to this environment are increasingly related to managing change and adopting change agent roles. Observations and conclusions in this chapter are primarily drawn from research on organizations that have initiated software process improvement initiatives.

Christopher Landauer and Kirstie Bellman describe, in "Generic Programming, Partial Evaluation and a New Programming Paradigm," a new approach to generic programming that uses integration results together with recent progress in partial evaluation methods for adaptation. Their approach to partial evaluation provides an adaptation mechanism by having much more information than is usually available, including explicit meta-knowledge about the program fragments and their intended execution environments.

Software risk-management practices acknowledge the vital, albeit difficult imperative of communicating the status of project risk to stakeholders while attempting to mitigate and/or control risk manifestations. The problem is that risks are typically dynamic, unpredictable, and may be outside the purview and control of the project manager. In "Communicating Project Drift Through Cost/Benefit Scenarios," authors David McComb and Jill Smith Slater present a communication mechanism to explain the phenomenon of "project drift" through a series of abstract cost/benefit scenarios. The scenarios may be used either separately or in various combinations to continually reassess risk both at project inception and in light of project history to date.

To be counted in the ranks of world-class software engineering firms is very difficult. There are relatively few deserving such distinction and those that do are continually raising the stakes at an ever increasing rate of change. The challenge is to not only match their rate of productivity improvement but to catch up to their performance levels. A widely-accepted process practice used by world-class software engineering firms is inspections. Thomas Rodgers, Conan Albrecht and Douglas Dean explore group-enabled software inspections as a software process improvement activity in "Group-Enabled Software Inspections." Past and present of software inspections are first explored as a basis for discussing several research concepts and their applications to future software inspections. The concepts addressed include primary collaborative process, feedback, distributed inspections, and knowledge management. The chapter concludes with a discussion of current research agendas and rationalization of why software inspection is a software improvement activity.

In "A Technical Infrastructure for Process Support" Shirley Becker and Daniel Ladino describe the use of database and Web technology in the development of a technical infrastructure to support process activities. A framework for process support is described that is the basis for the discussion on database and Web technology. The authors admit it is not their intention to recommend a specific data management architecture but to provide an illustration of what can be done to develop automated process support.

In summary, these chapters represent some important ideas and current work in the area of software process improvement. They are indicative of a much larger body of high-quality work in an area that is garnering renewed interest as SPI efforts are being undertaken by organizations of all types and sizes as they attempt to deal with the challenges of quality, complexity and competitiveness.

Chapter 1

Software Process Modeling

Rick Gibson
American University, USA

As an emerging technology, the effectiveness and potential impact of process improvement efforts have been debated, but not fully tested or validated. At the very core of this technological evolution is the idea that the quality of a software product is highly dependent on the quality of the process used for its development. Branching from this central idea are three categories of innovations: process models, modeling techniques, and the novel concept of process maturity assessment. The purpose of this chapter is to examine the current state-of-the-practice regarding software process models, modeling techniques, and assessments. Particular attention is directed at the most recent process improvement initiative, Humphrey's Personal Software Process.

Software Process Models

All engineering disciplines depend on reliable processes to create products. The term process as used herein conforms to its accepted definition as a written description of a course of action to be taken to perform a given task. It follows that a software process is as a set of activities, methods, and practices for the activities associated with the production and maintenance of software. Many scholars (Gibbs, 1994) contend that unlike the more mature, professional engineering disciplines, software engineering is deficient in the areas of scientific theory, mathematical modeling, proven design solutions and rigorous quality control. These deficiencies are clearly not from lack of effort—the origins of software process models can be traced back as far as software itself. Among the earliest software process model to gain widespread acceptance was Royce's (1970) waterfall model, considered to have been first utilized by IBM in development of the eminently successful System/360.

Alternative models of the software development process have continued to evolve. Examples include: prototyping, operational, concurrent, reuse, and spiral models. The most recently proposed solutions to the software crisis, software process improvement models, represent a major innovation—perhaps better described as a revolution than just another evolutionary step. In contrast to the ease with which new process models are accepted, the adoption of process improvement innovations has been slow. In fact, Balzer (1991) stated that process improvement problems continue to overshadow the progress made. Major obstacles to software process improvement include the attitude and culture of the people involved in the software development process. Whereas adoption of any new process model can be accomplished by individual developers, successfully implementing new software process improvement processes requires top management support, a culture of accepting change as a way of life, and significant financial investment (Curtis and Paulk, 1993). If any these elements are missing, the software process improvement effort is sure to fail.

Some of the software process improvement models currently in use include: the Software Engineering Institute (SEI) Capability Maturity Model (CMM), the International Standards Group for Software Engineering's Software Process Improvement and Capability Determination (SPICE) model, and the Quality Improvement Paradigm (QIP). This paper will focus on the CMM, which has had a profound impact on the global software industry, in spite of mild criticism by many experts (Bollinger and McGowan, 1991; Jones, 1995), largely due to a lack of emphasis on technology or automation. Detailed discussions of SPICE (Dorling, 1993) and QIP [6] are readily available along with descriptions of other approaches such as: Model-Based Process Assessment (McGowan and Bohner, 1993) and the Software Productivity Research assessment approach (Jones, 1995)].

The Capability Maturity Model (CMM) was developed under a federally funded program by the SEI as a common-sense application of process management and quality improvement concepts to software development and maintenance. As the name suggests, the CMM identifies five levels of maturity for measuring the capability of an organization's software development process.

The CMM provides a framework for organizations to determine the current level of maturity for their software development process, and the steps to take to increase their maturity level. Curtis and Paulk (1993) comment on the maturity concept by contrasting mature and immature process impacts on organizations.

Other maturity-based models have been developed for use in process assessment and supplier evaluation, such as Bell Canada's Trillium (1992). The Trillium model is used to develop a questionnaire and methodology for use in pre-contractual negotiations. It built upon and enlarged an earlier model, the Software Development Capability Assessment Method. It is intended for use both for the purposes of supplier evaluation and for in-house assessment as part of a planned process improvement activity.

Trillium is based on the CMM and bears a strong resemblance to it, but rather than providing a result in terms of a single maturity level, it is intended as a road map and the outcomes of assessment are provided as a profile across all evaluated process areas.

Before proceeding, it is pertinent to mention the International Organization for Standardization (ISO) 9000 series, which have become the most widely recognized and accepted quality standards in the world. For software development companies, the pertinent component of the ISO 9000 series is ISO 9001, entitled Quality Systems — Model for Quality Assurance in Design/ Development, Production, Installation and Servicing. It is noteworthy, however, that the focus in ISO 9001 is on process management, not process quality or improvement. The ISO 9000-3 guideline for the application of ISO 9001 to software interprets the standard and is written in the language of software development.

It is important to note that ISO 9000-3 does not tell software suppliers how to analyze, design, code, test, or document software products. Instead, it states that the suppliers must have a process that is defined, clearly documented, and followed. ISO 9000-3, which is an official ISO guidance standard developed to be used with the ISO 9001 requirements standard, is based on the assumption that, by following a defined engineering process and having a quality management system, higher-quality software can be consistently brought to customers in a more timely manner (Kehoe and Jarvis, 1996).

Oskarsson and Glass (1996) express concern that the differences between the ISO 9000-3 guideline and good software practice are profound. They assert that the quality perspective of ISO 9000 concerns management, not technology; much on what shall be done, less on how. It is more a tool for buying software than building it; and provides necessary but not sufficient goals.

ISO 9000-3 is only one of many interpretations of the ISO 9000 series to the software development environment. The British software industry and the British Department of Trade and Industry worked toward unified certification with TickIT ("tick" = "check" in British English and "IT" for Information Technology). TickIT is a guide to the implementation of ISO 9001 requirements for theinformation technology industry (TickIT, 1992).

The Personal Software Process (PSP) is a scaled-down version of a state-of-the-art industrial software process that is suitable for individual use. As with most emerging technologies, the theoretical underpinnings of PSP are pulled from more established models. By design the PSP incorporates many of the Software Engineering Institute (SEI) Capability Maturity Model (CMM) practices, which have been proposed, debated, applied and reviewed for the past several years by thousands of software engineers. Documented evidence exists for organizational benefits from CMM adoption, ranging from productivity to defect prevention, schedule improvement and return on investment (Paulk et al., 1995). It is anticipated that the PSP will provide comparable success at the individual level.

Humphrey (1996,79-80) explains the CMM—PSP relationship as fol-

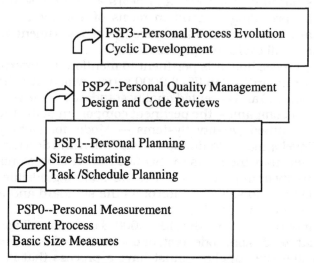

Figure 1. PSP Process Evolution

lows: "The CMM is an organization-focused process improvement framework. While the CMM enables and facilitates good work, it does not guarantee it. The engineers must also use effective personal practices. This is where the PSP comes in, with its bottom-up approach to process improvement...To be effective, engineers need support of a disciplined and efficient environment, which means that the PSP will be most effective in software organizations near or above CMM Level 2."

As with the CMM, where organizations start at Level 1 and progress in maturity to Level 5, individual engineers using the PSP start at PSP0 with no change to their current methods, except to capture measurements about those methods, whatever they are. An overview is shown in Figure 1. The objective is to reach PSP3, which like CMM Level 5 is not a stopping point, but rather an accomplishment that permits continuous improvement without bound.

A description of the process steps in Figure 1 is provided in Humphrey [20] as follows: Personal Measurement (PSP0)-This first step introduces forms and scripts for measuring development time and defects to establish benchmarks. PSP0 is the same process currently used, enhanced by measurements. PSP0.1 adds a coding standard, size measurement and process improvement proposal form. Personal Planning (PSP1)-This step introduces a regression-based method to develop estimates of program size and development time based on personal data. Task and schedule planning are added in PSP1.1, along with earned-value tracking. Personal Quality(PSP2)-This step introduces defect management via the use of checklists for code and design review. The checklists are developed from gathering and analyzing defect data from earlier programs. PSP2.1 adds a nontraditional approach emphasizing design completeness criteria, design verification, and consistency techniques. Cyclic Development (PSP3)-This final step, the highest process level, couples multiple processes in a cyclic fashion to scale up the PSP methods to larger programs.

Humphrey (1995) explains that the PSP is new, but based on five proven principles as follows: 1) defined and structured process can improve working efficiency; 2) defined personal processes should fit individual skills and preferences; 3) professionals must be involved in a process definition to ensure a fit with personal needs; 4) as professionals skills and abilities evolve, so should the process; and 5) continuous process improvement is enhanced by rapid, explicit feedback.

Several formal methods are used in the PSP. In planning, engineers follow a proxy-based estimation (PROBE) method and use their personal data and linear regression to make statistically sound estimates. Size proxies in PSP are objects and methods that enable engineers to effectively visualize program size. They also learn how to derive a prediction interval as a measure of the accuracy of their estimates. Schedule and task planning templates are introduced, and projects are tracked with the earned-value method, that helps determine project status and predict project completion. Planning accuracy is measured by a cost-performance index, which is a ratio of planned to actual development cost

The PSP measures are defined using the Goal-Question-Metric paradigm of Basili and Weiss (1984). With PSP quality management, engineers track their own defects, find their defect removal yields, and calculate cost-of-quality (COQ) measures. Further comment on quality is pertinent-while the COQ metric is traditionally associated with organizational efforts, the PSP emphasizes tracking individual COQ with three components: failure costs (diagnose, repair, re-test) appraisal cost (reviews and inspections), and prevention costs (identification of causes). Pareto defect analysis is used to derive personal design and code review checklists, which the engineers update with defect data from each new project. The PSP also addresses design quality, another potential area of defect prevention. Traditional software design methods focus on producing designs but fail to specify exactly what a design is and what it must contain when completed. Without this specification it is difficult to perform effective design reviews or to evaluate and improve design quality.

By using personal data and linear regression, programmers learn to make statistically sound estimates and derive prediction intervals that indicate the accuracy of their estimates. In order for software engineers to accept and use process improvement techniques, they must first believe them to be effective. Realizing that software engineers would demand data in support his assertions, Humphrey initially wrote a textbook and presented the PSP to computer science students. Student data combined with later results from seven industrial projects showed that PSP-trained software engineers completed projects on or ahead of schedule, and none of the industrial products had any defects reported during several months of customer use (Ferguson et al., 1997).

Since the experimental introduction of the PSP three years ago there is, as yet, relatively little data available to properly judge its effectiveness. As impressive as the initial published results have been, they could be subject to a number of evaluation pitfalls that Pfleeger (1997) reminds us of, including chance, selection bias, or short-term effects. PSP is now being taught at more than 20 universities in the Europe, North and South America, and Australia (Ferguson et al., 1997). Along with this small but growing number of graduate computer science programs, our university now offers a PSP course.

Before leaving this brief overview of process models, it is important to consider current process model options in general. Cusumano (1991) suggests that process options are rooted in product options, of which there are three. For high-end products (high-price, unique design, medium size systems) the process strategy involves full satisfaction of user requirements and highly skilled workers with custom tools. For middle-end products, a software factory process that balances user requirements with production costs and a standard development process. Low-end, mass replicated, systems use a process that maximizes functionality for the average user. Keeping theses options in mind helps to explain a contradiction pointed put by Curtis et al. (1987)—existing software process models fail to provide for the sub-processes most critical to success, such as opportunistic design, technical communication, and customer interaction.

In contrast, software process improvement models incorporate these critical success factors. Heineman et al. (1994) suggest that competitive pressures on the software development industry in the early 1980s led many organizations to examine their software development processes and to realize that the key to improving the results of their software development operations was to focus on the software process by which the operations were performed. Lai (1993) contends that the next logical step—an emphasis on improved modeling of the software process—is a direct consequence of the mutable nature of software development. As organizations attempted to examine their software process, they realized that it made no sense to talk about any single software development process as it is, given that it will change. It is therefore important to examine trends and capabilities regarding process modeling techniques, as outlined in the next section.

Process Modeling Techniques

Osterweili (1987) provided the seminal contention that there is a need for information systems practitioners to become as proficient at modeling software processes as they are at modeling applications. Ramamoorthy and Tsai (1996) suggest that changes to software process are a natural consequence of the increasing complexity of the domain of the applications. For example, techniques for modeling objects in an object-oriented development process emerged from the application-driven need to incorporate modularity, abstraction and reuse. Similarly, processes in real-time application domains emphasize formal, rigorously verified requirements to ensure safety and reliability. This has led to use of a Cleanroom process, first proposed by IBM's Harlan Mills, which makes use of a box structure technique for process modeling. The newest approaches to modeling the process of software design accommodate the need for creativity by techniques that treat software patterns. An example of using patterns to model software process is the need to locate errors in a telecommunication switching system. The software solution is modeled on patterns from hardware design. Dutton (1993) proposes a universal process definition notation in which processes are represented in an iconic dataflow-based graph language. His rationale stems from his belief that a dataflow model is the way most people think about processes. Ovals represent tasks, which consume and modify artifacts. By specifying the artifacts needed and produced, project control is achieved in a manner analogous to use of entry/ exit criteria in the waterfall process model.

In contrast, Yourdon (1996) suggests that real-world software developers do not work in terms of graphical abstractions of software, such as data flow diagrams or entity relationship diagrams. Instead they use mental models (based on experience, intuition, folklore, and myth). He contends that what is needed to accurately reflect this mental process are dynamic models such as pioneered by Abdel-Hamick and Madnick (1989), which make use of cloud boundaries, flow through pipelines with rectangular reservoirs and bubble regulators. By use of this dynamic modeling, a large telecommunications firm discovered that due to a high software defect rate, no successful work products would ever emerge from the defined process—bad work circulated and restricted the product flow.

Curtis et al. (1992) assert that in order to establish software process modeling as a unique area of practice and research it is necessary to identify conceptual boundaries that distinguish the work from other modeling, such as computer hardware or information science. They suggest that the differences emerge from the need to have humans enact the process. They then reviewed five categories of process modeling techniques to demonstrate that the process being modeled can be viewed from four perspectives: Functional (process steps), Behavioral (process states), Organizational (who performs), and Informational (structure and relationships). Existing modeling techniques adopt only a subset of these perspectives, as shown in Table 1.

A few of the techniques in Table 1 require additional commentary. Process programming approaches represent the process to be modeled in the form of a program, using programming notion and formalism. Lending support to Osterweili's (1987) observation that "software processes are software too." Although inherently complex, this technique permits either procedural (e.g., APPL/A and CML) or rule-based (e.g., MARVEL and MELMAC) languages to be used. Petri Net approaches use mathematically based graphical notion to model dynamic and distributed software processes. Although useful for validation, understandability is a concern.

IDEF0, a subset of SADT, is the most widely used functional modeling

	F	B	O	I
Integrated Definition (IDEF0)	✔		✔	
Entity Process	✔	✔	✔	
Process Programming	✔			
Petri Nets	✔	✔	✔	
System Dynamics	✔		✔	
Structured Analysis and Design Technique (SADT)	✔		✔	✔
Procedural Programming Languages	✔	✔		✔
Precedence networks		✔		
Object modeling			✔	✔
Data modeling				✔

Table 1. Modeling Perspectives

approach. Although lacking the details needed for concurrency, resource conflict, or state-oriented behavior, its understandability is useful for identification of missing process steps-important to process immature organizations.

Curtis et al. (1992) stress the important fact that process model information must be combined with project specific information to create plans and products in order for process enaction (execution of the plan) to occur. They demonstrate the importance of the often overlooked human element by the results of a survey on process modeling techniques using a scale of (0-4), with 0 being the worst, shown in Table 2.

Arnold(1996) suggests the ETVX (test Entry criteria, perform Task, Verify result, test eXit criteria) paradigm as a technique for process definition.. He applies the concept of a mixed initiative to accommodate the reality that developers typically operate with a balance of how much the process controls the practitioner and how much the practitioner controls the process. He suggests accommodating this mixed initiative by requiring rigid exit criteria (via a dependency network) to enable management control and

	Understandability	Learning Curve	Likelihood of Acceptance
SADT	4	4	3
IDEF0	4	4	4
Process Programming	1	2	1
System Dynamics	2	3	2
Petri Nets	0	0	0
Object Oriented	2	2	2
Entity Process	2	2	3

Table 2. Modeling Technique Evaluation

using flexible entry criteria, where appropriate, to allow developers to be creative and conduct many activities in parallel.

These provide a focus for assessment and improvement, thus mirroring the focus of the third process innovation category-assessment-discussed in the next section.

Process Assessment

Competitive pressures on the software industry have drawn attention to the need for judicial examination of software development processes. A necessary prerequisite for such an examination is the existence of a widely accepted standard with which to make comparisons. Although it is possible for firms to conduct process assessments of their existing software process, Davis and Wallace (1992) assert that the CMM provides a useful standard because it is based on time-proven quality principles applied specifically to software. Its roots are in statistical quality control, which was developed by Shewart in the 1930s and further developed and successfully demonstrated by Deming and Juran. The CMM casts these principles into a maturity framework, which consists of five maturity levels that describe the progression from a chaotic process to a well-controlled optimizing process. The levels lay successive foundations for continuous process improvement. By determining their position in this framework, organizations can readily identify the most fruitful areas for improvement actions. Each level establishes an intermediate set of goals toward higher levels of process maturity.

SEI assessments of the software industry are somewhat discouraging, suggesting that 75% of firms remain at the lowest level of maturity. Comparable results have been reported regarding from European firms. The ESPRIT program's Bootstrap assessment (uses the ESO process model and ISO 9000) results place 48% of firms at level 1 and 52% at level 2 of 5 possible levels. Experience has shown that it typically takes an organization committed to process improvement anywhere from a year and a half to three years to progress by one complete level of maturity; but the progression from level 1 to level 2 may require more on the order of three to five years.

Grady (1992) suggests that it is the organizational orientation of the CMM that limits rapid progression. Moreover, he reminds us that the CMM was not the first evaluative model, but it is the one that is gently forcing companies to look at software practices from an engineering perspective. Saiedian et al. (1995) suggest that because of the CMM's relatively recent arrival on the software process assessment scene, only time will tell if this effort will really work in terms of an overall improvement of software produced

While the CMM impetus has been primarily the defense industry, Rout (1995) reminds us that software process assessment methods have also been pioneered by telecommunications firms such as British Telecom, Bell Canada and Bellcore. Presently, firms may choose from among the many software process capability assessment and improvement models that have been developed, including a parallel evolution of proprietary and industry models. The proprietary ones (e.g., Andersen's Method/1, Pressman & Associates (1996), Gartner Group, Howard Rubin Associates) are still being refined by the vendors as a method of keeping the present users satisfied and thus avoiding transfer to the less profitable industry model process improvement environment.

Most software engineers learn to write programs in courses that focus on effective, efficient problem-solving but ignore discussion of plans, quality, or metrics. Not surprisingly, upon graduation they apply the accepted practice of writing code of unknown quality and rely on compiling and testing to find and fix the defects.

In contrast, Humphrey (1997) argues that developing high-quality software products requires more than writing code that will run on a computer—it requires delivery at an agreed cost and on schedule. Furthermore, he asserts that improving the personal software processes of individual developers is what is now needed.

Khajenoori (1994) describes a new Masters of Software Engineering program at Embry-Riddle Aeronautical University that incorporates process concepts, including Humphrey's Personal Software Process (PSP), as a means to introduce engineering discipline into software development. The PSP is data-driven: measurements and statistical techniques highlight process deficiencies and provide a focus for improvement. By providing a framework for data collection using assignment kits, PSP helps individuals develop a quantitative understanding of their process steps. It also demonstrates how process methods can improve quality and productivity. Evaluation of the new program is on-going, but reports are favorable from other students and faculty who, as a result of PSP, are more aware of rigor, process and variety.

Humphrey (1996) reports that a substantial number of industry and government groups currently use or are introducing the PSP. The SEI is working with many leading software organizations in both DoD and commercial industry. Some of the leading corporations currently introducing the PSP include: Advanced Information Systems, Citicorp, Ford Motor Co., Harris, Motorola, and Union Switch and Signal. As a result, data on their experiences are now becoming available. As an example of these findings, 104 engineers at Advanced Information Systems in Peoria, IL who completed the ten PSP course exercises reduced the interquartile range of the estimating errors by 40 percent. Further examples are available (Ferguson et al., 1997). On one development project three engineers guessed how long it would take to develop the first three components of a large product. Their initial estimating errors averaged 394 percent. One engineer estimated that his work would take six weeks when it actually took 26 weeks. Management stopped work, had the engineers trained in the PSP, then had them replan the project. After PSP training, these same engineers' estimates had an average error of negative 10.4 percent, that is, they finished an average of 10.4 percent early.

A key to estimating success with the PSP is that engineers use actual

Project	Staffing PSP/ non PSP	Planned Delivery	Actual Delivery
A	3/0	7 months	5 months
B	0/3	2 months	5 months
C	0/3	10 months	19 months
D	1/0	6 months	6 months
E	1/0	2 months	2 months
F	2/1	2 months	2 months

Table 3. Project Schedule Results

historical data to make plans. By comparing actual results with plans, they can see their mistakes and are more likely to make better plans in the future. Schedule performance data on six projects at Advanced Information Services (Ferguson et al., 1997) are shown in Table 3.

With qualified instructors, PSP training takes about 125 hours per engineer. Engineers should be encouraged to complete the full PSP course in order to acquire the personal data needed to convince themselves of the benefits of the PSP methods. The SEI offers instructor training for organizations that wish to train their employees themselves. When AIS first offered the course, it was given outside regular work hours using instructors not qualified. As a result only 1/2 the engineers completed the course. Since then, the course has been taught on company time. All the Madras, India subsidiary engineers and managers have been trained and 58% of U.S. so far, with all scheduled for this year. Motorola's Paging Products Group in Boynton Beach, FL has offered three classes committing 8 hours per week for training. Union Switch & Signal Automation and Information Systems business unit also tried class during regular work hours, but this proved too demanding, with only 1/2 of the participants completing the course. Subsequently, the classes were offered only during work hours with a full day allowed per assignment. All three companies followed course plans similar to, but shorter than, the 15 week academic course originally outlined by Humphrey. AIS has a 2-week course with lecture in morning and rest of day for program completion.

Our university adopted Humphrey's 15-week academic approach. The PSP is designed to be taught as a 15-lecture graduate university course during which the methods are practiced by way of 10 programming exercises and 5 analysis reports. To interpret the results from the course offerings, two approaches are used: trend analysis and GQM paradigm. As was done by Humphrey (1996), the data for this analysis was collected from several classes. Analysis of variance tests at the 5 percent level showed variances among individuals to be greater than among the class groupings. The analysis of variance test also examined potential differences caused by different programming languages, thus allowing that data to be pooled.

	1	2	3	4	5	6
Interrupt Time	15	10	24	6	19	14
% estimate error	33	20	33	5	15	24

Table 4. Interruptions

Both size and time estimates were somewhat erratic. Reported reasons ranged from difficulty with the statistical nature of the programming requirements to ever changing forms as the process scripts evolved. Additional factors discussed included unfamiliarity with reusability, which is imposed by the PSP exercises. Students initially overestimated both size and time and later used linear regression; but the initial overestimates compensation caused later underestimates. The early program estimates were merely guesses, but adequate given the simple nature of the early programs. In contrast the last program estimate was derived using prediction intervals—a guess would have been difficult. Also, the later programs reused a lot of code which improved estimation.

Time estimates for some students showed less of a trend than for others. One plausible explanation, supported by data in Table 4 (r2=.448), is that work interruptions introduce an associated difficulty in resuming at the same pace.

Most experts agree that lines-of-code (LOC) by itself is not a useful metric for productivity due to style differences (concise vs. verbose); but when examined in comparison with programs written by the same programmer and in the same language it can be effective in determining one's PSP. Moreover, LOC as a metric is useful in estimating development time. A test for correlation of the data from our students, which contains data from several engineers using a variety of languages, resulted in r2 values that ranged from .58 to .87, with values above .5 generally considered useful for planning purposes.

As explained in the preceding theory discussion, the PSP measures are defined using the Goal-Question-Metric paradigm. It has been shown to be particularly important for software organizations to understand the goals with respect to delivery of software. Once goals have been set through a process with internal and external agents, questions surrounding the goals are needed to add specificity to the implementation. The questions are geared toward setting specific paths to accomplishment. Measures are then designed into a framework to understand progress. As noted, several performance factors, reuse, and requirement's clarity drove the behavior of the projects in very acute ways.

As an example of the GQM applied to the PSP, one student expressed a goal of producing highly cohesive and loosely coupled programming code. The corresponding question that emerged was: What is the best methodology? As a metric, this individual chose to concentrate on minimizing interruptions. Another student goal was expressed as a desire for accurate postmortem reports. In answer to the question of best methodology, the data for the required metrics were consolidated in spreadsheets and templates. PSP data can be broken down into direct measurements and derived measurements. Direct include size time and defects. Derived include to-date values, productivity, and percentage reuse.

More experienced programmers enrolled in PSP classes state that their objective in not to learn a Personal Software Process, but rather to learn whether there are indicators and questions to ask that will allow for more accurate estimates. Upon completion, most agree that there are in fact two basic questions: 1) does the programmer have a process? and 2) does the process provide realistic estimates? Related questions are: what is the basis for the estimate, what methodology is used, and how extensive is the historical database? This last question demonstrates that the PSP provides a persuasive argument for the value of historical data to corroborate the time estimates. The discovered correlation between the time and size tells individual programmers about the stability of productivity metrics, and reminds them that if the size is properly estimated then the time can be also.

Pfleeger (1997) observes that the software engineering literature contains an abundance of research results, but the dilemma remains in deciding which of conflicting results apply to you. You may decide that you need to perform your own study—this the essence of the PSP. In conclusion, examining six projects is by no means sufficient to establish a process—personal or otherwise—however, familiarity with the PSP can be directly transferred to real-world conditions.

Two other assessment methods are in common use. McGowan and Bohner (1993) proposed the Model-Based Process Assessment (MBPA) as an alternative approach to the CMM for process assessment. As the name implies, MBPA involves creating a process model and using the model for the assessment. The MBPA focuses on a single project, takes twice as long, and lacks any baseline for comparison. It can be argued that this is not assessment, but rather classic systems analysis. Jones (1995) uses a five-level Excellence Scale for the assessment method of his firm, Software Productivity Research. Their results follow a more normal distribution of firms with the frequency of occurrence along the excellence scale being: Excellent 2%, Good 18%, Average 56%, Poor 20%, and Very Poor 4%

This chapter's focus on CMM is driven in part by the proprietary nature of most other schemes. An additional benefit of the CMM assessment efforts is the availability of software industry data. For example, a 1995 process maturity profile of the software community reveals a pattern of maturity level changes from the first to second assessment for sixty-three firms. The ever-increasing supply of assessment data provide countless opportunities for increasing our understanding of the software industry. For example, a simple application of Markov analysis to the assessment data suggests continued process improvement at an increasing rate.

One final issue regarding software process improvement assessment emerges from an observation that process improvement efforts have encountered many of the same productivity and payoff measurement problems as information systems in general. Investment payoff data are needed to establish an argument for adopting the CMM as a model to guide information systems investment decisions and fill the data vacuum. There is no other way to prove value of improving the software process.

Conclusions

This chapter has taken a first look at the foundation elements of a conceptual revolution that has substantially altered perceptions within the information systems industry. The three categories of software process innovations (modeling, techniques, and assessments) appear to be at different stages of development and use. The process modeling techniques appear to be farthest along the path toward widespread acceptance. Despite its obvious differences from traditional manufacturing, software is still a product and software development is an engineering process. Software engineering has practices, principles, and procedures that are used to perform and control analysis, design, implementation, test, and mainte- nance of the software product.

At the opposite end of the spectrum, it appears that information systems practitioners are far from agreement regarding a standard model for the process of software development. It is generally agreed that field of process modeling is still too young to expect consensus.

The work to date on process assessments holds great promise for software process improvement and other benefits. As standard practices begin to be defined and adopted for assessment purposes, it is only natural to expect the subsequent adoption of standards for process modeling. It will then be possible to rigorously evaluate process models and modeling methods by using the traditional quality characteristics of efficiency, verifiability, usability and reusability.

Although the PSP helps establish the trend toward acceptance of technical pluralism, the pragmatic essence of an engineering discipline requires a basis for choice. This concern is expressed most eloquently by Shapiro (1997,49): "If software engineering is to become an actuality rather than a wish, it will require more than simple acknowledgment of choice. It will also need a basis for choice...That basis, moreover, must consider the myriad of factors that characterize any particular software solution. A thoughtful basis, though, should not be taken to mean an exclusive reliance on science and mathematics. For while these will undoubtedly play important roles in software engineering, as they have in other engineering fields, they are no substitute for experience and aesthetics, intuition and heuristics."

Our results parallel related efforts described in the literature that detail experiences with project-based software engineering courses that attempt to utilize from-scratch assignments. Most such teams did poor design, documentation, testing and through heroic efforts submitted a fragile product. They knew that neither the process nor the product were correct. Instead, the PSP approach emphasizes the importance of planning, quality, documentation, and reuse.

References

Abdel-Hamid, T. & Madnick, S. (1989). Lessons learned from modeling the dynamics of software project management, *Communications of the ACM*, (December).

Abdel-Hamid, T. & Madnick, S. (1991). *Software Project Dynamics: An Integrated Approach.* Englewood Cliffs, NJ: Prentice-Hall.

Allgood, B., Clough, A., Cunha, G., & VanBuren, J. (1994). *Process Technologies Method and Tool Report,* Volume I, Technical Report, Software Technology Support Center Hill AFB, Utah. (March)

Arnold, P. (1996). Defining Processes for Automation. Presentation for 3rd International Conference on Cleanroom Software Engineering Practices, College Park, MD, (October).

Balzer, R. (1991). What we do and don't know about software process. In T. Katayama (Ed.), *Proceedings of the 6th International Software Process Workshop* (pp.61-65). Los Alamitos: IEEE Computer Society Press.

Basili, V.R. and Weiss, D.M. (1984). A Methodology For Collecting Valid Software Engineering Data. *IEEE Transactions on Software Engineering,* (November):728-738.

Bollinger, T.B. & McGowan, C. (1991). A Critical Look at Software Capability Evaluations. *IEEE Software* (July):25-45.

Curtis, B. Krasner, H. Shen, V. & Iscoe, N. (1987) Software process modeling under the lamppost. In *Proceedings of the ninth international conference on software engineering.* Washington, DC IEEE Computer Society Press 96-103.

Curtis, B., Kellner, M., & Over, J. (1992). Process modeling. *Communications of the ACM,* 35(9):75-90.

Curtis, B., & Paulk, M. (1993). Creating a software process improvement program. *Information & Software Technology,* 35, 381-386.

Cusumano, M. (1991). Japan's Software Factories. New York: Oxford University Press.

Davis, D. & Wallace, D. (1992). *The Capability Maturity Model for Software,* New York: DAZIX, An Intergraph Company.

Dorling, A. (1993). SPICE: Software process improvement and capability determination. *Information & Software Technology,* 35, 404-406.

Dutton, J. (1993). Commonsense approach to process modeling. IEEE Software, 10 (4):56-64.

Ferguson, P., Humphrey, W.S., Khajenoori, S., Macke, S. and Matvya, A. (1997). Results of Applying the Personal Software Process, *IEEE Computer,* (May):24-31.

Gibbs, W. (1994). Software's chronic crisis. *Scientific American,* (September): 86-95.

Grady, R. (1992). *Practical Software Metrics for Project Management and Process Improvement.* Englewood Cliffs, NJ: Prentice Hall.

Heineman, G. T., Botsford, J. E., Caldiera, G., & Kaiser, G. E. (1994). Emerging technologies that support a software process life cycle. *IBM Systems Journal,* 33, 501-529.

Humphrey, W. (1995). *A Discipline for Software Engineering.* New York: Addison-Wesley Publishing Company

Humphrey, W.S. (1996). Using a Defined and Measured Personal Software Process. *IEEE Software*, (May):77-88.

Humphrey, W.S. (1997). *Introduction To The Personal Software Process.* Reading, MA:Addison-Wesley.

Jones, C. (1995). Gaps in SEI programs. *Software Development*, (March), 41-48.

Kehoe, R. & Jarvis, A. (1996). *ISO 9000-3: A Tool for Software Product and Process Improvement.* New York: Springer-Verlag.

Khajenoori, S. (1994). Process-Oriented Software Education. *IEEE Software* (November):99-101.

Lai, R. (1993). The move to mature processes. *IEEE Software*, (July):14-17.

McGowan, C. & Bohner, S. (1993). Model based process assessments. *Proceedings of the 15th International Conference on Software Engineering*, IEEE Computer Society Press, Los Alamitos, CA. 202-211.

Oskarsson, O. & Glass, R. (1996). *An ISO 9000 Approach to Building Quality Software.* Upper Saddle River, NJ: Prentice Hall PTR.

Osterweili, L. (1987). Software processes are software too. *Proceedings of the International Conference on Software Engineering*, IEEE CS Press, pp. 2-13.

Paulk, M, Weber, C.V., Curtis, B., and Chrissis, M.B. (1995). *The Capability Maturity Model: Guidelines for Improving the Software Process*, Reading, MA: Addison-Wesley.

Paulk, M. (1993). Capability maturity model, version 1.1. *IEEE software*, 10, 18-27.

Paulk, M. (1995) How ISO 9001 Compares With The CMM. *IEEE software*, (January) 74-83.

Pfleeger, S.L. (1997). Guidelines for Applying Research Results. *IEEE Software*, (May/June):102-104.

Pressman, R. (1996). Software process impediment. *IEEE software*, (September) 16-17. [34]Ramamoorthy, C. & Tsai, W. (1996). Advances in software engineering. *IEEE Computer*, 29(10):47-58.

Rout, T. (1995). SPICE: A framework for software process assessment. *Software Process*, 1(1):67-78.

Royce, W. (1970). Managing the development of large software systems. *Proceedings of IEEE Wescon.*

Rozum, J. (1993). *Concepts on measuring the benefits of software process improvements.* Technical report CMU/SEI-93-TR-09.

Saiedian, H., Kuzara, R. & Hamilton, S. (1995). SEI capability maturity model's impact on contractors. *IEEE Computer*, (January) 16-26.

Shapiro, S. (1997). Splitting the Difference: The Historical Necessity of Synthesis in Software Engineering. *IEEE Annals of the History of Computing*, 19(1):20-54.

TickIT, (1992). *Guide to Software Quality Management System Construction and Certification* Using ISO 9001/EN 29001/BS 5750 TickIT Project Office.

Trillium. (1992). *Trillium — Telecom Software Product Development Capability Assessment Model*, Bell Canada, Draft 2.2, July.

Yourdon, E. (1996). *Rise & Resurrection of the American Programmer.* Upper Saddle River, NJ:Prentice Hall PTR.

Chapter 2

The Soft System Methodology as a Framework for Software Process Improvement

Peter D.C. Bennetts
Cheltenham and Gloucester College of Higher Education, UK

A. Trevor Wood-Harper
University of Salford, UK

Stella Mills
Cheltenham and Gloucester College of Higher Education, UK

The overall aim of this chapter is to argue that only a systems-based approach to information systems development (ISD) and software process improvement (SPI) are likely to cover all the recognised issues. This chapter will examine reports in the literature concerning problems associated with ISD and implementation. The characteristics of these problems are identified. It is noted that these problems have been known for many years. The responses to the problems fall into two broad areas which are characterised as paradigms. On the one hand, there is a belief that systems development should be considered to be a form of applied science or engineering (Dijkstra, 1976; Floyd, 1992; Hoare, 1982). This is also the approach behind Software Process Improvement. However, there are weaknesses with this approach which are identified below. These weaknesses are addressed by approaches from within the second paradigm or systems paradigm (Checkland, 1981; Checkland and Scholes, 1990). The systems paradigm has been developed from the traditional paradigm. Consequently, it is argued that fewer problems will be found if methodologies based on the systems paradigm are used. The foundations and nature of this approach are described. Further, it is shown that the Soft Systems Methodology (SSM), which is based on this paradigm, can be used as a metaphor or model of ISD. In this form it is recursive and so this model is characterised as Recursive SSM. SSM is offered as a useful framework for both ISD and software process improvement (SPI).

This chapter will therefore address the following major activities:

- Examining the possible causes of and responses to the problem area recognised as the 'software crisis'.
- Recognising that the above problems are not addressed by the science paradigm, *per se*. The science paradigm needs to be extended to address the outstanding issues. This extension is termed the systems paradigm.
- Identifying the support for the Soft Systems Methodology from the systems approach.
- Developing an understanding of the form of Recursive SSM.
- Recognising the use of SSM for ISD and SPI.

System Failures - Reasons and Responses

Software and its associated technologies and business processes are now transforming the opportunities for business organisations. Unfortunately, the promise of computer usage does not always bear fruit.

In 1968, a Study Group on Computer Science, established by the NATO Science Committee, responding to the perception of a "software crisis", recommended the holding of a working conference on Software Engineering (Naur, Randell and Buxton, 1976). The term "software engineering" was coined to be deliberately provocative, implying, as it does, the need for software development to be based on the principles and practices seen in engineering (Naur et al., 1976).

While the introduction of an engineering approach had an effect on the way software is developed we note that some years after the initial concept of software engineering, Pressman (1987) still commented that for "... the past decade managers and many technical practitioners have asked the following questions :

- Why does it take so long to get programs finished?
- Why are costs so high?
- Why can't we find all the errors before we give the software to our customers?
- Why do we have difficulty in measuring progress as software is being developed?"

Despite the problem represented by these questions being well known (in that these issues have been prominent in the literature for nearly thirty years), disasters are still happening.

While a common response to the software crisis has been to suggest that training should be improved (Canan, 1986; Hoare, 1982), practitioners and managers do not always do what they know they should. For example, Gibbs (1994) reports Larry E. Druffel, Director of Carnegie Mellon University's Software Engineering Institute as saying that unfortunately, "... the industry does not uniformly apply that which is well-known best practice." Even if "best practice" is enshrined in a methodology, this does not guarantee success. For example, a discussant (Eddie Moores) at the 1995 Information Systems Methodologies Conference, referring to some currently unpublished research of his, said that the most used methodology was "JDI" (Just Do It). It was also made clear in subsequent discussion that even when managers said a methodology was being used, this was no guarantee that this was so. Another example of managers not doing what is expected by the literature, is when they implement systems on time, but with known errors. As Pirsig (1984) notes, a quality product will only be produced if people care about quality.

The NATO Study Group's belief that the use of applied science would be an appropriate solution to the software crisis was echoed by Hoare (1982) when he said that "professional practice ... [should be] ... based on a sound understanding of the underlying mathematical theories and ... should follow closely the traditions of engineers in better established disciplines." Similarly, Dijkstra (1976) was interested in the mathematical basis of programming and considers the development of programs to be a scientific discipline. Gibbs (1994) still supports this view when he concludes that a disaster "... will become an increasingly common and disruptive part of software development unless programming takes on more of the characteristics of an engineering discipline rooted firmly in science and mathematics." This is the same recipe as reported by Naur et al. (1976) nearly twenty years earlier. It is also the spur towards software quality assurance and SPI.

From the above description we can characterise the software engineering perspective as deterministic and one that assumes that there is some definable, true and real set of requirements that can be elicited and formally specified. It concentrates on the production of a piece of software that conforms to a specification as efficiently as possible (Vidgen, Wood-Harper and Wood, 1993). However, this optimistic approach lacks the insight shown by Bronowski (1973) when he says "... There is no absolute knowledge. And those who claim it, whether they are scientists or dogmatists, open the door to tragedy. All information is imperfect. ... That is the human condition ...". While it might be overstating the issue to say an unnecessary business problem is a tragedy, this paper will demonstrate that this insight does apply to ISD. The problem of unsuccessful information system developments is seen as unnecessary as the problems and solutions are well known.

Even when a system is installed, there can still be difficulties and disappointments. Little (1993), for example, finds estimates of system failure in the literature running between 25% and 90%. In a major survey of the literature on why information systems fail, Lyytinen and Hirschheim (1987) identify four generic issues which give rise to such failures:

- Correspondence failure—the system, as implemented, does not correspond to what was required;
- Process failure—a system is not forthcoming within time or resource constraints;
- Interaction failure—systems, as implemented, which fail to satisfy the users;
- Expectation failure—systems which are unable to meet stakeholders' expectations.

The Process failure is clearly addressed (at least partly) by software engineering. However, the other three kinds of failures are not directly addressed by it. Recently, it has been recognised that it is important to recognise the way analysts are seen by the organisation and how they see themselves (Bell and Wood-Harper, 1992; Hirschheim and Klein, 1989). This can be identified by the use of metaphor. The software engineer is usually a technocrat who tries to deliver what is thought of as the user's requirements, but with minimal reference to the user. The other failure types are more likely to be addressed when the analyst acts as a facilitator. This change of emphasis from technocrat to facilitator is actually quite radical, as it reflects a major change in the background philosophy of the analyst. The facilitative approach is characterised as interpretative and contextual in outlook; it views models as a means of talking *about* reality rather than models *of* reality. This new philosophy cannot be supported entirely from within the current scientific framework. A way of encapsulating this form of framework is the concept of a paradigm. There are certain limitations to the science paradigm when considering individual members of staff and managers which are addressed by a related paradigm—the systems approach or systems theory (Checkland, 1981; Lyytinen and Hirschheim, 1987). A systems approach will reflect a concern to look at potential systems as a whole (holistically). This is in contrast to the scientific or engineering approach which tends to solve problems by breaking them down into smaller, more manageable fragments (reductionism). Further, and in particular, a systems approach will be expected to address the human and organisational issues which tend to be ignored in the traditional approaches.

Newman (1989) puts it quite strongly when he suggests that it is a myth that organisational issues are not the concern of its information systems professionals. The incorporation of social issues needs to be based on a systems approach (Checkland, 1981; Hitchman and Bennetts, 1994, 1995; Mitroff & Linstone, 1993). The systems approach is needed as it can incorporate these issues while a science or engineering-based approach cannot. Similarly, Bignell & Fortune (1984), examining failures in undertakings such as the building of the Humber bridge, also recommend a systems approach and also recognise the need to take human factors into account.

Today, even workers in safety critical systems, where very great technical demands are made on systems, recognise the need to include "human" aspects (Griffyth, 1995; Newman, 1995); software creation is recognised as a social activity (Price, 1995); similarly, Rogers (1995) identifies communication as crucial. Further, Prince (1993) reminds information system managers that "... quality assurance (QA) and related programs are first and foremost human resources programs. IS managers who attend to the human details succeed in a way that QA theorists never do." This has been recognised for some time. For example, Bostrom and Heinen (1977) in a comment that they recognise can be applied to any computer-based information systems effort, say "The major reason why management information systems (MIS) have had so many failures and problems is the way systems designers view organizations, their members and the function of an MIS within them." They argue for a "... more realistic view of organization", as in "Socio-Technical System design". Similarly, Earl and Hopwood (1980) recognise that "... lack of management support and involvement are [frequently] cited as causes of inadequate MIS". They urge "... a broader organizational perspective" for systems development. We therefore argue that an approach which is more than purely functionalist is required.

Others have recognised that software development is not just a purely rational process; for example Keen (1981); Kling and Iacomo (1984); Newman and Rosenberg (1985) see it as a social process. Lucas (1975) and Symons (1990) recognise how political the development of an information system can be. For example, a perceived benefit for one group is not necessarily a benefit for another group as increased access to information in one place may imply an eroded power base elsewhere (Symons, 1990). Lucas (1975) makes it quite explicit when he says "... information systems do not exist in isolation: they have the potential for creating major changes in power relationships and stimulating conflict." Similarly, "no one knows how many computer-based applications ... are abandoned or expensively overhauled because they were unenthusiastically received by their intended users" (Markus, 1983). Further, Markus (1983) argues that to "... design systems that will not be resisted or to devise ways to modify resisted systems ... technical system analysis must be augmented with a social or political analysis ...". It is clear that one key issue in ISD is organisational politics. Even so, Symons (1990) considers that despite often playing a key part in ISD, politics "... are generally ignored by researchers". Consequently, there is a possibility that a developer, creating a system through the use of a methodology which does not itself recognise the need for a political analysis, will avoid such an analysis.

This section has shown that the software crisis, first recognised well before 1976, is still an issue in 1996. Other problems of ISD have also been characterised. The issues giving rise to all these problems have been identified and seen to imply that human, social or organisational issues share much of the blame. We have noted above various problems associated with the development of information systems. These problems have been

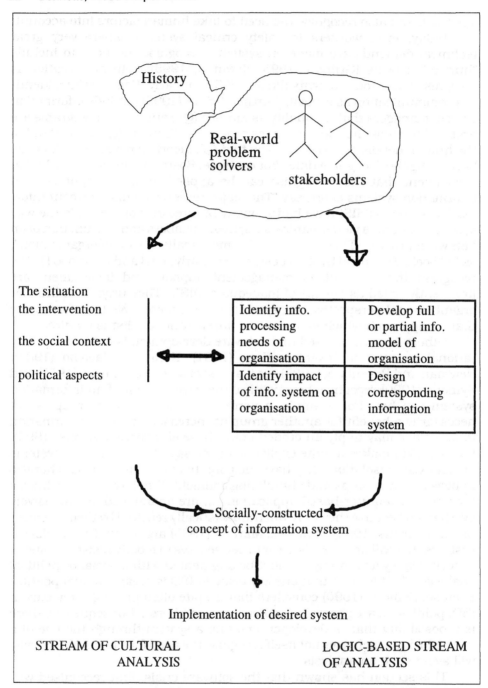

Figure 1. A framework for the ISD process (adapted from Bennetts and Wood-Harper, 1997 after Vidgen, Wood-Harper and Wood, 1993)

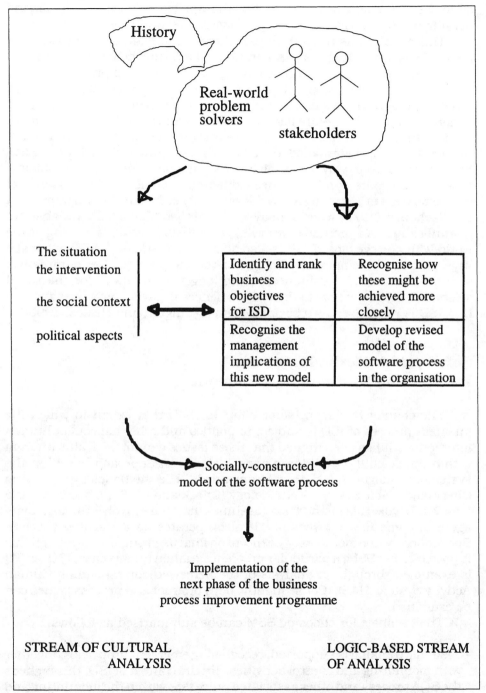

History

Real-world
problem
solvers

stakeholders

The situation
the intervention

the social context

political aspects

| Identify and rank business objectives for ISD | Recognise how these might be achieved more closely |
| Recognise the management implications of this new model | Develop revised model of the software process in the organisation |

Socially-constructed
model of the software process

Implementation of the
next phase of the business
process improvement programme

STREAM OF CULTURAL
ANALYSIS

LOGIC-BASED STREAM
OF ANALYSIS

Figure 2: A Framework for SPI

addressed by responses from within the applied science or engineering paradigm. However, these attempts have not resolved the problem.

This chapter has recognised that there are difficulties in the development of software. It is not clear from the literature how pervasive these difficulties are. For political reasons organisations would prefer to be able to say that they have no problems. While well-structured, clearly defined problems may well have no difficulties in their development, ill-structured or contentious problems are likely to have difficulties in their development. Some of these difficulties are intrinsic, some brought in by the behaviour of the developers or their managers or their clients. Software engineering has been offered as a way of resolving the intrinsic, technical problems. However, the other problems need different methods. Both classes of problems need to be resolved to achieve quality software. This is supported by Blackburn (1973) when he says "... by relying lopsidedly on abstract quantification as a method of knowing, scientists have been looking at the world with one eye closed." It is also supported by Hesse (1976) when she says that the "... empiricist account of science as objective, cumulative, success-oriented, and value-free, is no longer adequate ... for the social sciences." This reference to the social sciences is particularly relevant now that ISD is recognised as a social system (Ledington and Heales, 1993).

Soft System Methodology and Information Systems Development

The chapter has spent some effort to show that extent to which the business process of ISD is subject to politics and other aspects of human interaction. It has been argued that these issues cannot be dealt with from within the scientific tradition alone. Instead, an approach based on the systems paradigm has been recommended. The methodology chosen is Checkland's Soft System Methodology (Checkland, 1981; Checkland and Scholes, 1990). This methodology assumes that those involved in an activity agree to come to a consensus. It also operates as a learning process. Consequently, the methodology expects no final fixed outcome although this is possible. For SSM, a particular problem situation (in this case, ISD or SPI) is examined through an analysis of the perceived corresponding Human Activity System (HAS). Consequently, both product and process issues can be examined.

The rationale for choosing SSM can be summarised as follows:

• Systemic thinking is supported, recognising emergent properties, together with monitoring and control activities. (In the context of ISD, this embeds the SQA process and other associated processes within the monitoring and control activities of the methodology.)
• The social and organisational aspects of ISD are recognised in the form of a cultural stream of analysis which is continually being examined and

updated. (Hence, politics and human factors are explicitly recognised.)
• An in-built learning process is offered. (Software Process Improvement can only develop if learning takes place.)
• Participation by all stakeholders is assumed. (This is potentially very difficult to achieve in its ideal form. However, it does aid involvement and acceptance.)
• The processes to be invoked in the cultural and logic streams are not prescribed. (While this leaves organisations to make up their own minds, it does allow flexibility and change.)
• Historical information is expected. (How did the organisation get to its current state?)
• It does not assume that all answers are already known, but acts as a means of structuring a debate to identify the appropriate and feasible solutions in a particular organisation at a particular time. (Aids communication among stakeholders.)
• The context for development is determined by the stakeholders. (This allows ISD and SPI to reflect an organisation's business objectives, rather than an idealised set of objectives imposed from outside.)

Within SSM, models of purposeful human activity are generated and compared with perceived reality in order to gain insight. Cycles around the various phases of the methodology are repeated as required. The logic-based analysis involves the stages:

• Identify the information processing needs of the organisation;
• Develop an information model or models of the organisation;
• Design corresponding information systems;
• Identify the impact of these information systems on the organisation.

It should be noted that all these stages are ongoing. The information needs of any organisation are not fixed, but liable to change on an unpredictable basis. It has proved difficult, in practice, to achieve a usable information model of an organisation (Batra and Marakas, 1995; Reingruber and Gregory, 1994). The designs developed will be contingent on the resources, expertise and technology available. There may be external economic and political factors which affect which systems are implemented and how. This image of SSM in the context of ISD is summarised in Figure 1.

Recursive Soft System Methodology

Similarly, Bennetts and Wood-Harper (1997) and Lewis (1994) recognise that SSM can be seen as a metaphor for the process of data analysis. This is because the elements of the process of data analysis are covered either by the Logic Stream or by the Cultural Stream. Consequently, it is argued that any process which can be divided into elements that are dealt with by these two streams combined, can use SSM as a metaphor for its structure. It has already been noted that the process of ISD can be seen as a Human Activity System (HAS) and that many traditional developments fail precisely because they omitted to take note of organisational issues or political issues, preferring to respond only to the logical issues. This, therefore, establishes that a Social or Cultural Stream should be present in any methodology or combination of methodologies that address the whole process of ISD. It is already recognised that a Logic Stream is present. This Logic Stream, as represented by most methodologies, will concern itself with specific fragments of specific models of the systems life cycle. For example, SSADM defines its activities as covering the Requirements, Analysis, Design and Implementation phases of the Waterfall Systems Life Cycle. We are not concerned here with which methodologies might be considered, only with recognising that there are many ways of achieving the requirements of the ISD process' Logic Stream.

Checkland and Scholes (1990) develop SSM in the context of problem identification, right at the start of any systems life cycle. Further, Vidgen et al. (1993) show that SSM is an appropriate model for SQA, a monitoring and control process of ISD. Finally, Bennetts and Wood-Harper (1997) and Lewis (1994) show that SSM is an appropriate model for the process of data analysis. However, these are all fragments of the process of ISD which is itself modelled as an SSM process. Consequently, the process of ISD can be modelled as a recursive SSM process. This model is therefore called Recursive SSM.

Care is required here in interpreting the word "recursive". Two forms of recursion can be identified. The first one, found in mathematics and some programming languages, operates as a defined calculation together with a "stopping value". One common example of this form of recursion is the factorial function, where factorial (n) is defined by the calculation n * factorial (n-1) and 0 acts as the value at which the recursion stops, with factorial (0) defined as 1. We therefore call this form of recursion— mathematical recursion. The second form of recursion— schematic recursion - is structural rather than algorithmic and has no stopper. Instead, it is recognised that within a given model, parts of that model, which model specific sub-structures, have the same overall structure in relation to that sub-structure as the overall model has to the overall structure. Another example of this form of recursion may be found in Beer's concept of a Viable System (Beer, 1985). Recursive SSM has schematic recursion.

A Framework for SPI

This paper started with the difficulties of developing quality software. It was shown that a systems approach was required within ISD. Later it was shown that this supported SSM. However, by treating ISD as a HAS, it was shown that this can be modelled by a form of SSM (Recursive SSM).

A similar argument is developed by Curtis (1992), when he recognises that people had far more impact on the success of a software project than the tools used. He points out that nothing will be gained from using software tools if the project is already out of control. He uses this argument to support the use of the Capability Maturity Model (CMM). The critical issue is that organisations take the opportunity to learn from their mistakes. It is precisely this opportunity which is embedded in SSM. Further, the use of CMM is predicated on the use of TQM which not all organisations desire or can manage. Using SSM in the context suggested provides such organisations with a possible way forward.

As before, we can treat SPI as a HAS embedded in ISD. Cycles around the various phases of the methodology are repeated as required. In this case, the logic-based analysis can be seen to involve the stages:

• Identify and rank the business objectives for ISD;
• Recognise how these might be achieved more clearly;
• Develop a revised model of the software process in the organisation;
• Recognise the management implications of this model.

These stages are indicative only. Other ways of fragmenting the overall process are possible. Note that there is an implication, within this logic stream of analysis, of quantitative assessment of how well the identified goals have been achieved. Qualitative evaluation, covering issues reflecting the management and motivation of all members of the organisation, will take place within the social analysis stream on an on-going basis. The process improvement programme will, of course, be subject to the resources allocated and the determination of the participants. This image of SSM in the context of SPI is summarised in Figure 2.

Summary

The Soft Systems Methodology was specifically designed to assist in the resolution of ill-structured problems. It was also designed as an interpretative approach, allowing insights to be gained about this form of problem situation. The early sections of this chapter clearly show that ISD is not well structured. If it was it would be very much easier to control. Further, it was shown that politics and human factor issues are critical. Approaches based purely on the science paradigm have difficulty coping with these issues. SSM, however, is formulated specifically to include these issues. It does not force participants to dance a particular ritual, but it does ensure that the need for a dance of some kind is recognised. Consequently, this methodology is offered as a means of managing both ISD and SPI.

References

Batra, D. and Marakas, G.M. (1995). Conceptual data modelling in theory and practice; *Eur. J. Info. Sys.;* Vol. 4, p. 185-193.

Beer, S.; 1985; *Diagnosing the System for Organisations*; John Wiley & Sons.

Bell, Simon and Wood-Harper, Trevor (1992). *Rapid Information Systems Development: A non-specialist's guide to analysis and design in an imperfect world;* McGraw-Hill Book Company, Maidenhead.

Bennetts P.D.C. and Wood-Harper, A.T. (1997). Soft Systems Methodology: A Metaphor for the Process of Data Analysis; In Proceedings - UKSS97 (forthcoming).

Bignell, Victor and Fortune, Joyce (1984). *Understanding systems failures;* Manchester University Press, Manchester.

Blackburn, Thomas R.(1973) Sensuous-Intellectual Complementarity in Science; In Ornstein, Robert E., *The Nature of Human Consciousness - A Book of Readings;* Chapter 4, p. 27-40; Reprinted from *Science;* 1971; Vol. 172, p. 1003-1007.

Bostrom, Robert P. and Heinen, J. Stephen (1977). MIS Problems and Failures: A Socio-Technical Perspective - Part 1: The Causes; *MIS Quarterly;* September, p. 17-32.

Bronowski, Jacob (1973). *The Ascent of Man;* London, BBC Publications.

Canan, James W. (1986). The Software Crisis; *(US) Air Force Magazine;* Vol. 69, May, p. 46-52.

Checkland, P.B.(1981). *Systems Thinking, Systems Practice;* Chichester, John Wiley & Sons.

Checkland, P. and Scholes, J. (1990). *Soft Systems Methodology in Action;* Chichester, Wiley.

Curtis, Bill (1992). The Case for Process; In Kendall, Kenneth E, DeGross, Janice I. and Lyytinen, Kylle (eds.); *The Impact of Computer Supported Technologies on Systems Development* (Proceedings of the IFIP WG 8.2 Working Conference Minneapolis, Minnesota, USA, 14-17 June, 1992) (ISBN 0 444 89649 X) p. 333-343.

Dijkstra, Edsger W. (1976). *A Discipline of Programming;* Prentice-Hall, Inc., Englewood Cliffs, N.J.

Earl, Michael J. and Hopwood, Anthony G. (1980). From Management Information to Information Management; In Lucas, Henry C. Jr., Land, Frank F., Lincoln, Timothy J. and Supper, Konrad eds.; *The Information Systems Environment,* Proceedings of the IFIP TC 8.2 Working Conference on The Information systems Environment, Bonn, West Germany, 11-13 June 1979; Amsterdam, North-Holland Publishing Company; p. 3-13.

Floyd, Christiane (1992). Human Questions in Computer Science; In Floyd, Christiane, Züllighoven, Heinz, Budde, Reinhard and Keil-Slawik, Reinhard (eds.); *Software Development and Reality Construction* (Based on Conference "Software Development and Reality Construction", held at Schloß Eringerfeld, Germany, September 25-30, 1988); Berlin, Springer-Verlag; p. 15-27.

Gibbs, W. Wayt (1994). Software's Chronic Crisis; *Scientific American;* September, p. 72-81.

Griffyth, Jacqui (1995). Human factors in safety-critical software development - one perspective on the PRICES project; *Safety Critical Systems Newsletter;* Vol. 4, No. 3, p. 6-8.

Hesse, Mary (1976). Models versus paradigms in the natural sciences; In Collins, Lyndhurst (ed.); *The Use of Models in the Social Sciences;* Tavistock Publications.; p. 1-15.

Hirschheim, Rudy and Klein, Heinz K. (1989).Four Paradigms of Information

Systems Development; *Communications of the ACM*; Vol. 32, No. 10(Oct), p. 1199-1216.

Hitchman, S. and Bennetts, P.D.C. (1994). 'The Strategic Use of Data Modelling and Soft Systems Thinking' in *Proceedings of Information System Methodologies 1994* (Lissoni, C., Richardson, T., Miles, R., Wood-Harper, T. and Jayaratna, N. eds.), p.331 - 336.

Hitchman, S. and Bennetts, P.D.C. (1995).'Using Quality Issues in Inquiring Systems to Improve the Understanding and Use of Data Models', in *Proceedings of Information System Methodologies 1995* (Merali, Y., Probert S., Miles, R. and Jayaratna, N., eds.), p. 293 - 300.

Hoare, C.A.R. (1982). *Programming is an Engineering Profession;* Technical Monograph PRG-27; May 1982; Oxford University Computing Laboratory, Programming Research Group.

Keen, Peter G.W. (1981). Information Systems and Organizational Change; *Communications of the ACM;* Vol. 24, No. 1, January, p. 24-33.

Kling, Rob and Iacono, Suzanne (1984). The Control of Information Systems Developments After Implementation; *Communications of the ACM;* Vol. 27, No. 12, December, p. 1218-1226.

Ledington, Paul and Heales, Jon (1993). The Social Context of Information Systems Development: An Appreciative Field Perspective; In Avison, D., Kendall, J. E., and DeGroes, J. I. (eds.); *Human, Organizational and Social Dimensions of Information Systems Development;* Elsevier Science Publications B. V.; p. 455-473.

Lewis, Paul J. (1994). *Information-Systems Development*; Pitman Publishing, London.

Little, S.E. (1993). The Organizational Context of Systems Development; In Avison, D., Kendall, J. E., and DeGroes, J. I. (eds.); *Human, Organizational and Social Dimensions of Information Systems Development;* Elsevier Science Publications B. V.; p. 439-454.

Lucas, Henry C.Jr.(1975). *Why Information Systems Fail;* New York, Columbia University Press.

Lyytinen, Kalle and Hirschheim, Rudy (1987). Information systems failures - a survey and classification of the empirical literature; *Oxford Surveys in Information Technology;* Vol. 4, p. 257-309.

Markus, M. Lynne (1983). Power, Politics and MIS Implementation; *Communications of the ACM;* Vol. 26, No. 6, p. 430-444.

Mitroff, Ian I. and Linstone, Harold A. (1993). *The Unbounded Mind - Breaking the Chain of Traditional Business Thinking*; New York, Oxford University Press.

Naur, Peter, Randell, Brian and Buxton, J.N., eds. (1976). *Software Engineering - Concepts and Techniques;* Petrocelli / Charter, New York.

Newman, David (1995). Identifying the safety benefits associated with software; *Safety Critical Systems Newsletter;* Vol. 4, No. 3, May, p. 4-6.

Newman, Michael and Rosenberg, David (1985). Systems Analysts and the Politics of Organizational Control; *OMEGA, Int. J. of Mgmt. Sci.*; Vol. 13, No. 5, p. 393-406.

Pirsig, Robert M. (1984). *Zen and the Art of Motorcycle Maintenance;* William Morrow & Co., New York.

Pressman, Roger S. (1987). *Software Engineering - A Practitioner's Approach* (2nd edn.); McGraw-Hill.

Price, Stan (1995). Dijkstra or Mills and Boon?; *Safety Critical Systems Newsletter;* Vol. 4, No. 3, p. 1-2.

Prince, E.Ted (1993). Human Factors in Quality Assurance; *Information Systems Management*; Summer, p. 78-80.

Reingruber and Gregory (1994). *The Data Modeling Handbook;* John Wiley and Sons, Inc., New York.

Rogers, Jennie (1995). Safety needs communication; *Safety Critical Systems Newsletter;* Vol. 4, No. 3, p. 14.

Symons, Veronica (1990). Evaluation of information systems: IS development in the Processing Company; *J. of Information Technology;* Vol. 5, p. 194-204.

Vidgen, Richard, Wood-Harper, Trevor and Wood, Robert (1993). A Soft Systems Approach to Information Systems Quality; *Scandinavian Journal of Information Systems;* Vol. 5, p. 97-112.

Chapter 3

An Analysis of Excluded IS Processes in the Capability Maturity Model and Their Potential Impact

Russell L. Purvis
University of Central Florida, USA

Jose Santiago
University of Central Florida, USA

V. Sambamurthy
Florida State University, USA

Process improvement efforts are becoming pervasive within IS organizations as they attempt to meet the growing challenges of today's complex and dynamic environment. A popular framework often used in these efforts is the Capability Maturity Model (CMM) developed by the Software Engineering Institute. The model focuses specifically on software process improvement, neglecting the other functions of IS. This paper assesses which IS functions are excluded by the CMM by comparing it to a earlier, more comprehensive model, the Information Systems Management Architecture developed by IBM. The comparison of models is followed by a discussion of the potential ramifications of a model with such a narrow focus.

As an ever-larger number of businesses embrace the principles of quality management and process improvement, IS organizations are feeling growing pressure to follow suit and implement similar types of programs to improve systems development and operations services. IS organizations embarking in these programs often follow a standardized, step-by-step methodology to improve their processes.

The prevailing standardized process improvement methodology for IS organizations is Carnegie Mellon Software Engineering Institute's Software Process Maturity Framework. The original intent of the Software Process Maturity Framework was to provide a methodology for improving the software development processes and assess the software engineering capabilities of contractors (Humphrey, 1989). This framework has since undergone a number of revisions and become what is now known as the Capability Maturity Model (CMM), a model which applies the process management concepts of TQM to the software engineering processes (Paulk, 1995).

The CMM is specific to the management and development of software products and excludes the processes of the remaining IS organization. Paulk (1995) explains, "The CMM is not a silver bullet and does not address all of the issues that are important for successful projects (pg. 13)." He further explains, "Since the CMM is focused on software issues, there are a number of other issues that should be considered as part of an overall improvement program, but which are only touched on in the CMM (pg. 89)." The basic research question for this article is: what are the consequences of using an incomplete measurement tool when assessing quality improvement programs for an IS organization? More specifically:

RQ1: What IS processes outside of the management and development of software products are excluded from the CMM process improvement framework?

RQ2: What are the potential ramifications of focusing process improvement programs on systems development and not considering all IS processes?

To better understand these issues relating to the use of the CMM, this study will examine the key practices of the CMM and evaluate how they apply to the broader processes and functions operating within a typical IS operation. To identify what the "typical" IS processes and activities might be, we referred to an earlier, more comprehensive framework of IS processes: the Information Systems Management Architecture (ISMA). The ISMA was developed in the early 1980's by researchers working for IBM to identify generic business processes of an IS organization and assess the effectiveness of those processes (Van Schaik, 1985).

In the following section, we will describe the CMM and ISMA models and their original intentions. Next, we map the CMM key process areas and practices against the process definitions and descriptions of the ISMA. The chapter concludes with a discussion on the potential ramifications of using the CMM which is focused on systems development to improve quality within the IS organization.

Brief Overview of the CMM

The CMM "is a framework that describes the key elements of an effective software process (Paulk, 1995, pg. 4)." Its goal is to provide guidance

Initial Level
None

Repeatable Level

Requirements Management
To establish a common understanding between the customer and the software project of the customer's requirements to be addressed by the software project.

Software Project Planning
To establish reasonable plans for performing the software engineering and for managing the software project.

Software Project Tracking & Oversight
To establish adequate visibility into actual progress so that management can take effective actions when the software project's performance deviates significantly from the software plans.

Software Subcontract Management
To select qualified software contractors and manage them effectively.

Software Quality Assurance
To provide management with appropriate visibility into the process being used by the software project and of the products being built.

Software Configuration Management
To establish and maintain the integrity of the products of the software project throughout the project's software life cycle.

Defined Level

Organization Process Focus
To establish the organizational responsibility for software process activities that improve the organization's overall software process capability.

Organization Process Definition
To develop and maintain a usable set of software process assets that improve process performance across the projects and provide a basis for defining meaningful data for quantitative process management.

Training Program
To develop the skills and knowledge of individuals so they can perform their roles effectively and efficiently.

Integrated Software Management
To integrate the software engineering and management activities into a coherent, defined software process that is tailored from the organization's standard software process and related process assets.

Software Product Engineering
To perform consistently a well-defined engineering process that integrates all the software engineering activities to produce correct, consistent software products effectively and efficiently.

Intergroup Coordination
To establish a means for the software engineering group to participate actively with the other engineering groups so the project is better able to satisfy the customer's needs effectively and efficiently.

Table 1: Purpose of Key Process Areas Within the CMM

Peer Reviews
To remove defects from the software work products early and efficiently.

Managed Level
Quantitative Process Management
To control the process performance of the software project quantitatively.

Software Quality Management
To develop a quantitative understanding of the quality of the project's software products and achieve specific quality goals.

Optimizing Level
Defect Prevention
To identify the causes of defects and prevent them from recurring.

Technology Change Management
To identify beneficial technologies (i.e. tools, methods and processes) and transfer them into the organization in an orderly manner.

Process Change Management
To improve continually the software processes used in the organization with the intent of improving software quality, increasing productivity, and decreasing the cycle time for product development.

Table 1 (continued): Purpose of Key Process Areas Within the CMM

identifying the few key issues most critical to improving the ability of organizations to meet goals for cost, schedule, functionality, and product quality. The CMM is organized into five "maturity levels" which define the evolutionary plateaus leading to the achievement of a mature software process (Paulk, 1995). These maturity levels roughly parallel those defined by Philip Crosby (1979) in his Quality Management Maturity Grid (QMMG). The QMMG and the CMM define a mature organization as one that follows a disciplined process consistently and where the necessary infrastructure exists to support the processes. This in turn leads to process capability, which is the inherent capability of a process to produce planned results. The underlying premise of the CMM is that the quality of a software product is largely determined by the quality of the process used to develop and maintain it (Paulk, 1995).

The five software process maturity levels identified by Humphrey (1989) and incorporated into the CMM consist of the Initial, Repeatable, Defined, Managed, and Optimizing levels. During the Initial level the software process is characterized as ad hoc and chaotic. Few processes are defined and success depends on individual efforts and heroics. At the Repeatable level, basic project management processes are established to track cost, schedule, and functionality, and the necessary discipline is in place to repeat earlier successes on projects with similar applications. This discipline is further strengthened at the Defined level, when software processes are documented, standardized, and integrated into a standard software process for the organization. During the Managed level the organization begins collecting

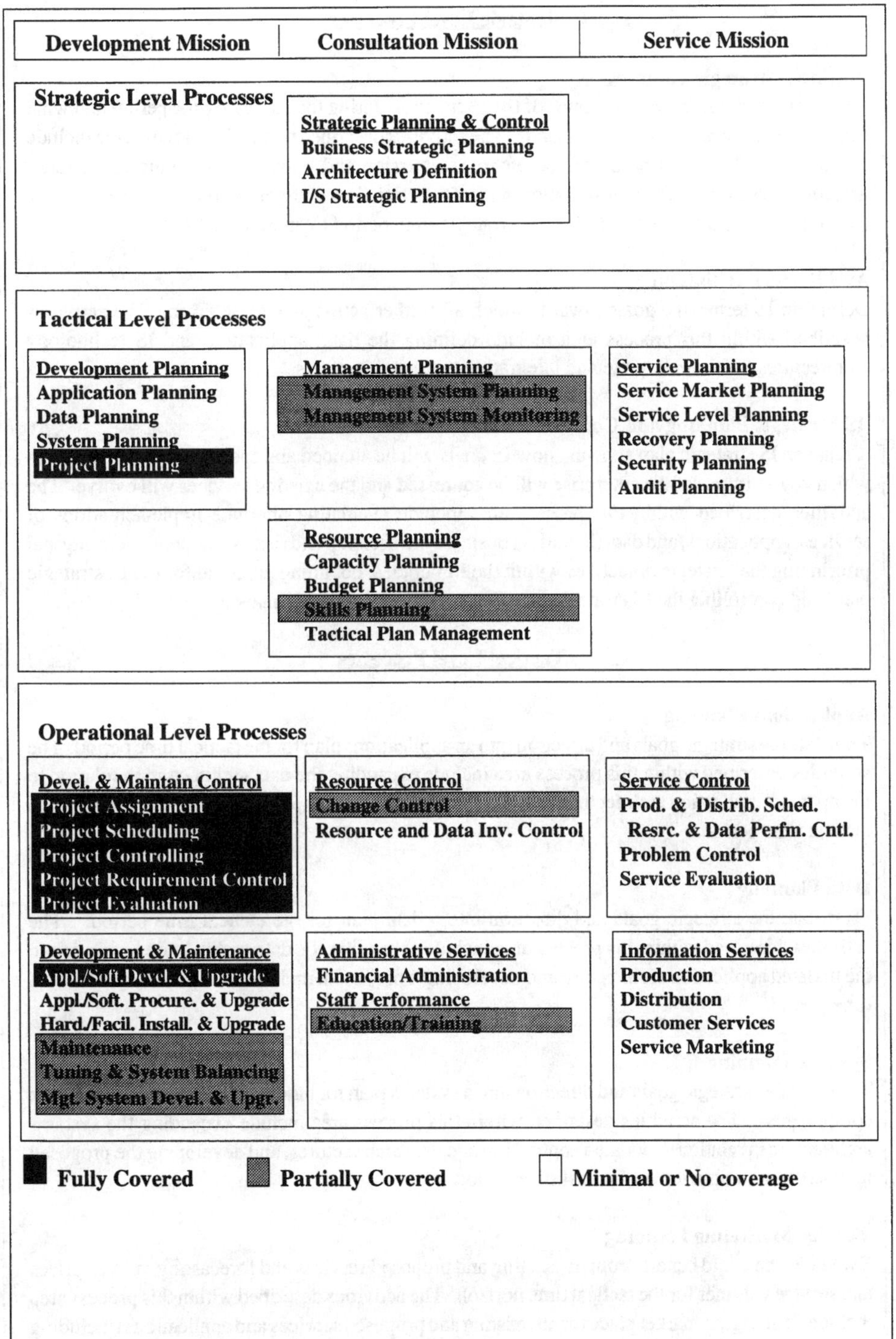

Development Mission	Consultation Mission	Service Mission

Strategic Level Processes

Strategic Planning & Control
Business Strategic Planning
Architecture Definition
I/S Strategic Planning

Tactical Level Processes

Development Planning
Application Planning
Data Planning
System Planning
Project Planning

Management Planning
Management System Planning
Management System Monitoring

Service Planning
Service Market Planning
Service Level Planning
Recovery Planning
Security Planning
Audit Planning

Resource Planning
Capacity Planning
Budget Planning
Skills Planning
Tactical Plan Management

Operational Level Processes

Devel. & Maintain Control
Project Assignment
Project Scheduling
Project Controlling
Project Requirement Control
Project Evaluation

Resource Control
Change Control
Resource and Data Inv. Control

Service Control
Prod. & Distrib. Sched.
Resrc. & Data Perfm. Cntl.
Problem Control
Service Evaluation

Development & Maintenance
Appl./Soft.Devel. & Upgrade
Appl./Soft. Procure. & Upgrade
Hard./Facil. Install. & Upgrade
Maintenance
Tuning & System Balancing
Mgt. System Devel. & Upgr.

Administrative Services
Financial Administration
Staff Performance
Education/Training

Information Services
Production
Distribution
Customer Services
Service Marketing

■ Fully Covered   ▨ Partially Covered   ☐ Minimal or No coverage

**Figure 1: Information Systems Management Architecture &
Capability Maturity Matrix Mapping**

Strategic Level Processes

Business Strategic Planning

Identify what the enterprise demands of the IS function during the strategic time period and what freedom IS has in meeting those demands. The activities described within this process area include defining the IS mission based on the enterprise mission and objectives, defining IS policies, defining business processes, information, and information flow of the enterprise, and the enterprise requirements for information during the strategic time period (Van Schaik, 1985).

Architecture Definition

Define, in IS terms, the goals towards which all further action should be taken. The activities described within this process area include defining the data, application, and IS technology architectures for the enterprise and integrating these architectures.

IS Strategic Planning and Control

Create an IS strategic plan showing how IS goals will be attained and specifying the sequence in which key activities of the enterprise will be addressed and the existing services will evolve. The activities described within this process area include evaluating alternate implementations of services, applications, and data (including business justification and risk assessment), defining and prioritizing the strategic objectives within the IS policies, obtaining approval for the IS strategic plan, and controlling the IS strategic plan against the tactical performance.

Tactical Level Processes

Applications Planning

Translate the strategic goals and direction into an applications plan for the tactical time period. The activities described within this process area include expanding the data architecture in relation to the updated application architecture, and developing a proposed updated applications plan for the tactical time period.

Data Planning

Translate the strategic goals and direction into a data plan for the tactical time period. The activities described within this process area include expanding the data architecture in relation to the updated application architecture and developing a proposed, updated data plan for the tactical time period.

Systems Planning

Translate the strategic goals and direction into a systems plan for hardware, software, and network components. The activities described within this process area include expanding the systems architecture in relation to updated application and data architectures, and developing the proposed updated system plan for the tactical time period.

Service Marketing Planning

Evaluate who could benefit from its existing and proposed services and forecasting market prices and service volumes for the tactical time horizon. The activities described within this process area include defining the market place for all existing and proposed services and applications (including

**Table 2: Areas in the ISMA That are Minimally or
Not Covered Within the CMM**

outside offerings), defining the services to be offered, forecasting service volumes by major classes of service, planning and publishing the basis for charging users, and planning the promotion of services sponsored by IS.

Service-Level Planning
Negotiate service agreements defining IS and user commitments and consolidating them into an overall tactical service plan. The activities described within this process area include negotiating service agreements (including recovery, security, and audit requirements), forecasting service volumes based on the service agreements, developing a preventive maintenance plan, reviewing agreed service agreements and defining the required consultation, help desk, and other support services, and defining a total service plan.

Recovery Planning
Collect individual requests for recovery to build an overall tactical recovery plan. The activities described within this process area include consolidating recovery requirements from all service agreements, defining business and IS recovery operating environment, identifying variances between operating environments and agreements, and developing an overall recovery plan.

Security Planning
Collect individual requests for security to build an overall tactical security plan. The activities described within this process area include consolidating security requirements of all service agreements, defining the business and IS security operating environment, identifying variances between the operating environment and agreements, and developing the overall security plan.

Audit Planning
Collect individual requests for auditability to build an overall tactical audit plan. The activities described within this process area include consolidating audit requirements of all service agreements, defining the business and IS audit environment, identifying variances between the operating environment and agreements, and developing an overall audit plan.

Capacity Planning
Define, in a capacity plan, how IS resources will cover the demand. The activities described within this process area include translating service requirements into a load forecast (for the hardware, software, network, facilities, and supplies), defining the capacity of existing and planned resources, comparing the load forecast against the planned capacity, evaluating and proposing alternate load and capacity forecasts, and documenting the capacity plan.

Budget Planning
Convert individual systems, service, project, capacity, personnel, and education plans into financial terms and identifying how funds will be obtained and allocated. The activities described within this process area include translating the service, project, capacity, personnel, education, and system plans into financial terms, reconciling sources of funds, establishing and evaluating alternative budgets, and documenting departmental budgets.

Skills Planning
Define (in the personnel and education plans) how the existing and planned skills will meet the

**Table 2 (continued): Areas in the ISMA That are Minimally or
Not Covered Within the CMM (Continued)**

demand. The activities described within this process area include defining the personnel required to support the planned services and projects, identifying existing and planned personnel, establishing and evaluating alternative personnel plans, defining an education plan, and documenting the personnel and education plans.

Tactical Plan
Management Merge individual plans, resolving any imbalances, and monitoring performance against the total plan and determining corrective actions when necessary. The activities described within this process area include balancing the service, project, capacity, personnel, education, budget, system, application, and data plans, obtaining management approval, publishing these plans, comparing actual attainment with the plan and analyzing variances, and rebalancing and republishing the plans if necessary.

Operational Level Processes
Change Control
Select, coordinate, group, and monitor all changes to the IS resources and procedures in such a way that there is either minimal impact on the IS operations or minimal risk. The activities described within this process area include recording change requests, prioritizing and grouping changes based on technical and business assessments, scheduling, deferring, or rejecting changes, monitoring the testing and installation of changes, and reporting and controlling the status of all changes.

Resource and Data Inventory Control
Build and manage inventories of all IS resources, including personnel and financial. The activities described within this process area include identifying system, application, data, personnel, supplies, and financial resources, updating the inventory status, maintaining security over all resources, administering access to all resources, and reporting and controlling the status of the inventory.

Production and Distribution Scheduling
Translate planned service agreements into schedules of work for the production and distribution functions. The activities described within this process area include planning the production and distribution service workload, developing a maintenance and measurement schedule, developing current work schedules, negotiating any deviations from the service agreements with users, publishing work, maintenance, and measurements schedules, and monitoring and modifying the schedule when necessary.

Resource and Data Performance Control
Quantify, measure, and report system performance levels to IS management. The activities described within this process area include measuring performance, analyzing trends, deviations, and thresholds, selecting predefined corrective actions based on the work and measurement schedules (when necessary), notifying problem control of any uncorrectable situations, and reporting the status of systems, data, and applications.

Problem Control
Collect and receive information on problems (including performance problems) and monitoring

Table 2 (continued) : Areas in the ISMA That are Minimally or Not Covered Within the CMM

their resolution. The activities described within this area include recognizing the problem, reporting and logging it, determining its nature, impact, and true extent, selecting predefined bypass and recovery procedures, initiating action to resolve it, and reporting and controlling the status of all problems in hand.

Service Evaluating

Collect performance status and problem impact reports, translating them into user terms, and comparing them with service agreements to identify any variances to users and management. The activities described within this process area include translating operational data (production, distribution, performance, and problem) into service-level terms, assessing user ratings of service, evaluating compliance to service agreements, identifying and reporting reasons for variances, and reporting service status and new service requests.

Hardware/Facility Integration and Upgrade

Select, install, and upgrade IS hardware, networks, and facilities. The activities described within this process area include defining detailed requirements, selecting hardware, networks, and facilities, lay out planning, defining hardware, network, and facilities recovery needs, and testing and installing new hardware.

Financial Administration

Apply service rates to IS resources to determine total costs applicable to individual users (including IS), accumulating the costs, charging the individual user organization, and matching this against the budget. The activities described within this process area include calculating charges for services, administering vendor and other contracts, executing cost accounting procedures, purchasing equipment, supplies, and services, reporting financial status, and tracking vendor performance.

Staff Performance

Track staff performance and report productivity. The activities described within this process area include collecting data on absences, accidents, attendance, and job performance, and comparing and reporting productivity.

Production

Schedule and execute jobs, transactions, and data, monitor the progress of work against the schedule and take corrective action when necessary. The activities described within this process area include receiving jobs, transactions, and input data from the distribution processes, setting up, initiating, and running jobs and transactions, making jobs, transactions, and output data available for distribution, monitoring the progress of production work against the production and distribution schedules (and taking corrective action if necessary), executing predefined or emergency production procedures for bypass, recovery, security, and/or performance, and recording and reporting information on status, incidents, actions taken and results.

Distribution

Receive, store, and ship data and information through the distribution network. The activities described within this process area include translating data into machine readable form, receiving, registering, and validating input from all sources, packaging, distributing, checking, and register-

**Table 2 (continued) : Areas in the ISMA That are Minimally
or Not Covered Within the CMM**

ing outputs, monitoring the progress of distribution work against the production and distribution schedules (and taking corrective action if necessary), executing predefined or emergency distribution procedures for bypass, recovery, security, and or performance, and reporting distribution status, incidents, actions taken, and results.

Customer Services
Provide an interface with the users to understand their expectations and help them realize those expectations. The activities described within this process area include publishing support service offerings (including contact persons and telephone numbers), providing help offerings for appropriate services, and forwarding all problems to the appropriate function.

Service Marketing
Market IS services to users and identify the need for future services. The activities described within this process area include selecting service offerings to match the client needs, marketing those services appropriately, reporting user needs for new services, initiating actions to provide services, and executing public service activities on behalf of the IS organization.

Table 2 (continued) : Areas in the ISMA That are Minimally or Not Covered Within the CMM

detailed measures of software process and product quality, and both the software process and products are quantitatively understood and controlled. Finally, at the Optimizing level continuous process improvement is enabled by the quantitative feedback from the process and from piloting innovative ideas and technologies.

Each maturity level of the CMM indicates a level of process capability and is composed of several key process areas. These key process areas, in turn, identify a cluster of related activities, referred to as key practices, that when performed collectively achieve a set of goals considered important for enhancing process capability (Paulk, 1995). The CMM assigns key process areas to each "maturity level" except the Initial level (see Table 1). At the Initial level the organization, by definition, has few consistent processes, most are ad hoc and are not repeated consistently by everyone. At the Repeatable maturity level the CMM identifies the Requirements Management, Software Project Planning, Software Project Tracking and Oversight, Software Subcontract Management, Software Quality Assurance, and Software Configuration Management key process areas. At the Defined level, it describes the Organization Process Focus, Organization Process Definition, Training Program, Integrated Software Management, Software Product Engineering, Intergroup Coordination, and Peer Reviews key process areas. During the Managed maturity level the key process areas identified are Quantitative Process Management and Software Quality Management. Finally, at the Optimizing level the CMM describes the Defect Prevention, Technology Change Management, and Process Change Management key process areas.

Brief Overview of the ISMA

The ISMA was developed from research beginning in the early 1970's on Business Systems Planning by IBM. The ISMA separates IS processes into three distinct missions: the Development Mission, the Service or Operations Mission, and the Consultation Mission (Van Schaik, 1985). Eleven IS management process groups are defined within these three missions which are further subdivided into 42 process areas. For each of these process areas the ISMA defines its function and purpose, followed by a description of the activities performed within it. In addition to identifying and describing the typical IS processes, the ISMA framework can be used to assess the effectiveness of those processes.

Depending on which IS processes have been effectively implemented, the ISMA designates the IS organization as being at one of five "Phases of Growth." The definition of these phases is based on Nolan's six "EDP Stages of Growth" model (Nolan, 1979). These ISMA phases consist of the Startup, Growth, Control, Planning, and Strategic Planning.

An IS organization is identified as being at the "Startup Phase" if its IS management system is fairly simple and information technology is used primarily to replace clerical work and save labor. IS in this phase typically has a minimal applications staff and has effectively implemented only a few processes, such as those responsible for production, distribution, maintenance and development.

At the "Growth Phase" the IS organization activities are greatly expanded, but the requirements typically exceed the time to grow. IS controls are informal and unenforceable and management is reluctant to delay projects that do not meet specifications. In general IS does not operate at a level satisfactory to users, but some activities start becoming repeatable. The activities becoming more standardized usually include requirements definition and project management.

An organization at the Control Phase has begun implementing controls to regain the stability of the IS function. Resource and change controls are implemented, as well as a number of Service Controls to monitor the ongoing delivery of services. Service agreements are negotiated with users and reporting systems are developed to quantify, measure, and report performance. Finally, Administration Services are put in place to manage the non-technical aspects of IS administration and development and maintenance controls, such as project reviews, are implemented to formalize the software processes.

At some point during the Control Phase, the IS organization shifts from a reaction driven mode to a plan driven mode. This is exemplified by its adoption of Development Planning, Budget Planning, Resource Planning, and Service Planning processes. The organization is then said to have entered the "Planning Phase", and begins using tactical plan management to track variances from these plans and initiate corrective actions if necessary.

Finally, the IS organization is said to have entered the Strategic Planning Phase when it starts showing concern with the decisions about future directions and has defined the IS mission, goals, scope, objectives, and responsibilities. At this phase the organization also begins to monitor the external environment and ties IS planning to the objectives and strategies of the business.

The ISMA framework is well-suited for the purposes of this study because of the similarities between it and the CMM. Both models, for example, have been adapted for use as assessment tools and both identify a series of business processes and key practices which the IS organization should be capable of effectively performing. The main difference is the comprehensiveness of the ISMA, which includes within its scope all of the IS processes, while the CMM is only interested in those processes directly related to the development of software.

In the next section, we map the CMM key process areas and practices to the process definitions and descriptions of the ISMA. We then discuss those processes not defined within the CMM.

Mapping of CMM Processes to the ISMA Processes

To identify those processes that are excluded from the CMM, the authors mapped the CMM processes with those identified within the ISMA. To control for the potential of bias in interpreting the processes, two of the authors independently mapped the CMM processes to the ISMA. There was a discrepancy within one process of 15 processes mapped to the ISMA. This process was included as being partially covered within the ISMA. The results of the mapping are given in Figure 1. There are a considerable number of processes not identified within the CMM that are recommended for an IS organization in the ISMA. These processes are defined in Table 1.

Discussion

As the number of establishments embracing the CMM framework continues to grow, it is important for managers to understand that the CMM is not a panacea that will solve all of their IS problems. Our analysis shows the CMM does not address the need for assessing and improving many very important IS processes. Because of these limitations, an organization whose software development process has reached the highest levels of maturity could potentially find itself hindered by an oversight in one of its critical operational areas not covered by the CMM. Further, focusing on the pursuit of optimizing software development for many IS organizations would not be in their best interest as software development is only a small function performed by IS. Many IS organizations spend most of their time maintaining legacy systems and purchase software instead of developing it in-house.

Functions Missing in the CMM

Processes only partially covered or not covered at all in the CMM are described in Table 2. Below we discuss the potential ramifications of the missing processes.

Strategic Level Processes. None of the strategic level processes are defined within the CMM. This group of processes focuses on the adjustments needed over time to meet the changing conditions and requirements of the environment (Van Schaik, 1985). It is comprised of three processes: Business Strategic Planning, Architecture Definition, and IS Strategic Planning and Control.

Strategic level processes are paramount to the successful delivery of information systems within an organization. Neidermann (1991) found these strategic level processes as the top issues in information systems management. It could be argued that poor strategic level processes could have more of a detrimental impact on the timeliness, cost, and quality of systems being developed than all of the processes covered within the CMM combined.

The CMM appears to be overestimating the effect that the software development processes have on their company's operations. Improving the quality of software development, for example, was ranked 9th in importance by the survey of senior IS executives (Niederman, 1991). One could contend that improving the effectiveness of the strategic level processes could have far greater consequences for the typical enterprise than the operational level processes assessed by the CMM. For all too often, those organizations that do not strategically plan and control their IS function find that they are disjointed and out of sync with the organization's overall mission, objectives, and strategies. While other IS organizations have found that decisions made concerning the data, application, and IT technological architecture without the benefit of strategic planning hinder or completely block expansion into needed IS services.

Tactical and Operational Level Processes. As shown in Figure 1, a wide range of tactical and operational IS processes are neither defined nor assessed by the CMM. Tactical processes not covered by the CMM include application, data, and system planning, service level planning, recovery, security, capacity, and budget planning. The CMM excludes virtually all processes in the operations functions such as production and distribution, resource and data performance control, service evaluation, production, distribution, customer services and service marketing.

Many of these processes are critical to the success of an IS organization. At a minimum, IS processes such as those responsible for security, capacity planning, and recovery, should also be good targets for assessment and improvement programs, as their inadequacy could have a detrimental impact on business operations.

Thwarting of Organizational Learning

It could be argued that the CMM could potentially thwart the learning of an IS development organization. Richard Nolan (1979) theorized that organizational learning is influenced by the environment in which it takes place. He described two possible environments: "control" and "slack." In the control environment all of the financial and performance management processes are directed at ensuring that IS activities are effective and efficient. In the slack environment, sophisticated controls are for the greater part absent. Instead, incentives to promote the use of IS in an experimental manner are present (for example, systems analysts may be assigned to users without any charge to the user's budgets).

Nolan's conclusions lead to the recognition of a potential risk from implementing the CMM framework. Nolan (1979) explains that management needs to be committed to much more than just strict control and that, although allowing organizational slack in the IS areas results in more resources being committed to the effort than are strictly necessary, the surplus serves to nurture innovation and the adoption of new technologies by the business process areas. The CMM, on the other hand, strives to create an environment of total control. The danger then is that as a result of implementing the CMM practices, the software development processes could become too rigid and inflexible, and relations with business users could be stifled.

Several researchers have agreed with Nolan on the issue of slack versus control. For example, in a comprehensive analysis of large IS shops, Boynton, et. al. (1994), found that to promote IT use an organization should favor an effective state of managerial information technology knowledge rather than an effective set of IS management processes. Rather than implementing programs, such as the CMM, which are aimed at increasing the structure and effectiveness of the IS management processes, the organization should instead concentrate on expanding managerial IT knowledge. The study also infers that an organic (flexible) IS management climate is more desirable than a mechanistic one which would probably result in a more mechanistic climate.

Improving the effectiveness of the IS processes, however, can often be beneficial to the enterprise. Boynton et al. (1994), for example, also observed that the successful application of IT in facilitating the introduction of new products or services and improving operational work processes is linked with the effective management of processes associated with the planning for, acquisition of, and implementation of technology for the organization. Unfortunately, as our analysis has shown, improving the effectiveness of these processes is not addressed by the CMM.

Conclusion

Although the CMM is characterized as a process improvement program, it should only operate as part of the IS organization's broader improvement efforts. And then only after the enterprise has evaluated and prioritized all of its needs and adequate resources have been assigned to improve the effectiveness of the most consequential IS operations.

A possible improvement to the CMM would be to expand the model to apply to all of the IS process areas as defined by the ISMA. This model could, in theory, take advantage of the strengths of the CMM while minimizing its weaknesses. The new framework could, like the Capability Maturity Model, be based on Philip Crosby's description of the five stages of quality management maturity, but would in fact be an Information Systems Management Maturity Model.

The proposed Information Systems Management Maturity Model should include steps to identify the goals of the enterprise and the IS organization and the firm's IS needs and wants based on the external customer's needs and wants. This information should then be used to prioritize and select the IS process areas to be improved first by the program.

A few other departures from the standard CMM framework could be advised during the construction of the new model. Its assessment tool should be modified, for example, to make it more suitable for use by incremental improvement programs. CMM assessments, for example, are often made several years apart, and the results for each level are stated in an "all or nothing" basis. In other words, the CMM algorithm takes into account the scores of the next level only if nearly all of the key criteria on the current level have been satisfied. This does not provide adequate information on the organization's true strengths and weaknesses. It was partly because of this deficiency that the European Software Institute began the Bootstrap project which refined the CMM assessment method to make it more fitting for incremental improvement (Haase, et al, 1994). The assessment tool should also be simplified to allow for more frequent assessments and self-assessments, perhaps by following the approach employed at Motorola to simplify the scoring and generate more valid information (Daskalantonakis, 1994).

Managers should also be aware of the deficiencies of the CMM's model for process improvement. As expounded by Garvin (1993), for example, continuous process improvement requires a commitment to learning. He described learning organizations as those skilled at creating, acquiring, and transferring knowledge, and at modifying their behavior to reflect new knowledge and insights. Although some might argue that the CMM's measurement and assessment activities facilitate organizational learning, the wisdom it creates is primarily of an internal nature. Far more significant gains could, for example, usually be achieved by investigating the operations and practices of other enterprises.

Although Activity 2 of the Technology Change Management key process area calls for the search and incorporation of new technologies, the model is silent as to the need to monitor the competitive environment or implement bench marking programs. A bench marking program, for example, could incorporate research and intelligence gathering to allow the concern to compare its operations to those of other firms (Shrednick, 1992). This process would involve studying the way that work gets done, rather than just the results, and often leads to the adoption of improved business practices (Garvin, 1993).

In conclusion, any model is not a panacea, but a discrete element of the overall quality improvement of the IS function. It must not stifle creativity, organizational learning of skill flexibility, but be an asset by channeling IS efforts into more efficient and effective efforts.

References

Allen, B.R. (1991), Information Architecture: In Search of Efficient Flexibility, *MIS Quarterly*, 435-445.

Blanton, J.E., Watson, H.J., and Moody, J. (1992), Toward a Better Understanding of Information Technology Organization: A Comparative Case Study, *MIS Quarterly*.

Boynton, A.C., Zmud, R.W., and Jacobs, G.C. (1994), The Influence of IT Management Practice on IT Use in Large Organizations, *MIS Quarterly*, 299-318.

Chase, R.B., and Hayes, R.H. (1991), Beefing Up Operations In Service Firms, *Sloan Management Review*, Fall, 15-26.

Crosby, P.B.(1979) *Quality Is Free*, New York:Mcgraw-Hill, 1979.

Daskalantonakis, M.K. (1994), Achieving Higher SEI Levels, *IEEE Software*, July, 17-24.

Earl, M.J. (1993), Experiences in Strategic Information Systems Planning," *MIS Quarterly*, 1-24.

Garvin, D.A. (1993), Building a Learning Organization, *Harvard Business Review*, July-August, 78-91.

Haase, V., Messnarz, R., Koch, G., Kugler, H., and Decrinis, P. (1994), Bootstrap: Fine-Tuning Process Assessment, *IEEE Software*, July, 25-35.

Humphrey, W.S., (1989) *Managing The Software Process*, Reading MA:Addison-Wesley.

Kaplan, R.S., and Norton, D.P., (1992), The Balanced Scorecard - Measures That Drive Performance, *Harvard Business Review*, January-February, 71-79.

Kaplan, R.S., and Norton, D.P., (1993), Putting the Balanced Scorecard To Work," *Harvard Business Review*, September-October, 134-142.

Moynahan, T., (1990), What Chief Executives and Senior Managers Want From Their IT Departments, *MIS Quarterly*, March, 15-26.

Niederman, F., Brancheau, J.C., and Wetherbe, J.C.(1991), "Information Systems Management Issues for the 1990s, *MIS Quarterly*, 475-495.

Nolan, R.L. (1979), Managing the Crises in Data Processing, *Harvard Business Review*, March-April, 115-126.

Paulk, M.C., Weber, C.V., Curtis, B., and Chrissis, M.B. (1995), *The Capability Maturity Model: Guidelines for Improving the Software Process*, Reading, MA:Addison-Wesley.

Perry, D.E., Staudenmayer, N.A., and Votta, L.G. (1994), People, Organizations, and Process Improvement, *IEEE Software*, July, 36-45.

Shrednick, H.R., Shtt, R.J., and Weiss M. (1992), Empowerment: Key to IS World Class-Quality, *MIS Quarterly*, December, 491-505.

Van Schaik, E.A. (1985) *A Management System For The Information Business: Organizational Analysis*, Englewood Cliffs, NJ:Prentice-Hall.

Chapter 4

Linking Strategies and Operational Goals

Shirley A. Becker
Florida Institute of Technology, USA

Mitchell L. Bostelman
American Management Systems, Inc., USA

An organization is comprised of strategic and operational management systems, both of which are essential in maintaining maturity, profitability, and competitiveness. A strategic management system defines the industries and specific markets in which the organization competes. An operational management system makes explicit the goals, the processes, and the feedback mechanisms on how to attain the desired competitive position. Each of these management components plays a role in the long-term success of an organization.

What is missing is a link between the strategy formulation and the implementation of an operational management system. This link would tie together the strategic and operational systems so that an organization would have a support mechanism for achieving a higher-level of maturity as defined in the Capability Maturity Model (CMM) (Paulk et al., 1995). A higher level of maturity is achieved when an organization is focused on a common vision supported by operational goals, as well as metrics that would provide feedback on the organization's strengths and weaknesses.

Organizational techniques and strategic perspectives have been proposed for the analysis of industries, markets, and strategies (Porter, 1985; Mintzberg, 1987; Prahalad & Hamel, 1990; Hax & Majluf, 1996; and others). These approaches not only provide valuable insights but also offer techniques for effective strategic planning and management. What is also important from a process improvement perspective, however, is the enhancement of strategic planning in terms of goal setting, evaluation, and measurement techniques. The link between the strategic and operational management systems is embodied in the organization's process of goal setting, tracking, and assessment.

Process support at this high level would provide a straightforward mechanism for linking operational goals to the strategies proposed by the organization. One technique, the Goal Question Metric approach has been used successfully in industry for operational goal setting, tracking, and assessment (Basili, 1992; Caldiera & Rombach, 1996; Rombach, 1997). GQM is described in this work as a technique for linking the strategic and operational aspects of an organization.

This chapter will describe the dimensions of strategic management in order to develop a foundation upon which an organization establishes it operational goals. The chapter discusses the use of a structured goal setting approach in order to identify a comprehensive set of goals and metrics to support strategic management. Then, the chapter is concluded with future research opportunities in strategic management and operational implementation.

Strategy Dimensions

Strategy is the fundamental basis by which an organization can facilitate the management of current operations and adaptation to a changing environment. The development of a strategy establishes the opportunity for profitability while taking into account the culture, tradition, and history of the organization's approach to doing business.

Strategy is a multidimensional concept that embraces all of the critical planning and assessment activities of the organization. It should provide a sense of unity, direction, and purpose and serve as a vehicle to facilitate changes induced by the organization's environment (Porter, 1985). For example, a strategy focused on leadership in a particular market would address its competitive positioning in the industry.

Hax and Majluf (1996) have identified nine critical dimensions that contribute to a unified definition of the concept of strategy. These nine dimensions are briefly described as they provide a basis for developing a strategic plan and will play an important role in establishing a foundation for operational goal setting.

1. Strategy reveals the organization's purpose in its long-term goals. This view identifies a strategy as a foundation upon which long-term organizational goals are developed. The organization's goals may be considered *operational extractions* from the strategies that have been formulated. The strategy becomes the basis for action programs to develop projects and products in order to enter new markets, maintain or improve existing marketshare, and satisfy stakeholders. It provides a basis for long-term resource utilization to promote the development of a skill-base and expertise necessary for continued growth.

Once defined, these goals are considered permanent and not modifiable unless an organization's external or internal conditions call for a re-examination. Goals that are constantly changing have a trickle-down effect in the organization. Some of these effects include wasted or underutilized resources, low-quality, poor performance, and missing or unnecessary functionality, as well as others. Through the good use of a re-examination process, the negative impacts of constantly changing goals (e.g., customers changing suppliers, employees leaving the organization, and stakeholders selling stock) will be reduced.

2. Strategy drives the products or services that are (or intend to be) developed by the organization. One of the key components of strategic management is the definition of the organization's competitive domain. Strategy formulation in terms of product/service development is necessary for an organization to address issues of growth, diversification, and divestment.

In order to formulate a strategic plan, it is important to perform an evaluation of the organization's business segments in order to identify target markets, opportunities, and threats, among others. This requires an organization to review lower level business units in order to answer important questions such as: *"What business are we in?"*, *"What business are we in but we should not be in?"*, and *"What businesses are we not in but should be?"* There is a wealth of information that can be gathered from past experiences to support this strategic planning activity.

Business segmentation is the key for business analysis, strategic positioning, resources allocation, and portfolio management. Segmentation consists of selecting a business unit, identifying the customers served by the unit, and determining its competition. In the past, end products typically have been the starting point for business segmentation, but this may no longer be relevant. Core-products (recipients of organizational core competencies) may be a more appropriate means for business segmentation activities. Core products would support economies of scale, promote reusability, and provide for effective resource utilization.

3. Strategy attempts to achieve a long-term, sustainable advantage within each business unit by responding to the opportunities and threats within the organization's environment. An important aspect of strategy is the development of a long-term, sustainable advantage over key competitors for each of its business units. Competitive advantage results from a thorough understanding of the external and internal forces that impact the organization. The organization must identify industry attractiveness, trends, and the characteristics of the major competitors in order to understand the external environment surrounding it. The organization must assess its internal environment in terms of its competitive capability. This includes an internal evaluation of resources utilization, productivity, technological advances, expertise, product quality, and process maturity, among others.

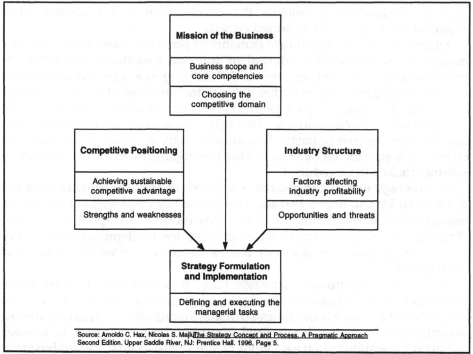

Figure 1: Framework of Business Strategy

Strategy supports a matching of the organization's external environment and its internal capabilities. A fundamental framework of business strategy has been developed to support this requirement (Hax & Majluf, 1996). The framework, as shown in Figure 1, is composed of three areas: the *business unit*, the central subject of analysis; the *internal competencies*, which define the ways in which the organization competes; and, the *industry*, which determines the environmental trends.

This framework identifies the relationships among the three areas as a synergistic force for strategy formulation and implementation. The long-term goals, the strategic action programs, and the allocation of resources should be based on the business units' goals, the trends in the industry structure, and the internal capabilities needed to achieve the desired competitive position.

4. Strategy identifies the distinct managerial tasks at the corporation, business, and functional levels. Strategy identifies three distinct yet interconnected areas of work that need to be management effectively. These areas; corporate, business, and functional, may be considered abstracted views of the organization as each level provides a more granular distinction of work necessary to support organizational goals. The corporate area of work deals with issues regarding the definition of organization's mission statement, validation of proposals from the business and functional levels, the identification and exploration of relationships among business units, and the allocation of resources. The business area of work includes activities necessary to enhance the competitive position of the individual business units. The functional area of work addresses the functional competencies in finance, administrative   structure, human resources, technology, procurement, logistics, manufacturing, distribution, marketing, sales, and service.

It is important to recognize the boundaries of these three areas in order to manage strategic work appropriately at each level and across the levels. As such, management can set specific work goals and ensure that these goals are consistent with higher and lower level ones.

5.   Strategy is a coherent, unifying, and integrative pattern of decisions. Strategy may be considered a mechanism for providing a comprehensive and integrated blueprint of the organization's long-term growth. The organization's strategy is decomposed into lower level building blocks that drive the work efforts at each level. These lower level blocks may be project or product (service) driven in terms of planning, tracking, and measurement requirements. It is important to ensure consistency of lower level goals and implementation plans with the strategy and organizational goals so that the organization as a whole will be working together towards a common vision.

It is important that decision-making throughout the organization is driven by the strategies and goals that have been put in place.   Each decision relating to a particular level in an organization should have measurement capability in order to assess its short and long-term impact on the organization at local and global levels.

6.   Strategy defines the nature of the economic and non-economic contributions made to the stakeholders. An organization's strategy must focus on maximizing the economic and non-tangible wealth of the stakeholders. The economic component is apparent by financial achievement and reward goals that have been set by the organization.

The intangible aspect of organizational contributions recognizes that the organization's strategy is a means of establishing a social contract relevant to its external environment. As a result, the organization's strategy is impacted by society as a whole including cultural, behavioral, and other aspects of social interchange.

7.   Strategy is an expression of the strategic intent of the organization. The ultimate objective of any strategic plan is to develop an organization of excellence and maturity. The strategic intent of an organization identifies its leadership position within a given industry and the criteria that will measure its success in achieving this goal (Hamel, 1989). Hax and Majluf (1996, p. 8) state that strategic intent encompasses an active management process that creates a sense of urgency, focuses the organization on the essence of winning, and motivates people through actions such as:

• developing a competitive focus at every level through widespread use of competitive intelligence,
• providing employees with the skills needed to work effectively, leaving room

for individual and team contribution,
- guiding resource allocation through the consistent use of intent,
- giving the organization time to digest one challenge before launching another; and,
- establishing clear milestones and review mechanisms to track progress and ensure that internal recognition and rewards reinforce desired behavior.

The central focus of strategic intent is to encourage the organization and its members to set high but achievable goals, promote learning for ongoing process improvements, develop new mechanisms for eliminating competitor's advantages, make investments in core competencies, develop core product capabilities, and develop an organizational allegiance of strategic intent.

8. Strategy is aimed at developing and nurturing the core competencies of the firm. The organization's strategy focuses on developing the core competencies of an organization. This shifts the strategic focus from lower level business units to the corporate level. By doing so, the business units will be integrated into a corporate whole based on a common strategy instead of working as autonomous units (Prahalad & Hamel, 1990). What distinguishes the performance of an organization from others is the capabilities and internal resources developed to support core competencies. This is what differentiates an organization from its competitors.

9. Strategy provides a means for investing selectively in tangible and non-tangible resources that are necessary for a competitive advantage. This resource-based view postulates that the central sources of competitive advantage are dependent on the organization's ability to develop resources and capabilities.

In particular, DeMarco points out that too often organizations do not evaluate human capital in terms of investment opportunities and losses (DeMarco, 1996). Though valuable human resources need to be viewed as capital assets, often times they are simply viewed as expenses. Strategic planning must include human capital investments in order to maintain a competitive advantage especially in this technology-driven era.

These strategic dimensions play an important role in establishing the high-level goals of an organization. Though these dimensions are broad in their scope of coverage, it is recommended that they be used as a basis for establishing completion conditions at the end of the strategic planning phase.

Strategy Planning

Strategy planning deals with organizational decision-making at the highest level. An organization's strategy will encompass decisions regarding all resources, products, projects, and personnel over time and geographic location. The decisions related to the strategy cannot be decentralized; managers who operate at lower levels do not have the proper vantage point for decision-making at the organizational level.

King (1978) refers to the set of decisions that are made at this level as the organizational strategy set. The organizational strategy set consists of the organization's mission statement, strategy, and other strategic organizational attributes (information supportive of a particular strategy). The mission statement of the organization is typically the driving force behind decision-making at this level. The strategy set provides the foundation for decision-making at lower levels (business and functional strategy components).

A firm's strategic plan is a collection of strategies that must be unified into a cohesive, organization-wide plan of action. The pieces of the organization's strategy should fit together like pieces of a puzzle with consistency among corporate, business, and functional strategies. It is important to note that strategic planning is not the end; it is the beginning of a more comprehensive process of goal setting and assessment at lower levels in the organization.

Table 1 summarizes the justification for strategic planning and presents the benefits associated with it. It is apparent from this table that the strategic planning phase is critical for organizational commitment and buy-in by all participants. All stakeholders including employees, customers, investors, and society would have access to the organization's vision, which is necessary for long-term stability and growth opportunities.

It is proposed that strategic planning be enhanced by providing a structured approach to operationalizing goal setting and assessment activities. The intent is to provide a mechanism whereby a strategy is expressed as one or more organizational goals with appropriate metrics for continuous assessment. This approach would also be used to decompose organizational goals into lower level goals (business and function) in order to ensure a common focus by all participants in the organization.

The Goal Question Metrics (GQM) method is introduced as a structured approach to setting goals and identifying appropriate metrics for goal assessment (Basili, et al., 1994). Though it is beyond the scope of this chapter to demonstrate its application to granular levels of planning and assessment, we describe its use at the organizational level. A brief introduction to GQM is provided in the next section (refer to (Rombach, 1997; Caldiera & Rombach, 1996) for a comprehensive discussion of all of the components of the GQM approach).

Goal Question Metric Approach

The application of the GQM approach results in the specification of a measurement system targeting a particular set of issues and a set of rules for the interpretation of the measurement data. GQM guidelines have been established to help managers focus on a goal and then refine it into a list

Why Plan?	• To unify corporate directions. • To establish stability in an uncertain world. • To capitalize on the rapid changes in technologies. • To evaluate limitations. • To look for opportunities. • To maintain competitive advantages.
What Strategic Planning Delivers	• An assessment of business trends—How the functional mission is changing? • An assessment of corporate trends —How components of the corporation are changing? • An assessment of technological trends—What will be economically feasible for the future? • An educational device and an opportunity for personal interactions and negotiations at all levels. • A discipline for long-term thinking in the organization. • A plan that is aligned with the vision and goals of the organization. • A plan to satisfy the critical information requirements of the organization.
Benefits for the Organization	• Appropriate focus on critical areas for mission success. • Improved segmentation of the organization. • Improved resource utilization. • Improved flexibility of resource use. • Reduced redundancy of development efforts. • Established business priorities for product (service) development. • Established buy-in and commitment by all employees.
Cost of Poor Planning	• Loss of competitive edge in marketplace. • Crisis management, reactive rather than proactive to changing environment. • Loss of strategic focus resulting in haphazard decision-making. • At the mercy of outside influences (e.g., competition). • Technological advances that make current technology obsolete.

Table 1: Benefits and Risks of Strategic Planning (DOD, 1997; Porter, 1985; Hax & Majluf, 1996)

of questions. In turn, these questions suggest specific measures to be collected.

The GQM paradigm is based upon the assumption that for an organization to measure in a purposeful way, it must: (1) specify the goals for itself and its projects (products); (2) trace those goals to the data that are intended to define those goals operationally; and, (3) provide a framework for interpreting the data with respect to the stated goals (Basili, et al., 1994).

Process support is essential to the successful application of the GQM approach. The process that has been described includes methodological steps of identifying a goal, decomposing it into structured components, asking a set of questions related to goal attainment, and then identifying metrics that would answer the questions (Rombach, 1997). This process is very briefly described in this section.

Each goal is formalized in a statement that is decomposed into basic sources of information: purpose, issue, object, and viewpoint. From the specification of each goal, meaningful questions can be derived that characterize each goal in a quantifiable way. Once the questions have been developed, each question is associated with an appropriate metric.

There are some factors that need to be considered when doing this association. One important point is whether there is sufficient and high-quality data available. Secondly, objective measures are applied to more mature measurement objects and subjective measures tend to be used when dealing with informal or unstable objects.

The GQM process for a particular goal and metrics setting activity is completed by ensuring a sufficient number of metrics are in place to evaluate the object of measurement. It is also important to ensure that a sufficient number of metrics has been identified to evaluate the reliability of the GQM model that has just been developed. The GQM approach should not be considered a static process but instead will require iterations and adaptation as more information becomes available.

Table 2 illustrates the decomposition for a goal that has been identified in a real world example. In this example, the high-level goal is based on the customer (academic engineering institutions) viewpoint. The goal is supported by a set of questions would be answered by one or more metrics. A metric may be used to answer more than one question though this example does not illustrate this capability. The hierarchical decomposition of the goal, questions, and metrics provides an effective mechanism for ensuring a higher level strategy is operationalized in the products (or services) being developed.

Strategic Planning and GQM

Strategic planning is comprised of work activities including strategy formulation and goal setting. Strategy formulation is intended to encompass all of the strategic issues of the organization by integrating corporate, business, and functional perspectives. The planning tasks associated with each perspective require an analysis of the external and internal environment.

Once this analysis process has been completed, the organization initiates the goal setting activity. A strategy is expressed as one or more organizational goals and appropriate measurements. Each goal statement is rephrased in terms of its purpose, issue, object, and viewpoint statements. For example, a strategy may be refined in a GQM format based on customer, management, shareholder, society, or other viewpoints.

The nine strategy dimensions provide an opportunity to develop a template for ensuring a sufficient and necessary set of organizational goals has been identified. Each of the strategy dimensions may be expressed in terms of a purpose, object, issue, and view. This template would be used to initiate the organizational process of setting goals and identifying

Assess the supply from accredited American and Canadian academic engineering institutions.		
Goal	Purpose	To assess the supply of engineers produced from accredited American and Canadian academic engineering institutions.
	Issue	The supply of engineers from accredited U.S. and Canadian institutions for each academic year since 1950.
	Object/Process	Survey data of accredited institutions located in the U.S. and Canada.
	Viewpoint	Accredited academic engineering institutions.
Question		What is the supply of engineers from accredited academic institutions located in the U.S. and Canada since 1950?
Metric		Total number of engineers that have a terminal degree in an engineering field from an accredited institution in the U.S. and Canada categorized by academic year since 1950.
Metric		Total number of students currently enrolled (1998-99) in U.S. and Canada institutions with accredited engineering programs.
Question		What is the change in supply of engineers from accredited academic engineering institutions in the U.S. and Canada since 1950?
Metric		Percent increase (decrease) per year from 1950 to 1998
Metric		Overall trend for the previous 38 years.
Question		How many new and lost accreditations from U.S. and Canadian accredited academic engineering institutions have occurred each academic year?
Metric		Total number of new and lost accreditations by academic year.
Metric		Percentage change in accreditations by academic year.

Table 2: Example of GQM Structural Decomposition [Bostelman 1998]

appropriate metrics at lower levels in the organization. Table 3 presents a component of this generic template for strategic planning use (since the focus is from the view of the organization, the view column is not listed in the table).

A strategy statement associated with a particular dimension listed in Table 3 could be decomposed into one or more operational goals that would be expanded into a set of questions and supporting metrics. Table 4 illustrates a GQM table that contains a structured decomposition to support the second strategy dimension, *"Strategy drives the products or services that are (or intend to be) developed."*

Table 5 has identified a set of questions that would be applied to all products as they relate to the strategies of the organization. Then, Table 2 shows the GQM approach used at a lower, operational level. The GQM structural decomposition shown in Table 2 describes a specific product in order to demonstrate the decomposition process. The product that is being evaluated is the survey and its data *(assessment)*. In this case, the organization has defined a goal that operationalizes the strategy as defined in the higher-level GQM table.

This approach of linking strategic planning and goal-setting processes promotes a wealth of individual commitment and participation within the organization. At the organizational level, management has identified clearly defined goals and metrics. This information is used at the business

Dimension Goal	Purpose	Object	Issue
1 Strategy reveals the organization's mission in its long-term goals.	Reveal	Long-term goal	Organization's mission
2 Strategy drives products (services) that are developed.	Drive	Products (services)	Strategic development
3 Strategy attempts to achieve long-term advantage in each business unit by responding to threats/ opportunities.	Respond	Threats & opportunities	Long-term advantage in each business unit
4 Strategy identifies distinct managerial tasks at each organizational level.	Identify	Each organizational level	Distinct managerial tasks
5 Strategy is a coherent, unifying, & integrative pattern of decisions.	Ensure	Decisions	Coherent, unifying & integrative
6 Strategy defines nature of economic/non-economic contributions to stakeholders.	Define	Contributions to stakeholders	Nature of economic or non-economic
7 Strategy is an expression of strategic intent of organization.	Express	Organization	Strategic intent
8 Strategy is aimed at developing & nurturing core competencies.	Aim	Core Competencies	Developing & nurturing
9 Strategy provides a means for investing selectively in tangible/non-tangible resources for competitive edge.	Provide	Tangible/ non-tangible resources	Investing selectively for competitive edge

Table 3: Generic Template for Categorization of Strategic Dimension

and functional units to define goals appropriate to the level of work. This approach not only unifies the organization but provides a vehicle by which the organization would move towards achieving its common goals.

Conclusion

The strategic plan provides a basis for producing a set of corporate, business, and functional goals that are expressed in terms of the stakeholders' needs. The strategic plan and operational goals are essential components for the successful pursuit of the organization's vision. The strategic plan and its goals define the essence of why the organization exists, who it will serve, what needs it will fulfill, and under what terms it will operate.

Strategy drives products (services) that are (or intend to be) developed by the organization.		
Goal	Purpose	Drive
	Issue	Strategy-based development
	Object/Process	Products (services)
	Viewpoint	Organization
Question		Is the business that we are in recognized in the strategy statement? ("What is our business?")
Metric		List of core competencies.
Metric		Profile of competitive domain.
Question		Are we in the right business?
Metric		Profile of competitive domain.
Metric		Market trends, societal, and cultural changes.

Table 4: Illustration of GQM Structural Decomposition at the Organizational Level

Identify the success factors of the products that we currently offer.		
Goal	Purpose	Identify
	Issue	Success factors
	Object /Process	Products (services)
	Viewpoint	Organization
Question		What products are we currently offering?
Metric		Tangible products by business segment for fiscal period.
Metric		Intangible products by business segment for fiscal period.
Question		What products are we currently offering?
Metric		Consumer satisfaction survey results by product and target market.
Metric		Total and projected sales by product and target market for fiscal period.

Table 5: Illustration of GQM Structural Decomposition to an Operational Level

Without an effective strategic planning mechanism, it is difficult to focus on the identification of strategies for the organization, function, and business units. A structured approach is needed to identify goals and metrics at each operational level in the organization.

The Goal Question Metrics approach has been shown to be an effective support mechanism for establishing operational goals in an organization. Though it has been primarily used to support software development, it is illustrated in this chapter as a tool to support strategic planning.

References

Basili, V. R. (1992). Software Modeling and Measurement: The Goal Question Metric Paradigm, *Computer Science Technical Report Series*, CS-TR-2956 (UMIACS-TR-92-96), University of Maryland, College Park, MD.

Basili, V. R., Caldiera, G. & Rombach, H.D. (1994). Goal Question Metric Paradigm, *Encyclopedia of Software Engineering*, John C. Marciniak, editor, Volume 1, John Wiley & Sons, 528-532.

Bostelman, Mitchell (1998). *Integration of Strategic and Operational Management Systems into a Goal-driven Communicable Framework for Organizational Change.* Master's thesis, American University.

Caldiera, G. R. & Rombach H.D. (1996). *The Goal Question Metric Approach.* Institute for Advanced Computer Studies and the Department of Computer Science, University of Maryland (Basili, Caldiera), Universitëitt Kaiserslautern, Kaiserslautern, Germany.

U.S. Department of Defense. *Functional Process Improvement Fundamentals, Introduction to Strategic Planning.* The Electronic College of Process Innovation, <http://www.dtic.mil/c3I/ bprcd/0113c3.htm> Accessed October 1997.

DeMarco, T. (1996). Human Capital Unmasked, *The New York Times*, Sunday, April 14, p. 13.

Hamel, Gary & C.K. Prahalad (1989). Strategic Intent, *Harvard Business Review.* May-June.

Hax, Arnoldo C. & Majluf, S. N. (1996). *The Strategy Concept and Process. A Pragmatic Approach.* Second Edition. Prentice Hall, Upper Saddle River.

King, W. (1978). Strategic Planning for Management Information Systems, *MIS Quarterly*, 2(1).

Mintzberg, H. (1987). Crafting Strategy, *Harvard Business Review*, July-August.

Paulk, M. C., Weber, C.V., Curtis, B., & Chrisses, M.B. (1995). *The Capability Maturity Model: Guidelines for Improving the Software Process*, Addison-Wesley, Reading Mass.

Porter, Michael E. (1985). *Competitive Advantage. Creating and Sustaining Superior Performance.* New York, NY: The Free Press, Inc.

Prahalad, C.K. & Hamel, G. (1990). The Core Competence of the Corporation, *Harvard Business Review*, May-June.

Rombach, H. D. (1997). *GQM Process Model.* FB Informatik, Universitëit Kaiserslautern. <http://www.iese.fhg.de/ Services/Projects/Cemp/GQM-Process-Model/pm_2.html> Accessed August 1997.

Chapter 5

Software Development and Organizational Viability: An Account of the Impact of Organizational Issues Upon Software Quality

P. Kawalek
University of Manchester

D.G.Wastell
University of Manchester

This chapter seeks to understand the impact of organizational issues upon software development. It utilises the Viable System Model (VSM) which has been developed from cybernetic theory. The chapter describes the VSM and presents two case studies of its application. These case studies provide evidence of how software development can be affected by organizational issues. On the basis of this evidence it is concluded that the VSM can be used to assist the optimal organization of software development.

As software systems have become ever more ubiquitous and critical to our daily lives, it has been widely acknowledged that the successful development of software has become increasingly difficult and more urgent. As a consequence of this, the discipline of software engineering has developed several different perspectives from which issues of software development can be addressed e.g. quality standards and awards, structured methods, process maturity and formal methods. The work described in this chapter starts with a broader vantage point than many of these existing investigations. We consider organizational issues such as the identity of different operational teams, their relations with each other, the sharing of resources, the ability to alert management to crises and the effective formulation of policy objectives. These represent a wide-range of issues that affect many forms of cooperative human enterprise (e.g. managing a hospital ward, running a business).

The premise underpinning this work is that these organizational factors can have an impact upon how successfully teams are able to develop software. The organization of any particular team will depend upon what it seeks to achieve and the business environment in which it seeks to achieve it. It follows from this that not all of the variables are under the control of the development team itself. They might find themselves in a changing business environment which threatens to undermine their effectiveness. These observations suggest that it can be valuable to be able to diagnose the organizational effectiveness of a software development team and to be able to adapt the way it is organized in order to address new aims or business environments.

The theoretical foundations of our work come from cybernetics. This has been dubbed "the science of effective organization" (Beer 1985; see also Wiener 1961). Fundamentally cybernetics is concerned with structures of communication and control. Our work utilises a detailed cybernetic model known as the Viable System Model (VSM) (e.g. Beer 1979). Further details of the VSM are set out below. In this chapter two case studies of its use are described. The case studies concern two software development teams which faced changing business environments. The studies showed that the ability of the teams to develop quality software was threatened by organizational issues arising in these environments. As operational conditions changed, so the teams needed to adapt the way in which they organized their work. We conclude from the case studies that there is merit in taking an organizational perspective upon software development and that the VSM is effective as an analytical and diagnostic device.

The Viable System Model (VSM)

In a series of original and challenging books, Beer has proposed a cybernetic theory of organization (Beer, 1979; Beer, 1981; Beer, 1985). In these, he sets out a model of what he terms a *viable system*, i.e. a system (an organization of some kind) which is capable of maintaining separate existence, of surviving on its own (1979, p.113). This is the central idea in Beer's philosophy. Organizations (at whatever level) are to be seen as systems (i.e. goal directed entities made up of interacting parts, operating in an environment of some kind). The issue is: what form of internal "architecture" is required if these systems are to be viable? Flood and Jackson (1991) have emphasised that VSM studies constitute a diagnostic of organizational fitness-for-purpose (or viability). This is akin to, and possibly complementary to, a CMM assessment of process maturity (e.g. Paulk et al., 1993).

The present section will briefly describe the VSM, further details may be gleaned from the previously referenced texts of Beer as well as other academic writings (e.g. Beckford, 1998; Espejo and Harnden, 1989).

System and Meta-system

The concepts of operational system and meta-system are fundamental. All viable systems comprise these two elements: an *operational system* which performs productive work, and a *meta-system* which is the means of regulating the operational system. These concepts are recursive in that the combined structure of operational system/meta-system at one organizational level together constitute the operational system at another 'higher' level in the hierarchy (e.g. project teams organised in departments, departments nested in enterprises). At each level, though, the relationship of operational system and metasystem is invariant. Note that the use of the terms 'lower' and 'higher' does not infer a conventional, hierarchical structure of command and control. VSM proposes a distinctive view of control in organizations which emphasises the need for self-organization and localised management. Hierarchy simply denotes the referential context of a particular level of "organizational recursion," not some other notion of significance or authority.

The role of the meta-system is to manage the operational systems under its jurisdiction. This brings us to a fundamental concept in cybernetic thinking, namely the Law of Requisite Variety (Ashby, 1965). This law stipulates that the "variety" of the regulator must equal or exceed the variety of that which is being regulated (variety is defined as the number of possible states of whatever it is whose complexity we want to measure). It follows from this that organizations can be understood to be structures for handling variety. Therefore the structure of an organization seeking to survive in a particular environment must be attuned to the variety of the environment. For example, as an environment becomes more complex so the organization will require to adapt itself in order to manage this variety and to preserve its viability. This simple idea is depicted at Figure 1.

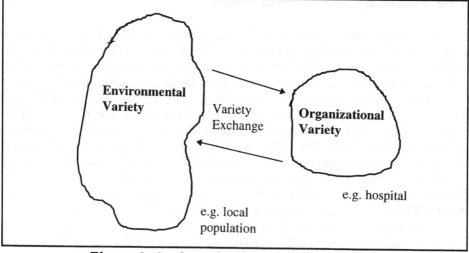

Figure 1: An Organization and its Environment

The operational system in VSM is referred to as System One. The rest of the model is made up of four further functional elements (referred to as Systems Two to Five) and the control and information loops between them. Each of these components is shown in Figure 2 and then described in more detail in the later sub-sections.

Figure 2 follows the diagrammatic conventions established by Beer. The environment is shown to the left of the diagram by the cloud like shapes. The operational teams are represented as circles. The operational management, like all management units, is represented by a square. Upright triangles denote System Two which stands outside both the System One operations and outside the metasystem. An inverted triangle represents the System Three audit. "Squiggly" vertical lines between system one elements represent informal interactions (the "grapevine"). Straight vertical lines represent formal interactions between the various elements: the two lines connecting System Three and the team leaders in System One (i.e. operational management) symbolise the regulation of System One through the resource bargain; goals/resources are propagated downwards though "variety amplifying" links whilst aggregated management information is transmitted upwards through "variety attentuating" channels.

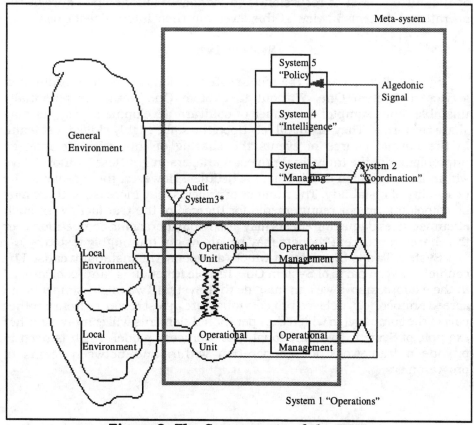

Figure 2: The Components of the VSM

System One

System one is the basic building block of VSM. It comprises a collection of operational systems, each comprising an area of operational activity (*operational unit*) and the local management structure responsible for directly managing the operational unit (*operational management*). System One constitutes the set of these systems visible *at the current level of analysis*. This latter emphasis is absolutely crucial. VSM is a recursive model of viable organization: organizations are seen as nested arrangements of systems within systems. Given that a particular level of analysis has been chosen (the "system-in-focus" in Beer's terminology), internal details of the next level down are not visible, the next level is a "black box". For example, if our system-in-focus is a software department, we are not concerned with the internal organization of the project teams that make up the "operational systems" working within the department. These are viable systems in their own right, and are properly opaque to management at this level (this follows from Ashby's law: management at the departmental level simply does not have the detailed knowledge to intervene at the next level down). The issue at the current level of recursion is to manage relationships between the operational systems in view at this level, nor their internal workings.

System Two

System Two is part of the meta-system which acts as a co-ordination service to System One. Without it, System One would be potentially unstable. For example, a number of software development projects may share resources. They might all rely upon the same highly skilled test team. In the normal course of events the sharing of this resource may be unproblematic, the individual project managers might "lose" minor delays within their specified development schedules. However, there remains the possibility of instability. The number of projects may increase or there may be coinciding urgent requirements for the use of the test facility. In such circumstances damaging effects may arise from increasing competition over the shared resource: Products may be late or not thoroughly tested.

System Two is the element which 'dampens' the instability caused by conflict between parts of System One; its sole function is "anti-oscillatory." In the example above we can imagine that System Two might simply be an agreed protocol (e.g. delayed projects must hire in test resource from another part of the company) to which the operational elements will comply. Another example of System Two functionality is a process model which is used to provide a framework for cooperation within and between teams of programmers.

System Three

The role of System Three is to steer the organization towards its current objectives. It interprets the policy decisions of higher management and maintains the operations of System One. To System Three, the internal operations of System One are opaque; perforce, the management of System One is based upon a resources-results basis.

There are three information loops in VSM between Systems One and Three. These are: legal and corporate requirements, resources and accountability. Legal and corporate requirements cover those matters that are bound into the organization through legislation (e.g. Companies Acts) or the organization's own constitution with regard to matters such as the scope of operations, safety standards and so forth. The resource and accountability loops together form what Beer calls the "resource bargain". This bargain represents a continuous process of negotiation between central and operational management about the balance of central and local control: it embodies an agreement stipulating that, in return for certain resources, System One will achieve certain goals. It is, of course, a matter for System One to "amplify" these goals into operational targets and to set up internal structures with sufficient variety to regulate performance. This is properly beyond the competence of System Three.

Having said this, there will be times when System Three will want more knowledge of how System One operations are accomplished. This special and important prerogative of System Three is known as an audit. Through this mechanism, System Three by-passes operational management in order to gain knowledge of operations directly. There are two important constraints upon the process of audit. First, it must be sporadic. Secondly, it must be used to enable more informed decision making and not to interfere in the operations and management at a lower level.

System Four

System Four is concerned with enabling the organization to learn and adapt. It is an intelligence gathering and reporting function that seeks useful information about the environment of the current system-in-focus. It searches the environment for opportunities and threats. It provides a model of the organization and the environment. This serves as a basis upon which hypotheses are explored and changes proposed to the organization as a whole (e.g. "move into object oriented development"). The significance of System Four can be highlighted by the fact that the modern business environment is often regarded as generating an unprecedented rapidity of business and technological change (a state of affairs which is especially true of software development.) In these circumstances, the ability to perceive opportunities and threats quickly, and to foster appropriate responses, is clearly critical to the well-being of the organization.

System Five

We have noted that System Three gives the organization the ability to steer itself towards current objectives and System Four allows it to generate alternative directions and objectives. System Five sets policy. The values and beliefs espoused through System Five should be shared with all other elements of the organization. An important part of this role is thus to arbitrate between System Three and System Four. Conflict can arise because of the different functional emphases on the *status quo* (System Three) and change (System Four).

Similarly, System Five should be open to the other elements of the viable system. It should be able to respond to all significant signals that pass through the "complexity filters" of Systems One, Two, Three and Four. A special kind of signal is the algedonic signal which by-passes all the normal communication channels and reaches directly from System One to System Five. In a well-functioning organization the signal will simply say that all is well, but it can also quickly alert System Five to a sudden crisis (e.g. "new product specification cannot be met.")

A Case Study of Daffodil Systems

The first case study concerns Daffodil Systems (DS)[1], a medium-sized software development department in a large chemical company. DS consists of two teams of sixteen programmers. The first team specialises in mainframe based applications whilst the second team is responsible for PC based applications. Each team has a leader who reports to a more senior manager who oversees the whole operation of DS.

Many of the applications developed by DS are safety critical. DS had achieved a reputation for producing high quality software and had been consistently scoring highly in internal and external quality appraisals. Anecdotal evidence gathered during the study also supported the team's claim to be a high quality supplier.

At the time of the study the department was undergoing fundamental organizational change. Traditionally it had been entrusted with producing the vast majority of the software developed for major projects undertaken by the company. This was enforced through corporate procedures which required project leaders in the company to obtain software through DS if at all possible. These procedures were about to be changed. In the future project leaders would be allowed to buy in software services from outside the company and, as a result, DS would have to compete with outside contractors for work. Our study sought to evaluate the likely impact of these changes on the validity of the current organizational structure of DS and, in particular, to identify any threats to viability.

The VSM of DS relied on information gained through interviews with users. The aim was to be able to describe the features of DS by reference to the VSM. A diagrammatic depiction of DS was developed at the same time.

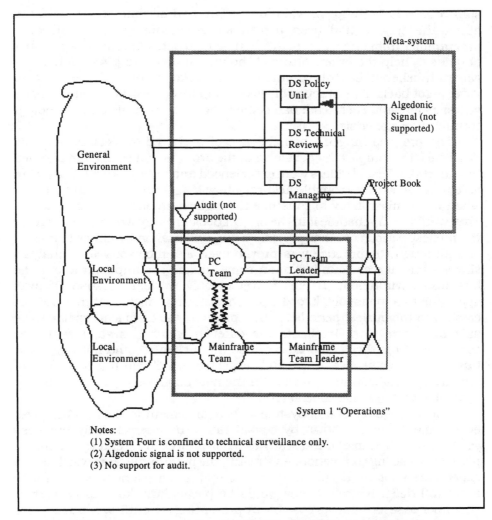

Figure 3: Level One of the VSM of Daffodil Systems Example

Part of this is given in Figure 3.

Creating the model and comparing the characteristics of DS with those set out in the VSM provided a diagnostic of the department's viability. The diagnostic highlighted several features of DS's operation which were considered to be problematic. Of these, one posed an especially pernicious threat to the viability of DS. This is presented below.

The Inadequacy of Coordination Protocols

In the new business environment, DS was likely to be handicapped by an ineffective System Two capability. There was a need for a new approach to the shared management of resources of all kinds, but most especially the staff resource. In the past, when one group had become busier than the other, the custom had been to ask for assistance from the other. A programmer from one team might then be instructed to take on a number of tasks to help the other. Although no formal measuring was done, it is generally believed that this resource sharing balanced out. What each team gave, it got back. This practice of 'give and take' had worked well for many years; as a result, each team had come to depend upon the other to help it through times of crisis.

The practice hinged upon the use of a shared 'project book'. This described (in a simple bar chart format) the projects that each team planned to undertake. Team leaders were experienced and highly skilled. They were able to judge with reasonable accuracy how long a project would take and when it was most likely to consume the highest amount of person hours. They would then schedule it in the project book in a way which tried to avoid the busiest periods of other projects being undertaken by either team.

Although the practice was proven over a number of years, analysis showed that it was founded upon some unsafe assumptions about the business environment. In short, it had only worked because DS was operating as a monopoly. In order to schedule projects so that they did not clash with the busiest periods of other projects, the team leaders had to be able to dictate to their clients the date on which a system would be completed. This they could do because these clients could not take their business anywhere else. It was fully expected by DS that this informal co-operation would continue to work in the new business regime where they competed with outside contractors.

The inadequacy of this System Two arrangement in the new business environment can be shown by considering a number of likely business scenarios. At the time of the study a major project to extend the chemical plant was nearing completion. As a result, the mainframe team was likely to experience a notable decline in the number of commissions they receive. As a natural defensive reflex they would be particularly keen to keep their customer base as broad as possible by preventing the outflow of business to the software houses with whom they now have to compete. In such circumstances they would no longer be able to dictate completion dates to their clients. The project managers would gain much greater influence and be able to insist upon earlier completion. The completion of the plant extension was likely to put the PC team in exactly the same situation. However in its case the situation was likely to be further exacerbated by the fact that, in order to replace the lost work, the team might find itself competing more and more to produce general applications (i.e. non-safety critical) on PCs. The competition with external suppliers is likely to be at its most intense in this non-safety critical sector where DS will be less able to rely upon its existing reputation for high quality. Therefore the PC team will also be unable to dictate completion dates. In such circumstances it is highly likely that the cooperation between the teams over resources will be replaced by competition as both struggle to meet coinciding urgent deadlines. They may with-hold resource from each other and may sacrifice quality procedures (e.g. peer reviews, testing) simply in the interests of getting the job done on time.

A Case Study of Violet Computing

The second case study considers Violet Computing (VC), a large operating systems development team of over fifty staff. VC have achieved a reputation for high quality, their product is well known and highly regarded in its market sector. Their efforts to engender a culture of quality amongst staff had gained recognition through a number of prestigious quality awards. However, the organization of VC had been rationalised and revised over a number of years and at the time of the study a further set of initiatives was proposed. These changes were contentious and provoked some opposition from within VC. The VSM diagnostic sought to identify whether the changes were likely to have any implications for the ability of the organization to continue to successfully develop software.

Creating the VSM models proved to be difficult. It was clear that VC were used to surviving in a state of organizational flux and there was some difficulty in clearly defining what the implications of the proposed changes would be. Nonetheless, as the study progressed several significant issues emerged. This presentation highlights the most critical of these; the meta-systemic management of technical strategy in VC.

The Management of Technical Strategy
in the Metasystem of VC

The review that VC undertook of their organizational structure was motivated by their wish to improve customer responsiveness and to control the number of product enhancements. This latter concern was especially acute. Despite the maturity of the product, even the best understood and most proven product functions continued to undergo a greater number of enhancements than had been anticipated. This was felt to endanger product quality and cost. Using the VSM we were quickly able to identify the reason why this was the case. The System One operational system is made up of a number of semi-autonomous 'function teams,' each of which is responsible for developing a defined part of the product. The teams had the power to propose enhancements to their part of the product in order to ensure that it was able to satisfy renewed technical and market expectations. It became obvious that these teams were exploiting this power to propose enhancements in order to generate work for themselves. In other words, even where there was insufficient technical or market justification, the function teams still argued that their part of the product should be enhanced. This is an example of what Beer regards as "pathological autopoiesis" (Beer, 1979; p.412). It was in the interests of the function teams to behave in this way so that they were able to secure resource from management and, ultimately, to ensure that their team continued to exist.

In order to address this problem, VC decided to reduce the power of the function teams by putting greater emphasis on a project structure of organization. This meant that in the future, resource would be allocated only in response to customer requirements which were grouped and organised into defined work packages (i.e. projects). Although the function teams would continue to exist and would have sole responsibility for the technical standards within their remit, they had lost their power to argue for product enhancements on technical criteria alone.

These changes were part of the programme of organizational change that was under way as our VSM study was carried out. Although many parts of the programme were contentious, the VSM diagnostic helped to reveal their rational basis and we were generally supportive of them. However, we

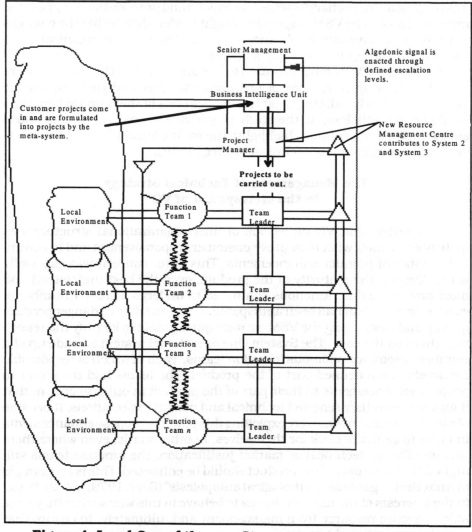

Figure 4. Level One of the new Structure Proposed by VC

were concerned about the change to a project structure of organization. One implication of this would be that there would be no metasystemic ownership of technical issues. The management at this level of concern was to be focused only on market issues. As a result it would be unable to arbitrate between conflicting technical objectives at the operational level and, in the face of sudden market opportunities or threats, it would be unable to organize any radical reworking of the product. This shortcoming was felt to threaten organizational viability.

The new project arrangement is depicted as a VSM diagram at Figure 4. The bold black arrows are used to interpret the flow of customer requirements from the business environment, through the metasystem and to the operational system.

The rational analysis facilitated by the VSM revealed the precarious nature of this new arrangement. The ownership of technical issues was entrusted to the function teams. However none of these had a holistic view across different parts of the product and all were prohibited from proposing enhancements on technical criteria alone. Clearly then, the market would become the sole source of technical enhancements and yet, if ever these enhancements were wide-ranging, there was no mechanism to provide holistic management of them. Product quality would be endangered by this. At the same time VC would have no mechanisms for promoting enhancements on technical criteria or in anticipation of market benefit. Thus, technical management would be fragmented and reactive. A retrospective analysis of VC helped us to understand why this state of affairs had come about. It was instructive because it revealed how the team had responded to changes in the business environment over a number of years and how as change was laid on change, ultimately, the integrity of the organizational structure was compromised.

Perhaps the most prominent feature of the traditional organization of VC was the role played by a 'technical commission.' This commission, which was headed by a single individual, was made up of a number of team members who were selected for their technical and personal skills. The principal goal of the technical commission was to maximise product quality and integrity. In the language of the VSM, the commission dominated System Three, Four and Five functionality and to as great a degree as possible made long-term technical values preordinant. The prime responsibility of the commission was to prepare and update the functional specification for the product. This was done through the monitoring of technical possibilities and requirements (System Four), the evaluation of their potential benefit vis-à-vis current practice (Systems Three and Four) and the arbitration of conflicts between the two (System Five). Control of the functional specification certainly afforded the technical commission considerable power in the organization, however the VSM exercise suggested that the uncompromising way in which the commission were able to wield this power actually depended upon a transitory set of environmental conditions that existed at that time.

In order to ensure that their technical standards were adhered to, the commission took a strategic role in the organization by providing the interface between the business environment (i.e. customers, salesmen etc.) and the function teams (i.e. detailed designers, programmers, testers). From this vantage point the technical commission were able to work in two interdependent ways. First, they were able to provide an environment of relative stability for the function teams by insulating them from the worst fluctuations of market demands (e.g. changing requirements). This made it easier for the function teams to work to the specification and to concentrate upon achieving high quality. Secondly, they could filter out market requirements that threatened to undermine technical strategy. This was done by putting an alternative technical case to potential customers or even rejecting some demands. This latter role was crucial. It meant that as the technical commission were able to attenuate market variety from the point of view of the function teams, so too they were able to amplify the technical variety from the point of view of market. However the VSM study suggested that their ability to provide this amplification was only possible because of some temporary features of the business environment. In particular, in the market segment occupied by VC there was little competition. For many purchasers there was actually no practicable alternative to the Violet system and many of these purchasers were relatively uninformed about technical possibilities.

Today there is more competition and customers of VC have a higher level of market and technical awareness. This means that VC can no longer rely upon being able to put an alternative technical case to potential customers or to reject some of their demands. Therefore the environmental conditions within which VC seek viability are quite different to those they encountered earlier in the project. The VSM cogently describes the interconnection of environmental, managerial and operational variety and through this reveals such environmental change was likely to precipitate management and operational change within VC.

Indeed it became apparent that over a period of time the technical commission had been reduced in size and influence. Instead, greater authority was given to the function teams through the reformulation of the resource bargain between System Three and System One. The function teams were also allowed to be more directly involved with the customers of VC and, in this way, could be more responsive to market requirements. Thus, in empowering the function teams at the expense of the technical commission, VC had solved one set of problems only to find themselves in new difficulty when the "pathological autopoiesis" of the function teams became evident.

Clearly, VC needed to devise a way of ensuring that the function teams had sufficient power whilst preventing them becoming too powerful and promoting enhancements to their part of the product at the expense of the technical integrity of the product as a whole. We were able to highlight that the crux of the problem lay in the way the resource bargain was negotiated between Systems One and Three. Although the domination of this bargain by the technical commission had been untenable for some time, so too the prospect of awarding resource solely on the basis of customer requirements was a possible threat to viability. Instead we argued for a hybrid approach which would return some ownership of technical issues to the meta-system. We proposed that resource should then be distributed to the function teams either on the basis of customer requirements (the project stream) or technical issues (the technical stream). The balance between these streams should be determined by System Three acting in concert with the demands of Systems Four and Five. We further recommended that this two stream approach should be facilitated by a resource pool (a recent VC innovation, see Figure 4) acting in a System Two capacity to attach staff to function teams as needs arose. Through this, each function team could be reduced to notional status when there was no work to be done in that area. At other times, when enhancements were needed, the function team could be reactivated and staff placed within it. This design was felt to address the need for management of technical strategy whilst avoiding the pitfall of "pathological autopoiesis." Our proposals were arrived at through the use of the diagnostic capability of the VSM and were facilitated by the use of cybernetic terminology to clearly identify issues of concern. The proposals have gained considerable support amongst senior managers in VC and a further review of the organizational structure is now planned.

Analysis: The Implications for Software Development

Both DS and VC were known as high quality, successful software development teams. They had both undertaken a range of quality initiatives and reaped reward in good reputation which, in the case of VC, led to official industry recognition. However working from an organizational perspective, we were able to raise issues which it was felt would affect the efficacy of the organization's operations and, ultimately, could endanger their ability to continue to successfully develop software. Taken together, these two case studies suggest that there is merit in the further investigation of an organizational perspective on software development. One implication is that organizational issues can arise in spite of process or technological excellence when some environmental factor is acting to frustrate the best efforts of the team. As we stated earlier, not all of the variables that affect software quality are under the control of the software development team itself. There are secondary factors (i.e. environmental issues) that can be of profound consequence. It therefore follows that the ability of software development teams to establish and maintain product quality will be in part reliant on their ability to diagnose organizational effectiveness, to take cognizance of the business environment and to correct organizational defects.

DS is a particularly acute example of this. They had hitherto operated in an environment of relative calm, with a guaranteed market. The study suggested that the proposed changes to the business environment would have wide-ranging impact upon the organization of the team. This was not generally appreciated by DS at the time of the study. Although it was anticipated that the organizational changes would cause some perturbation to their operations, it was not generally expected that there would be any implications for the System Two coordination of team resources. The study suggested that the informal give and take arrangements based around the use of a shared 'project book' would not be appropriate in the new business environment. Both teams would be forced to offer shorter completion dates to customers and so, finding themselves more rushed, would be unable to rely upon support from the other team. The effect would be to heighten the impact of the shorter time scales. The resulting pressure could mean less rigorous application of the development process, worse time management, and the hurried introduction of new practices and technology. Inevitably then, this would carry a threat to quality and, in the longer term, to the viability of the team itself.

In VC the adaptations to environmental change were less sudden than those confronted by DS but had reached a critical and contentious stage. Over a number of years these changes had undermined the traditional dominance of the technical commission and lead, via the empowerment of functional teams, to a proposed project basis for the operation. The VSM study revealed the rationality of many of the new proposals. However, it also highlighted how the shift of power from the technical commission to the function teams had pushed technical issues out of the metasystem. This was a risky state of affairs which meant that the organization would be vulnerable in a number of ways (e.g. whenever conflict arose between function teams or if ever a wide-ranging re-working of the product was needed). In order to counter this difficulty, the VSM study proposed that the need for technical overview should be balanced against the need to have flexible and adaptive development teams. This could be done by instituting a new twin-stream arrangement for the System Three to System One resource bargain, and could be facilitated by a new System Two function.

Conclusion

This paper has introduced an organizational perspective upon issues of software quality. The general theoretical basis comes from cybernetics and from the Viable System Model in particular. The VSM constitutes a complete description of the functions (i.e. the internal architecture) that an organization must possess for it to be viable (i.e. able to survive on its own in some environment). Two case studies of the use of the VSM have been presented. DS's reputation for high quality was endangered by the profound changes taking place in their business environment. The ongoing rationalisation of VC, whilst generally assisting the viability of the team, ultimately began to raise issues in respect of the technical management of the product. It follows that these studies suggest that an organizational perspective on software development might usefully complement other perspectives (e.g. process, metrics, technology) in addressing the difficulties of producing high quality software systems. This organizational perspective allows researchers to consider how some generic human concerns (e.g. how teams are organized, how communication is facilitated) are manifest in the challenging endeavour of software development. The DS and VC studies also provide validation of the usefulness of the VSM which has proved valuable as a diagnostic device. It is proposed that the investigation can be developed by using the VSM to undertake further studies and especially those where a longitudinal perspective can be cultivated.

Endnote
[1] Daffodil Systems and Violet Computing are pseudonyms.

References.

Ashby, W.R. (1965). *Introduction to Cybernetics*, Chapman and Hall, London.

Beckford, J. (1998. *Quality: A Critical Introduction*, Routledge, Andover.

Beer, S. (1979). *Heart of Enterprise*, John Wiley & Sons, Chichester.

Beer, S. (1981). *Brain of the Firm*, Second Edition, John Wiley & Sons, Chichester.

Beer, S., (1985), *Diagnosing the System for Organisations*, John Wiley & Sons, Chichester.

Espejo, R., Harnden, R. (1989) *The Viable System Model, Interpretations and Applications of Stafford Beer's VSM*, John Wiley & Sons, Chichester.

Flood, R.L., Jackson, M.C. (1991) *Creative Problem Solving, Total Systems Intervention*, John Wiley & Sons, Chichester.

Paulk, M., Curtis, W., Chrissis, M., Weber, C. (1993) *Capability Maturity Model for Software, Version 1.1.*, *Technical Report* CMU/SEI-93-TR-24, DTIC ADA263404, Software Engineering Institute, Carnegie Mellon University, Pittsburgh, USA.

Wiener, N. (1961) *Cybernetics*, Second Edition, MIT Books and John Wiley, London.

Chapter 6

Using the Software CMM with Small Projects and Small Organizations

Mark C. Paulk
Software Engineering Institute, USA

The Software Engineering Institute (SEI) is a federally funded research and development center established in 1984 by the U.S. Department of Defense with a broad charter to address the transition of software engineering technology—the actual adoption of improved software engineering practices. The SEI's existence is, in a sense, the result of the "software crisis" —software projects that are chronically late, over budget, with less functionality than desired, and of dubious quality. (Gibbs, 1994). To be blunt, much of the crisis is self-inflicted, as when a Chief Information Officer says, "I'd rather have it wrong than have it late. We can always fix it later." The emphasis in many organizations on achieving cost and schedule goals, frequently at the cost of quality, once again teaches a lesson supposedly learned by American industry over twenty years ago and now enshrined in Total Quality Management (TQM).

To quote DeMarco (1995), this situation is the not-surprising result of a combination of factors:

- "People complain to us because they know we work harder when they complain."
- "The great majority [report] that their software estimates are dismal... but they weren't on the whole dissatisfied with the estimating process."
- "The right schedule is one that is utterly impossible, just not obviously impossible."

Level	Focus	Key Process Areas
5 Optimizing	*Continual process improvement*	Defect Prevention Technology Change Management Process Change Management
4 Managed	*Product and process quality*	Quantitative Process Management Software Quality Management
3 Defined	*Engineering processes and organizational support*	Organization Process Focus Organization Process Definition Training Program Integrated Software Management Software Product Engineering Intergroup Coordination Peer Reviews
2 Repeatable	*Project management processes*	Requirements Management Software Project Planning Software Project Tracking & Oversight Software Subcontract Management Software Quality Assurance Software Configuration Management
1 Initial	*Competent people and heroics*	

Figure 1. An overview of the Software CMM.

DeMarco goes on to observe that our industry is over-goaded, and the only real (perceived) option is to pay for speed by reducing quality.

The lesson of TQM is that focusing on quality leads to decreases in cycle time, increases in productivity, greater customer satisfaction, and business success. The challenge, of course, is defining what "focusing on quality" really means and then systematically addressing the quality issues. Perhaps the SEI's most successful product is the Capability Maturity Model for Software (CMM), a roadmap for software process improvement that has had a major influence on the software community around the world (Paulk, 1995). The Software CMM defines a five-level framework for how an organization matures its software process. These levels describe an evolutionary path from ad hoc, chaotic processes to mature, disciplined software processes. The five levels, and the 18 key process areas that describe them in detail, are summarized in Figure 1. The five maturity levels prescribe priorities for successful process improvement, whose validity has been documented in many case studies and surveys (Herbsleb, 1997; Lawlis, 1995; Clark, 1997).

Although the focus of the current release of the Software CMM, Version 1.1, is on large organizations and large projects contracting with the government, the CMM is written in a hierarchical form that runs from "universally true" abstractions for software engineering and project management to detailed guidance and examples. The key process areas in the CMM are satisfied by achieving goals, which are described by key practices, subpractices, and examples. The rating components of the CMM are maturity levels, key process areas, and goals. The other components are informative and provide guidance on how to interpret the model. There are 52 goals and 316 key practices for the 18 key process areas. Although the "requirements" for the CMM can be summarized in the 52 sentences that are the goals, the supporting material comprises nearly 500 pages of information. The practices and examples describe what good engineering and management practices are, but they are not prescriptive on how to implement the processes.

The CMM can be a useful tool to guide process improvement because it has historically been a common-sense application of Total Quality Management (TQM) concepts to software that was developed with broad review by the software community. Its five levels are simplistic, but when intelligently used they provide a lever for moving people such as the DOD program manager who bluntly stated, "The bottom line is schedule. My promotions and raises are based on meeting schedule first and foremost."

While the Software CMM has been very influential around the world in inspiring and guiding software process improvement, it has also been misused and abused by some and not used effectively by others. The guidance provided by CMM v1.1 tends to be oriented towards large projects and large organizations. Small organizations find this problematic, although the fundamental concepts are, we believe, useful to any size organization in any application domain and for any business context.

Are meeting schedules, budgets, and requirements important to small projects? To small organizations? It is arguable that in some environments, such as the commercial shrinkwrap segment, cost is comparatively trivial when compared to the market share available to the first "good enough" product to ship. If the employees of an organization are satisfied with the status quo, there is little that the CMM can provide that will lead to true change; change occurs only when there is sufficient dissatisfaction with the status quo that managers and staff are willing to do things differently. This is as true for small organizations as large.

The CMM provides good advice on desirable management and engineering practices, with an emphasis on management, communication, and coordination of the human-centric, design-intensive processes that characterize software development and maintenance. It should be considered a guidebook rather than a dictate, however, and the CMM user must apply professional judgment based on knowledge and experience in software engineering and management, plus the application domains and business environment of the organization. Because the CMM is focused on software, there are important aspects of TQM that are not directly addressed in the model, such as people issues and the broader perspective of systems engineering, which may also be crucial to the business. The CMM is a tool that should be used in the context of a systematic approach to software

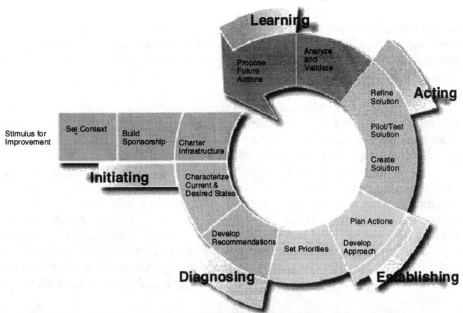

Figure 2. SEI's IDEAL approach to process improvement

process improvement, such as the SEI's IDEAL model, illustrated in Figure 2 (McFeeley, 1996).

Effective software process improvement occurs in a systematic fashion. The SEI's IDEAL model depicts the activities of an improvement program in five phases:

I   Initiating (the improvement program)
D   Diagnosing (the current state of practice)
E   Establishing (the plans for the improvement program)
A   Acting (on the plans and recommended improvements)
L   Learning (the lessons learned and the business results of the improvement effort)

The *Initiating* phase establishes the business reasons for undertaking a software process improvement effort. It identifies high-level concerns in the organization that can be the stimulus for addressing various aspects of quality improvement. Communication of these concerns and business perspectives is needed during the Initiating phase in order to gain visible executive buy-in and sponsorship at this very early part of the improvement effort. This is also where the tie-in to any existing TQM programs should be identified. Software process improvement efforts should be aligned with quality improvement initiatives since the goals are the same, even if the scopes initially differ.

The *Diagnosing* phase is used to baseline, through an assessment, the organization's software process maturity. This baseline will build a common understanding of the current processes of the organization, especially the strengths and weaknesses of those current processes. It will also help identify priorities for improving your software processes. This diagnosis is based on the SW-CMM (or one of the other CMMs).

The *Establishing* phase finalizes the strategy and supporting plans for the software process improvement program. It sets the direction and guidance for the next three to five years, including strategic and tactical plans for software process improvement.

The *Acting* phase takes action to effect changes in organizational systems that result in improvements in these systems. These improvements are made in an orderly manner and in ways that will cause them to be sustained over time. Techniques used to support and institutionalize change include defining software processes and measurements, pilot testing, and installing new processes and measurements throughout the organization. The SW-CMM provides guidance for the improvement actions in its informative components: the key practices and their subpractices and examples.

The *Learning* phase completes the process improvement cycle. Lessons learned from the pilot projects and improvement efforts are documented and analyzed in order to improve the process improvement program for the future. The business needs that were determined at the beginning of the cycle are revisited to see if they have been met. Sponsorship for the program is revisited and renewed for the next software process improvement cycle.

An opening question for software process improvement discussions should always be: Why is the organization interested in using the Software CMM? If the desire is to improve process, with a direct tie to business objectives and a willingness to invest in improvement, then the CMM is a useful and powerful tool. If the CMM is simply the flavor of the month, then you have a prescription for disaster. If the driver is customer concerns, ideally the concerns will lead to collaborative improvement between customer and supplier. Sometimes the supplier's concern centers on software capability evaluations (SCEs), such as are performed by government acquisition agencies in source selection and contract monitoring. DOD policies on the criteria for performing SCEs would exclude most small organizations and small projects (Barbour, 1996), but there are circumstances under which they may occur.

Many of the abuses of the Software CMM spring out of a fear of what "others" may do. If an organization applies common sense to the guidance in the CMM as guidance rather than requirements, then many of the interpretation problems of the model vanish. There are cases, however, where ignorance of good engineering and management practices is the problem. This is particularly problematic for good technical people who have been promoted into management positions, but who have little management experience or training. This contributes to the concerns identified by a DOD task force (DOD, 1987):

- "Few fields have so large a gap between best current practice and average current practice."
- "The big problem is not technical... today's major problems with military software development are not technical problems, but management problems."

Small Organizations and Small Projects

The focus of this chapter is on using the Software CMM correctly and effectively for small organizations because I am frequently asked, "Can the Software CMM be used for small projects (or small organizations)?" Yet the definition of "small" is challengingly ambiguous, as illustrated in Table 1. At one time there was an effort to develop a tailored CMM for small projects and organizations, but the conclusion of a 1995 CMM tailoring workshop was that we could not even agree on what "small" really meant! The result was a report on how to tailor the CMM rather than a tailored CMM for small organizations (Ginsberg, 1995). In a 1998 SEPG conference panel on the CMM and small projects (Hadden, 1998a), small was defined as "3-4 months in duration with 5 or fewer staff." Brodman and Johnson define a small organization as fewer than 50 software developers and a small project as fewer than 20 developers (Johnson, 1998).

Note that small to tiny projects are in the range being addressed by Humphrey in his Team Software Process[SM] (TSP) work, and the individual effort is in the range of the Personal Software Process[SM] (PSP) (Humphrey, 1995). TSP and PSP illustrate how CMM concepts are being applied to small projects. The "ridiculous" variant represents an interpretational problem. On the two occasions this variant has been discussed, the problem was the definition of "project." In both cases it was a maintenance environment, and the organization's "projects" would have been described as tasks in the CMM; the more accurate interpretation for a CMM "project" was a baseline upgrade or maintenance release... but the terminology clash was confusing.

One of the first challenges for small organizations in using the CMM is that their primary business objective is to survive! Even after deciding the status quo is unsatisfactory and process improvement will help, finding the resources and assigning responsibility for process improvement, and then following through by defining and deploying processes is a difficult business

Variant of "Small"	Number of People	Amount of Time
Small	3-5	6 months
Very small	2-3	4 months
Tiny	1-2	2 months
Individual	1	1 week
Ridiculous!	1	1 hour

Table 1. Defining a "Small" Project

decision. The small organization tends to believe
- we are all competent - people were hired to do the job, and we can't afford training in terms of either time or money
- we all communicate with one another - "osmosis" works because we're so "close"
- we are all heroes - we do whatever needs to be done, the rules don't apply to us (they just get in the way of getting the job done), we live with short cycle times and high stress.

Yet small organizations, just like large ones, will have problems with undocumented requirements, the mistakes of inexperienced managers, resource allocation, training, peer reviews, and documenting the product. Despite these challenges, small organizations can be extraordinarily innovative and productive. Although there are massive problems that may require large numbers of people to solve, in general small teams are more productive than large teams—they jell quicker and there are far fewer communication problems. The question remains, however, is process discipline needed for small teams? To answer this CMM mantra, we need to consider what discipline involves—and that leads to the heart of this chapter's CMM interpretation discussion.

One last precursor, however. When assessing "small" organizations, it is advisable to use a streamlined assessment process; the formality of a two-week CMM-based appraisal for internal process improvement (CBA IPI) is probably excessive (Strigel, 1995, Paquin, 1998, Williams, 1998). The emphasis should be on efficiently identifying important problems, even if some are missed due to lack of rigor. I recommend focusing on the institutionalization practices that establish the organization's culture: planning, training, etc.; and explicitly tying process improvement to business needs.

Interpreting the CMM

Where does the Software CMM apply? The CMM was written to provide good software engineering and management practices for any project in any environment. The model is described in a hierarchy

```
Maturity levels                                      (5)
    → Key process areas                             (18)
        → Goals                                     (52)
            → Key practices                        (316)
                → Subpractices and examples      (many)
```

In my experience over the last decade of software process work, environments where interpretation and tailoring of the CMM are needed include:

- very large programs

- virtual projects or organizations
- geographically distributed projects
- rapid prototyping projects
- research and development organizations
- software services organizations
- small projects and organizations

The interpretation guidance for small projects and small organizations is also applicable to large projects and organizations. Intelligence and common sense are required to use the CMM correctly and effectively (Paulk, 1996). It is simultaneously true that all (software) projects are different and all (software) projects are the same. We are required to balance conflicting realities: similarity versus uniqueness, order versus chaos. Those who succeed build lasting organizations (Collins, 1994) that are truly capable of organizational learning (Senge, 1990); the rest must derive their success elsewhere.

The "normative" components of the CMM are maturity levels, key process areas, and goals. All practices in the CMM are informative. Since the detailed practices primarily support large, contracting software organizations, they are not necessarily appropriate, as written, for direct use by small projects and small organizations - but they do provide insight into how to achieve the goals and implement repeatable, defined, measured, and continually improving software processes. Thus we prevent such "processes" as the estimating procedure that was simply "Go ask George."

The CMM does not tell organizations "how" to do software engineering or management, and it can be characterized as a descriptive model as a result. The CMM is a prescriptive model, however, in that it identifies improvement priorities via the five maturity levels that have been demonstrated to be effective. This improvement roadmap identifies what engineering and management practices should be the primary focus of improvement efforts.

My most frequent interpretation recommendation is to develop a mapping between CMM terminology and the language used by the organization. In particular, terms dealing with organizational structures, roles and relationships, and formality of processes need to be mapped into their organizational equivalents to prevent misunderstandings such as the "ridiculous one-hour project." Examples of organizational structures include "independent groups" such as quality assurance, testing, and configuration management. Appropriate organizational terminology for roles such as project manager and project software manager should be specified. People may fill multiple roles; for example, one person may be the project manager, project software manager, SCM manager, etc. Explicitly stating this makes interpretation of the CMM much simpler and more consistent.

Once the terminology issues are understood, we can think about what the "invariants" for a disciplined process are and which practices depend on the context. In general we assume that key process areas and goals are always relevant to any environment, with the exception of Software Subcontract Management, which may be "not applicable" if there is no subcontracting. In contrast, I can conceive of no circumstances under which Peer Reviews can be reasonably tailored out for a Level 3 organization. This is a matter of competent professional judgment, although an alternative practice such as formal methods might replace peer reviews. Professional judgment and trained, experienced assessors are crucial, even for small organizations (Abbott, 1997).

I have never seen an environment where the following were not needed (though implementations differ):

- documented customer (system) requirements
- communication with customer (and end users)
- agreed-to commitments
- planning
- documented processes
- work breakdown structure

Some practices, however, deal with "large-project implementations." A small project is unlikely to need an SCM group or a Change Control Board... but configuration management and change control are always necessary. An independent SQA group may not be desirable, but objective verification that requirements are satisfied always is. An independent testing group may not be established, but testing is always necessary. We thus see that even for context-sensitive practices, the intent is critical even if the implementation is radically different between small organizations and large. Many of the context-sensitive, large-project implementation issues relate to organizational structure. If one reads the CMM definition of "group," it states that "a group could vary from a single individual assigned part time, to several part-time individuals assigned from different departments, to several individuals dedicated full time," which is intended to cater to a variety of contexts.

The issue of providing resources for process improvement—both to formally identify problems and systematically address them—is a challenge for small organizations. Frequently these resources will be part-time rather than full-time, depending on how "small" is defined.

In addition to these, specific questions that arise repeatedly, especially for small organizations, relate to:

- management sponsorship
- measurement
- planning
- SEPGs
- documented processes
- "as is" processes
- tailoring
- training
- risk management

• peer reviews

Trite though it may seem, obtaining senior management sponsorship is a crucial component of building organizational capability. As individuals, we can exercise professionalism and discipline within our sphere of control, but if an organization as a whole is to change its performance, then its senior management must actively support the change. Bottom-up improvement, without sponsorship and coordination, leads to islands of excellence rather than predictably improved organizational capability. It should be noted, however, that for small organizations, while the president (or founder) is the primary role model, a respected "champion" frequently has the influence to move the entire organization—including the president.

Management by fact is a paradigm shift for most organizations, which must be based on a measurement foundation. To make data analysis useful, you need to understand what the data means and how to analyze it meaningfully. This implies the necessity of beginning by collecting a simple set of useful data. You also have to be sensitive to the potential for causing dysfunctional behavior by what you measure (Austin, 1996). The act of measuring identifies what is important, but some things are difficult to measure. Management needs to ensure that attention is visibly paid to all critical aspects of the project, including those difficult to measure, not just those it is easy to measure and track. At the same time, the effort of collecting the data has to be minimized so the small organization is not overwhelmed by overhead. This is also a problem for large organizations, but the margin for error is razor-thin for small organizations.

The #1 factor in successful process definition and improvement is "planfulness" (Curtis, 1996). Planning is needed for every major software process, but within the bounds of reasonable judgment, the organization determines what is "major" and how the plan should be packaged. A plan may reside in several different artifacts or be embedded in a larger plan.

In most organizations, a software engineering process group (SEPG) or some equivalent should be formed to coordinate process definition, improvement, and deployment activities. One of the reasons for dedicating resources to an SEPG is to ensure follow-through on appraisal findings. Many improvement programs have foundered simply because no action resulted from the appraisal. Small organizations may not have full-time SEPG staff, but the responsibility for improvement should be explicitly assigned and monitored.

Document your processes. The reasons for documenting a process (or product) are to 1) communicate— to others now and perhaps to yourself later; 2) understand— if you can't write it down, you don't really understand; and 3) encourage consistency— take advantage of repeatability.

Documented processes support organizational learning and prevent reinventing the wheel for common problems— they put repeatable processes in place. Documentation is therefore important, but documents need not be lengthy or complex to be useful. Keep the process simple because we live in a rapidly changing world. Processes do not need to be lengthy or complex. The CMM is about doing things, not having things. A 1-2 page process description may suffice, and subprocesses and procedures can be invoked as needed and useful. Use good software design principles, such as locality, information hiding, and abstraction, in defining processes. Another useful rule of thumb is to track work at 2-3 tasks per week at most. Order is not created by complex controls, but by the presence of a few guiding formulae or principles (Wheatley, 1992, page 11).

The degree of formality needed for processes is a frequent challenge for both large and small organizations [Comer, 1998]. Should there be separate procedure for each of the 25 key practices at Level 2 that mention "according to a documented procedure?" (Hadden, 1998a, Pitterman, 1998). The answer, as discussed in the section "Documentation and the CMM" of the CMM book (Paulk, 1995), is a resounding NO! Packaging of documentation is an organizational decision.

Begin with the "as is" process, not the "should be" process, to leverage effective practices and co-opt resisters. Mandating top-down that everyone will follow the new "should be" process, particularly if not developed by empowered workers, is a common recipe for failure. The "as is" process evolved because the people doing the work needed to get the job done - even if that meant going around the system. The "should be" process may, or may not, be feasible in the given culture and environment. With an organizational focus on process management and improvement, the "as is" and "should be" processes will converge, resulting in organizational learning. This is less of a problem for small organizations since, unlike large, established companies, they have usually not had the opportunity to accrue value-free practices over time and there is a more direct realization that processes need to be focused on providing value.

Processes need to be tailored to the needs of the project (Ginsberg, 1995, Ade, 1996). Although standard processes provide a foundation, each project will also have unique needs. Unreasonable constraints on tailoring can lead to significant resistance to following the process. As Hoffman expresses it, "Don't require processes that don't make sense" (Hoffman, 1998).

Documented processes are of little value if they are not effectively deployed. To achieve buy-in for the documented, process implementers must be part of process definition and improvement. Training, via a wide variety of mechanisms, is critical to consistent and effective software engineering and management. Management training is particularly important because ineffective management can cripple a good team. People who are promoted to management because of their technical skills have to acquire a new set of skills, including interpersonal skills (Mogilensky, 1994, Curtis, 1995, Weinberg, 1994).

The reason for training is to develop skills. There are many "training mechanisms" other than formal classroom training that can be effective in building skills. One that should be seriously considered is a formal mentoring program. In this case, formality means going beyond assigning a mentor and hoping that experience will rub off. Formality implies training people on how to mentor and monitoring the effectiveness of the mentoring.

Training remains an issue after the initial deployment of a process or technology (Abbott, 1997, Williams, 1998). As personnel change, the incremental need for training may not be adequately addressed. Mentoring and apprentice programs may suffice to address this issue, but they cannot be assumed to be satisfactory without careful monitoring.

Some argue that software project management is really risk management. In one sense, the CMM is about managing risk. We attempt to establish stable requirements so that we can plan and manage effectively, but the business environment changes rapidly, perhaps chaotically. We try to establish an island of order in the sea of software chaos, but both order and chaos have a place. As Wheatley suggests, "To stay viable, open systems maintain a state of non-equilibrium, keeping the system in balance so that it can change and grow" (Wheatley, 1992, page 78). Although we can establish processes that help us manage the risks of a chaotic world, we also need to change and grow.

This implies that you should use an incremental or evolutionary life cycle. If you want to focus on risk management, the spiral model may be the preferred life cycle model. If you want to focus on involving the customer, perhaps rapid prototyping or joint application design would be preferable. Few long-term projects have the luxury of the stable environment necessary for the waterfall life cycle to be the preferred choice. Yet it is probably the most common life cycle. Note, however, that for small projects, the waterfall life cycle may be an excellent choice. It is also worth noting that in some extreme cases the risk to the organization if a small project fails may be comparatively small, and formal risk management is not worth the overhead.

Although you can argue over the best kind of peer review, the simple fact is that the benefits of peer reviews far outweigh their costs. The data suggests some form of inspection should be used (Ackerman, 1989), but any form of collegial or disciplined review, such as structured walkthroughs, adds significant value. Recognizing the value of peer reviews does not mean, unfortunately, that we do them systematically. We need to "walk the walk," not just "talk the talk." This is very frustrating for technical people who do not understand the emphasis on management in the CMM, yet poor management leads to abandoning good engineering practices such as peer reviews.

There are other issues that have been identified for small organizations and projects. Paquin (1998) identifies five:

- assessments
- project focus
- documentation
- required functions
- maturity questionnaire

We have not directly discussed the project focus of Level 2 as being a challenge for small organizations. Software process improvement involves overhead that may be excessive for a small project. Some recommend attacking small project process improvement from an organizational perspective (Comer, 1998, Paquin, 1998), which is certainly a reasonable approach, even if it does seem to mix Levels 2 and 3. This is a consideration for any size organization or project (Paulk, 1996). Although an organization can achieve Level 2 without an organization process focus, the most effective organizational learning strategy will be one that stresses organizational assets that lessen the overhead of projects. At the same time, it must be recognized that there may be resistance to change at the project level, perhaps based on valid concerns, and addressing resistance needs to be considered part of the organization's learning process.

Required functions are an issue because there may be more CMM functions than there are people. This issue has been discussed as terminology or role mapping. The maturity questionnaire is a concern because it uses CMM terminology, thus it may be confusing to those filling it out. Expressing the questionnaire in the terminology of the organization is thus a desirable precursor to even an informal assessment or survey.

Abbott (1997) identifies six keys to software process improvement in small organizations:

- senior management support
- adequate staffing
- applying project management principles to process improvement
- integration with ISO 9001
- assistance from process improvement consultants
- focus on providing value to projects and to the business.

If applying good project management to software projects is the best way to ensure success, then the same should be true for process improvement, which should be treated like any other project. ISO 9001 is more frequently an issue for large organizations than small, so it is interesting that Abbott points this out for his small company.

Brodman and Johnson (Johnson, 1998) identify seven small organization/small project challenges:

- handling requirements
- generating documentation
- managing projects
- allocating resources
- measuring progress
- conducing reviews
- providing training

Brodman and Johnson have developed a tailored version of the CMM for small businesses, organizations, and projects (Johnson, 1996, Johnson, 1997, Brodman, 1994). Although the majority of the key practices in the CMM were tailored in the LOGOS Tailored CMM, they characterized the changes as:

- clarification of existing practices
- exaggeration of the obvious
- introduction of alternative practices (particularly as examples)
- alignment of practices with small business/small organization/small project structure and resources.

Therefore the changes involved in tailoring the CMM for small organizations should not be considered radical.

Abusing the Software CMM

Using the CMM correctly means balancing conflicting objectives. CMM-based appraisals require the use of professional judgment. Although the CMM provides a significant amount of guidance in making these judgments, removing subjectivity implies a deterministic, repetitive process that is not characteristic of engineering design work. The CMM is sometimes referred to as a set of process requirements, but it does not contain any "shall" statements. That is why it is an abuse of the CMM to check off (sub)practices for conformance.

Some are unwilling or unable to interpret, tailor, or apply judgment. It is easy to mandate the key practices, but foolhardy. This foolishness is frequently driven by paranoia about customer intentions and competence. On more than one occasion I have heard someone say they were doing something that was foolish, but they were afraid that the customer was so ignorant or incompetent that they would be unable to understand the rationale for doing things differently than literally described in the CMM. This is particularly problematic for SCEs. It is true that judgments may differ - and sometimes legitimately so. What is adequate in one environment may not suffice for a new project. That is why we recommend that process maturity be included in risk assessment rather than using maturity levels to filter offerors [Barbour96]. Small organizations should have less of a concern with this problem since it is unlikely that SCEs for small organizations are cost-effective. It is more of a problem for large organizations with many small projects.

Unfortunately I have no solution for this problem. "Standards" such as the CMM can help organizations improve their software process, but focusing on achieving a maturity level without addressing the underlying process can cause dysfunctional behavior. Maturity levels should be measures of improvement, not goals of improvement. That is why we emphasize the need to tie improvement to business objectives to continually remind us of the end goal since, to quote George Box, "All models are wrong; some models are useful."

Conclusion

The bottom line is that software process improvement should be done to help the business - not for its own sake. This is true for both large organizations and small. The best advice comes from Sanjiv Ahuja, President of Bellcore: "Let common sense prevail!"

Building software is a design-intensive, creative activity. While the discipline of process is a crucial enabler of success, the objective is to solve a problem, and this requires creativity. Software processes should be repeatable, even if they are not repetitive. The balance between discipline and creativity can be challenging (Glass, 1995). Losing sight of the creative, design-intense nature of software work leads to stifling rigidity. Losing sight of the need for discipline leads to chaos.

The CMM represents a "common sense engineering" approach to software process improvement. Its maturity levels, key process areas, goals, and key practices have been extensively discussed and reviewed within the software community. While the CMM is neither perfect nor comprehensive, it does represent a broad consensus of the software community and is a useful tool for guiding improvement efforts, and it can be used to help small software organizations improve their processes (Abbott, 1997, Hadden, 1998b, Hoffman, 1998, Pitterman, 1998, Sanders, 1998).

Small organizations should seriously consider PSP and TSP (Ferguson, 1997, Hayes, 1997). Having taken the PSP course, I can highly recommend it for building self-discipline. Note that the effect of reading the book is not the same as taking the course and doing the work! Where the CMM addresses the organizational side of process improvement, PSP addresses building the capability of individual practitioners. The PSP course convinces the individual, based on his or her own data, of the value of a disciplined, engineering approach to building software.

This work is sponsored by the U.S. Department of Defense. (CMM is a registered trademark of Carnegie Mellon University. SM Capability Maturity Model, IDEAL, Personal Software Process, PSP, Team Software Process, and TSP are service marks of Carnegie Mellon University.

References

Abbott,John J. (1997). "Software Process Improvement in a Small Commercial Software Company, *Proceedings of the 1997 Software Engineering Process Group Conference* , San Jose, CA, 17-20 March 1997.

Ackerman, A.F., L.S. Buchwald, and F.H. Lewski (1989). "Software Inspections: An Effective Verification Process," *IEEE Software*, Vol. 6, No. 3, 31-36.

Ade, Randy W. and Joyce P. Bailey (1996). "CMM Lite: SEPG Tailoring Guidance for Applying the Capability Maturity Model for Software to Small Projects," *Proceedings of the 1996 Software Engineering Process Group Conference*: Wednesday Papers,

Atlantic City, NJ, 20-23 May.

Austin, Robert D. (1996). *Measuring and Managing Performance in Organizations*, Dorset House Publishing, ISBN: 0-932633-36-6, New York, NY6.

Barbour, Rick (1996). Software Capability Evaluation Version 3.0 *Implementation Guide for Supplier Selection*, Software Engineering Institute, Carnegie Mellon University, CMU/SEI-95-TR-012, April.

Brodman, J.G. and D.L. Johnson (1994). "What Small Businesses and Small Organizations Say About the CMM," *Proceedings of the 16th International Conference on Software Engineering*, IEEE Computer Society Press, Sorrento, Italy, 16-21 May, 331-340.

Clark, Bradford K. (1997)."The Effects of Software Process Maturity on Software Development Effort," PhD Dissertation, Computer Science Department, University of Southern California, August.

Collins, James C. and Jerry I. Porras, (1994). *Built to Last*, HarperCollins Publishers, New York, NY, 1994.

Curtis,Bill, William E. Hefley, and Sally Miller (1995). *People Capability Maturity Model*, Software Engineering Institute, CMU/SEI-95-MM-02, September.

Curtis, Bill (1996). "The Factor Structure of the CMM and Other Latent Issues," Proceedings of the 1996 Software Engineering Process Group Conference: Tuesday Presentations, Atlantic City, NJ, 20-23 May 1996.

DeMarco, Tom (1995). *Why Does Software Cost So Much?*, ISBN 0-932633-34-X, Dorset House, New York, NY, 1995.

Department of Defense (1987)."Report of the Defense Science Board Task Force on Military Software," Office of the Under Secretary of Defense for Acquisition, Washington, D.C.

Ferguson, Pat and Jeanie Kitson (1997). "CMM-Based Process Improvement Supplemented by the Personal Software Process in a Small Company Environment," *Proceedings of the 1997 Software Engineering Process Group Conference* , San Jose, CA, 17-20 March.

Gibbs,W. Wayt (1994). "Software's Chronic Chrisis," *Scientific American*, September, 86-95.

Ginsberg, Mark and Lauren Quinn (1995). *"Process Tailoring and the Software Capability Maturity Model,"* Software Engineering Institute, CMU/SEI-94-TR-024, November 1995.

Glass, Robert L. (1995). *Software Creativity*, Prentice Hall, Englewood Cliffs, NJ.

Hadden,Rita (1998). "How Scalable are CMM Key Practices?" *Crosstalk: The Journal of Defense Software Engineering*, 11(4), 18-20, 23.

Hadden, Rita (1998). "Key Practices to the CMM: Inappropriate for Small Projects?" panel, Rita Hadden moderator, *Proceedings of the 1998 Software Engineering Process Group Conference*, Chicago, IL, 9-12 March.

Hayes, Will and James W. Over (1997). *The Personal Software Process (PSP): An Empirical Study of the Impact of PSP on Individual Engineers*, Software Engineering Institute, Carnegie Mellon University, CMU/SEI-97-TR-001, December.

Herbsleb, James, David Zubrow, Dennis Goldenson, Will Hayes, and Mark Paulk (1997)."Software Quality and the Capability Maturity Model," *Communications of the ACM*, Vol. 40, No. 6, 30-40.

Hoffman, Leo (1998). "Small Projects and the CMM," in "Key Practices to the CMM: Inappropriate for Small Projects?" panel, Rita Hadden moderator, *Proceedings of the 1998 Software Engineering Process Group Conference* , Chicago, IL, 9-12 March 1998.

Humphrey, Watt S. (1995). *A Discipline for Software Engineering*, ISBN 0-201-

54610-8, Addison-Wesley Publishing Company, Reading, MA.

Johnson, Donna L. and Judith G. Brodman,(1996). *The LOGOS Tailored Version of the CMM for Small Businesses, Small Organizations, and Small Projects,* Version 1.0, August 1996.

Johnson, Donna L. and Judith G. Brodman,(1997). "Tailoring the CMM for Small Businesses, Small Organizations, and Small Projects," *Software Process Newsletter,* IEEE Computer Society Technical Council on Software Engineering, No. 8, Winter, 1-6.

Johnson, Donna L. and Judith G. Brodman,(1998). "Applying the CMM to Small Organizations and Small Projects," *Proceedings of the 1998 Software Engineering Process Group Conference,* Chicago, IL, 9-12 March..

Lawlis, Patricia K., Robert M. Flowe, and James B. Thordahl (1996). "A Correlational Study of the CMM and Software Development Performance," *Crosstalk: The Journal of Defense Software Engineering,* 8(9), 21-25. Reprinted in *Software Process Newsletter,* IEEE Computer Society Technical Council on Software Engineering, No. 7, Fall 1996, pp. 1-5.

McFeeley, Bob (1996). "IDEAL: A User's Guide for Software Process Improvement," Software Engineering Institute, CMU/SEI-96-HB-001, February.

Mogilensky, Judah and Betty L. Deimel (1994). "Where Do People Fit in the CMM?," *American Programmer,* 7(9), September, 36-43.

Paquin, Sherry (1998). "Struggling with the CMM: Real Life and Small Projects," in "Key Practices to the CMM: Inappropriate for Small Projects?" panel, Rita Hadden moderator, *Proceedings of the 1998 Software Engineering Process Group Conference,* Chicago, IL, 9-12 March..

Paulk, Mark (1996). Carnegie Mellon University, Software Engineering Institute (Principal Contributors and Editors: Mark C. Paulk, Charles V. Weber, Bill Curtis, and Mary Beth Chrissis), The Capability Maturity Model: Guidelines for Improving the Software Process, ISBN 0-201-54664-7, Addison-Wesley Publishing Company, Reading, MA.

Paulk, Mark (1996)."Effective CMM-Based Process Improvement," *Proceedings of the 6th International Conference on Software Quality,* Ottawa, Canada, 28-31 October 1996, 226-237.

Pitterman, Bill (1998)."Key Practices to the CMM: Inappropriate for Small Projects?" panel, Rita Hadden moderator, *Proceedings of the 1998 Software Engineering Process Group Conference,* Chicago, IL, 9-12 March 1998.

Sanders, Marty (1998). "Small Company Action Training and Enabling," in *The CMM and Small Projects,* Society for Software Quality Roundtable, Washington, DC, 26 January.

Senge, Peter M. (1990). *The Fifth Discipline: The Art & Practice of the Learning Organization,* Doubleday/Currency, New York, NY, 1990.

Strigel,Wolfgang B. (1995). "Assessment in Small Software Companies," *Proceedings of the 1995 Pacific Northwest Software Quality Conference,* 1995, pp. 45-56.

Weinberg, Gerald (1994). *Quality Software Management, Volume 3: Congruent Action,* ISBN 0-932633-28-5, Dorset House, New York, NY.

Wheatley, Margaret J. (1994). *Leadership and the New Science,* Berrett-Koehler Publishers, San Francisco, CA.

Williams,Louise B. (1998). "SPI Best Practices for 'Small' Projects," in The CMM and Small Projects, Society for Software Quality Roundtable, Washington, DC, 26 January.

Chapter 7

IS Change Agents in Software Process Improvement

Eugene G. McGuire
American University, USA

Kim A. Randall
Department of Defense Education Activity, USA

This chapter examines the complex organizational and software development environment in which IS professionals commonly function today. Skills and competencies appropriate to this environment are increasingly related to managing change and adopting change agent roles. These skills and competencies are discussed in relation to complex and changing environments and a survey of IS professionals evaluates their perceptions of the importance of these competencies and their own capability in these areas. Observations and conclusions in this paper are primarily drawn from research on organizations that have initiated software process improvement initiatives (McGuire 1996a; 1996b; 1997).

The growing global economy for software products and services has driven many organizations to redefine the very paradigms by which they operate. A larger and more demanding customer base, the necessity for reduced cycle time, the growing complexity of software systems, and the increased mission-critical status of these software systems are only some of the factors that are pressuring organizations to deliver higher quality, more complex software products in the face of an ever turbulent and competitive global environment.

According to Waldrop (1992), many organizations are operating at or approaching the "edge of chaos" as the complexity of their environment increases and as the metabolic rate of their functions and processes escalates to keep pace. "The edge of chaos is where new ideas and innovative genotypes are forever nibbling away at the edges of the status quo, and where even the most entrenched old guard will eventually be overthrown....The edge of chaos is the constantly shifting battle zone between stagnation and anarchy, the one place where a complex system can be spontaneous, adaptive, and alive." (Waldrop 1992, p. 12). Successfully operating at the "edge of chaos" requires first recognizing the environmental, organizational, structural, and process elements that lead to this state and then identifying appropriate professional skills that are appropriate for this state.

Managing Complex Change

It would appear that if an organization is operating at or near the "edge of chaos" that traditional models of managing innovation and change within that organization are quickly becoming outmoded. The literature shows a strong call for new models of change management that are more appropriate for organizations operating in complex, chaotic environment.

Orlikowski and Hofman (1997) note that traditional models of change as characterized by Lewin's three-stage model of "unfreezing, change, and refreezing" are appropriate only for organizations that are relatively stable and bounded and whose functionality is fixed. These models, however, are not appropriate in the more turbulent, flexible, and uncertain organizational and environmental conditions that often exist today.

Orlikowski and Hofman suggest that a more appropriate way of thinking about change would be an approach that reflects the "unprecedented, uncertain, open-ended, complex, and flexible nature of the technologies and organizational initiatives involved." Such a model, they note, would enable organizations to systematically absorb, respond to, and even leverage unexpected events, evolving technological capabilities, emerging practices, and unanticipated outcomes. This type of approach would accommodate and encourage ongoing and iterative experimentation, use and learning. The proposed model relies on two assumptions: first, the changes associated with technology implementations are an ongoing process; and second, not all of the technological and organizational changes made during an ongoing process can be anticipated ahead of time.

New change models suggest the need for new roles for change agents. Markus and Benjamin (1996) have recently addressed the need for an expanded definition of the traditional model of IS change agency. They conclude that the traditional IS model wherein the IS change agent views the technology as the agent of change is rapidly becoming unviable. They further state that IS professionals should probably begin integrating aspects of the "facilitator" model of change agency wherein the facilitator views people as the agent of change but views himself/herself as the expert in the process of change and the "advocate" model of change agency wherein the advocate views his/her role as one of influencing others' behaviors in certain directions into their Traditional IS role. They note that IS professionals need to become better organizational change agents "because change agentry will most likely become the largest and most important part of interorganizational IS work in the future" as more information technology is implemented into organizations.

One area in which IS professionals are finding new challenges today is that of software process improvement. With the focus equally on people, process, and technology, effective software process improvement initiatives require IS professionals to have the ability to acquire and use an expanded skill set within a fast-cycle software development project operating in a highly complex and changing organizational environment. Implications of this situation are discussed in the following sections of this paper.

Organizational Complexity

McMaster (1996) notes that between 1970 and 2000 there will be an approximately 500 million-fold increase in the ability to access, move create, and process information. This shift is made possible by computers and includes increasingly extensive and effective use of information technology, but the shift is not really about computers. It is about information itself and includes communication technology, organizing work practices, organizing information, accessing information and generating information.

Compared to the increase in the capacity to move, process and store information, methods of organizing and working together have not been adequately transformed to meet that increase. This era requires new capacities for transforming chaotic data into useful information and new levels of innovation capable of designing practical applications for that information.

Software professionals, in particular, appear to frequently confront complexity and the changes associated with this environment. They are, however, not always confident in their ability to effectively deal with these situations. For example, a recent study by Zelkowitz (1996) examines how the software engineering discipline deals with technological change. In studying NASA software development projects, Zelkowitz concluded that:

1) most software professionals are resistant to change thereby decreasing the likelihood of rapid adoption of new technology;
2) technology transfer is more than simply understanding the new technology and may involve multiple instances of training and pilot projects;
3) technology infusion is part of the total environment of the consumer organization — it does not occur in a vacuum;
4) the government can have an impact on technology infusion, although more by utilizing advocates in key positions than by imposing rules mandating certain technologies;
5) people contact is the main transfer agent of change and finding the appropriate advocate to act as gatekeeper or guru for the technology is a

crucial component of any technology transfer mechanism;
6) timing is a critical decision and may be either a positive or negative influence on the overall technology infusion process.

These findings are not surprising given the nature of software development environments. While never particularly stable, these environments have become increasingly complex and non-linear and new organizational structures and thinking are being proposed by many observers.

Nonlinearity in Software Development Organizations

Nonaka and Takeuchi (1995) address the successful management of the new product development process that is characteristic of software organizations. They state that organizations must maintain a highly adaptive and flexible approach to new product development because it rarely proceeds in a linear or static manner and instead involves an iterative, dynamic, and continuous process of trial and error. They cite the software industry as best embodying this spiral approach and reference a recent study by Cusumano and Selby (1995) showing that software developers move around in phases, iteratively designing, coding, and testing as the project progresses.

In addition, Nonaka and Takeuchi believe that self-organizing project teams should oversee new-product development. Organizations should be willing to give a high degree of autonomy to such teams especially as they cope with ambiguity, fluctuation, and creative chaos in the startup phases of new-product development where little prior knowledge exists and taking initiatives and risks are necessary.

Nadler, et al (1992) view the future organization in much the same way. One of the characteristics they see becoming prevalent for organizations is that organic, adaptable teams will be the norm at all organizational levels. Not only will this provide the capability for faster response time but these teams will be relatively autonomous in comparison to previous organizational eras. Teams will have far greater latitude to be innovative and solve problems than before and management will assist rather than direct this process.

In addition, Nadler et al see an emphasis on system-level learning to be one of the cornerstones of the new organizations. This will enable organizations to greatly increase their capacity to innovate and learn because they will require members to seek out new ideas and adapt them to internal use. Increased innovation and experimentation will result in successes and failures that will be analyzed to extract knowledge that can be applied to new situations.

Leonard-Barton (1995) sees much the same thing happening to organizations. Certain types of tool implementation such as intensive codevelopment with user groups leads to the opportunities for mutual adaptation of both technology and user work environment. Mutual adaptation is the reinvention of the technology to conform to the work environment and the simultaneous adaptation of the organization to use the new technical system. Two major aspects of mutual adaptation are: (1) it occurs in small and large recursive spirals of change and (2) it often requires attention to all four of what Leonard-Barton identifies as the organization's core capabilities — employee skills and knowledge, physical technical systems, managerial systems, and values and norms. She integrates these two aspects of mutual adaptation into a vision of the new organization addressing all of its activities in an "iterative, return-loop nature" that is characterized by prototypes of all different kinds and a "try-it-and-learn" attitude. Nonlinearity and higher-order learning (learning beyond the current operating level and problems of the organization) become organizational norms.

The concept of organizational nonlinearity is also explored by Goldstein (1994) who describes one of the advantages of a nonlinear system as its potential for self organization since change does not need to be imposed but just released under appropriate conditions. Linear systems, in contrast, do not have this potential. He notes that the radical organizational change that strategies such as reengineering, cycle time management, concurrent engineering, TQM, and continuous improvement call for are more congruent with the spontaneous system reorganization of nonlinear systems than with the more stable nature of linear models. He reasons that if organizations are nonlinear, then only a nonlinear strategy takes advantage of organizational nonlinearity with its evolutionary potential.

Nonlinearity is also seen as the norm in software development by Olson (1993) who argues that "highly detailed linear development processes" don't match the way real software development is done but plans and schedules are nevertheless constructed according to this model. He states that the failures in software development are the result of applying valid and significant disciplines (such as linear process models) in areas where the base assumptions of the disciplines don't match the problems that are to be solved or the organizations that are involved.

Olson believes that software development is characterized by a chaotic approach where "there's always another way. You should achieve a fit between the discipline, the problem, the people, and the organization." (p. 54). He claims that the fundamental stages of software development such as problem solving, requirements gathering, system design, user interface design, coding and data structures are all chaotic in nature as they involve multiple iterations and feedback loops that result in a maturing sequence of mental models. The progression from model to model, he states, is not linear but instead proceeds in fits and starts as software developers study and worry about problems, find solutions, and then discover new problems. These mental models, explains Olson, behave like drops of water, with change over time, internal dynamics, and feedback between cycles. Chaotic behavior, therefore, should be expected.

Within these increasingly complex organizational and software development environments there is a call for higher quality and reliability in software systems. Software process improvement issues have recently gained much visibility in the industry and software professionals are being asked to adopt new work practices in addition to working in complex environments.

Software Process Improvement

One model of software process maturity that has received considerable attention is the Capability Maturity Model (CMM) developed by the Software Engineering Institute (SEI) at Carnegie Mellon University in Pittsburgh (Paulk et al , 1993). The SEI was established in the mid 1980s at Carnegie Mellon University to develop a better understanding of software design and development. Although the CMM and the quality principles it embodies are well known in the software industry there are still many challenges to overcome in successfully implementing a sustainable, quality software development culture.

Software process improvement as typified by the CMM provides guidelines for an organization to employ a structured approach to strategically improve all aspects of a software development operation and dramatically changes or extends concepts previously employed under recognized systems development models such as the waterfall and spiral approach (Royce, 1970; Boehm, 1988). Organizations previously would often attempt to improve performance in an ad-hoc manner by using technology driven approaches instead of addressing root problems. For example, organizations would often assign more staff or more tools to an already late and over-budget development project rather than addressing the reasons why the project had problems.

In contrast, in a mature organization (as measured under the CMM framework), managers use metrics to quantitatively measure the quality of a software product. Schedules and budgets are based on historical performance and are realistic; the predicted results for product cost, schedule, functionality, and quality are routinely achieved. Based on the predictability of the project results, reliable management decisions can be made about tradeoffs among these outcomes. Models such as the CMM are designed to contribute toward lower costs and reduced intervals because they specify high quality processes. These processes are capable of predictable results (producing high quality software products) which in turn help with the planning and management of projects.

The maturity framework underlying the CMM applies quality management practices to the process of software development. A major theme of the CMM's maturity framework is that a software activity can be improved if the same activity can be predictably repeated. This philosophy pertains to all the people, processes, and technologies that comprise the software activity.

Part of the reason for the recent attention to quality in software development is that empirical research consistently shows that many software development projects suffer from a lack of proven and well established methods. Many organizations, nevertheless, employ talented software engineers and managers and produce successful software products even though they are not operating with a strong process focus. In such organizations, it is appropriate to examine if team and management issues arise as those software development groups move towards a more structured, process-oriented environment.

Most improvement programs to date have emphasized process or technology and not people. People management practices in many organizations, despite a significant amount of literature addressing people-related issues (Demarco & Lister, 1987; Rasch & Tosi, 1992; Humphrey, 1997), do not address people issues in a systematic and structured manner. In addition, most managers are untrained or inadequately trained in implementing corrective solutions once people problems are identified (Statz, 1994; Zahniser, 1993). Also, organizational factors, while widely cited (Constantine, 1993; McIntyre, 1992, 1994) are often not systematically analyzed for their effect on process improvement efforts.

The characteristics of the CMM levels show that information systems professionals who work on software engineering projects must be capable of being highly productive in complex, team-oriented environments with strong emphases on process control and overall quality (Walz et al, 1993; Zultner, 1993). These requirements are critical but may not always be present in current information systems professionals. The lack of appropriate team and process control skills can greatly contribute to internal organizational volatility.

The CMM requires that organizational management, users, customers, and software development professionals communicate and collaborate frequently and effectively to achieve quality and repeatable processes. In fact, team training is specifically required to fully satisfy the requirements of some key process areas in the CMM.

Teams can be created for the purpose of continuous improvement any level in the organization. For these teams to be successful, however, they require clear identification of their mission and agenda, facilitation for effective team development, and guidelines concerning improvement areas and implementation plans. Mohrman et al (1995) note that the primary focus of improvement teams within an organization should not be on transforming core processes but instead on improving the organization's current capability to deliver products and services. These teams typically focus on issues such as quality improvement of chronic problems, redesigning existing processes to better meet market demands, and solving new problems as they develop (Mohrman et al, 1995). Clearly these issues can overlap and all can be addressed by one team. This is often the situation for software process improvement teams, whether they be at a development level within an individual project or at an organizational level as typified by a Software Engineering Process Group (SEPG) or a similar group.

For example, most software development organizations find that the high cost associated with discovering and fixing software defects late in the project life cycle is a chronic problem that can be initially addressed by increased focus on the testing process. It is unlikely, however, that improving testing will be an entirely adequate solution to excessive software defects. Redesigning the software development process is usually necessary to insure such things as requirements traceability and formal peer reviews of design and code. Further complications such as the demand for reduced cycle time can compel the improvement team to develop innovative solutions for new problems, i.e. increased overall quality in less time.

Process improvement teams must address several important areas in their activities. These areas involve focusing on process, quality, teams, change models and change management, organizational learning, strategic alignment and environment stabilization. Following is a brief discussion of each of these areas.

Process Focus

Organizations with a process focus work to prevent crises from occurring instead of reacting to them after they occur. User satisfaction is actively monitored and the quality of the process is quantitatively measured so all aspects of the process can be continuously improved. As the focus on process and process maturity increases, institutionalization of organizational processes is achieved via policies, standards, and organizational structure. Individual approaches to problem solving are integrated into the process focus rather than used instead of a process focus. The maturity framework underlying the CMM applies quality management practices to the process of software development. A major theme of the CMM's maturity framework is that a software activity can be improved if the same activity can be predictably repeated. This philosophy pertains to all the people, processes, and technologies that comprise the software activity.

Quality Focus

One of the most important issues affecting the software development profession is that of quality. Over the past twenty years there have been thousands of articles addressing the issues of quality. However, views about quality have been shaped to a considerable degree by five major writers: Crosby, Deming, Feigenbaum, Juran, and Taguchi. Crosby's (1979) views of quality may be expressed by three concepts: the notion of "zero defects;" the definition of quality as "conformance to requirements;" and the view that quality is assured by a highly structured, step-by-step program focused on improving quality.

Deming (1986), arguably the most influential proponent of quality, stresses the idea that processes are subject to variation, that statistical measurement can be used to determine if a process is in control, and that the emphasis should be on minimizing variation in the process. Feigenbaum (1983) first coined the term "total quality control in 1951 and takes an engineering approach to managing quality wherein he defines four stages for quality-control activities: new-design control; incoming-material control; product control; and special process studies.

Juran (1979), similar to Crosby, defines quality as "fitness for use." Juran points out that much effort can be wasted on controlling quality if one attempts to control all factors. Instead he points out that there are a "vital few" factors to address and that the remainder are the "trivial many" which can consume much effort but contribute little to the ultimate quality of a product or service. Taguchi (1989) argues that a total life cycle cost enables a designer to see the societal loss over the product's lifetime and that this loss function can be minimized by the proper selection of design parameters.

Team Orientation

This is perhaps the most commonly cited characteristic of successful process and quality environments. A team orientation is often necessary throughout an organization when reengineering efforts cross functional and disciplinary boundaries. Ramifications of this structural change includes requiring that employees not adopt or retain insulated work modes but instead develop business, managerial, and political skills to successfully negotiate with multiple constituencies and integrate their work and decision making with the strategic plans of the organization. Increasingly effective teams have to be interdisciplinary and cross functional because they have to know the tasks of others and can provide backup and feedback capabilities to other members of their team and related teams.

Team attributes include such factors as the composition of the team, whether contributors are dedicated, whether team members are co-located, the reporting relationships of team members, how often meetings are held, etc. Multi-team linkages may be established to handle interdependencies among teams and across the organization. In knowledge-work settings, it has been shown that teams are generally not self-contained. Both team attributes and multiteam linkages are structural responses that must fit with the task, and both contribute equally to performance facilitators and effectiveness. There is often a considerable emphasis placed on training and education in the transition phase to a team-based organization. Empowerment of teams requires that they receive direction and have the capability to make a difference in the attainment of goals.

Change Model

It is useful to frame change management strategies in a model. Many such models are available. One widely applicable model developed by Stokes (1991) entails seven steps: 1) external and/or internal pressures to change are perceived by the organization; 2) a vision for the future state is created; 3) benefits of the change for people and for the organization are developed and made explicit; 4) key variables which will impact the change (e.g., peoples' previous experience with change in that organization) are determined and their impacts assessed; 5) reasons for possible resistance to the proposed change (based on analysis of key variables) are determined and ways to deal with the resistance are planned; 6) strategies for introducing and managing the change are designed and implemented; and 7) post-change follow-up, reinforcement and support to help solidify the change and prepare people for further on-going changes.

Change Management

Change management strategies must be utilized from the beginning of a process improvement effort to first anticipate possible causes of resistance to the change and then to have strategies in place to overcome individual and group resistance. Benefits of the change must be clearly articulated and reward systems implemented that recognize the shift from individual effort to team- and process-driven effort. Barriers that inhibit the change from successfully occurring must be removed. Management may find it appropriate to adopt a coaching and facilitating style instead of a command and control style in dealing with employees when change is occurring. If so, management needs to be trained in this area.

Organizational Learning

Many organizations are realizing that continual learning patterns must become institutionalized for that organization to achieve maximum use of people and remain competitive. This learning is not achieved simply through training and education opportunities for people although these are important, particularly if they promote substantive professional development. Learning organizations as defined by Senge (1990) and others are more than this however. These organizations work hard at facilitating systems thinking (seeing the organization as a whole); enhancing existing mental models of existing processes and procedures (thinking outside the box); and team learning (where collaboration and group success are the norms). These characteristics can serve as useful guidelines for organizations as they establish change management strategies.

Strategic Alignment

The goals, objectives, values, beliefs, and actions of the organization, management, teams and work units, and individuals should be kept in alignment throughout a process improvement effort. Too often one or more of these areas suffers as the change effort in instituted.

Environment Stabilization

Change management and strategic alignment activities should help people maintain or regain stability in the face of the current change. Change management strategies, therefore, should address the following areas:

Organizational Context (e.g., clear mission and shared vision, supportive culture, rewards consistent with objectives, information and feedback); Group Structure (e.g., clear goals, clearly defined roles, appropriate group membership, effective group culture); Group Process (e.g., problem solving, decision making, conflict management, communication, boundary management); and Group Effectiveness (e.g., service that meets or exceeds performance standards, meeting team members' needs).

Successfully implementing process improvement efforts requires attention to many organizational, people, process, quality, and methodological factors. The factors discussed in this section are directly applicable to technical environments where software professionals are facing increasing demands for higher quality with reduced cycle time to meet global competition.

Competency Needs of IS Professionals

New competency needs of IS professionals will be shaped by the complex organizational and systems development environment discussed above. A summary of desirable competencies includes:

Communications

IS professionals must communicate in a variety of settings using oral, written, and multimedia techniques. Change agent roles, in particular, require the ability to effectively articulate both strategic and tactial planning to multiple levels of an organization during the life cycle of a project or program.

Problem Solving

IS professionals must be able to choose from a variety of different problem solving methodologies to analytically formulate a solution. IS professionals must think creatively in solving problems. IS professionals must be able to work on project teams and use group methods to define and solve problems.

Organization and Systems Theory

IS professionals must be grounded in the principles of systems theory. IS professionals must have sufficient background to understand the functioning of organizations since the information system must be congruent with, and supportive of the strategy, principles, goals, and objectives of the organization. IS professionals must understand and be able to function in the multinational and global context of today's information dependent organizations.

Quality

IS professionals must understand quality, planning, steps in the continuous improvement process as it relates to the enterprise, and tools to facilitate quality development. As the IS field matures, increasing attention is being directed to problem avoidance and to process simplification through reengineering. Error control, risk management, process measurement and auditing are areas that IS professionals must understand and apply. IS professionals must possess a tolerance for change and skills for managing the process of change. Given the advancing technology in the IS field, education must be continuous. IS professionals must understand mission-directed, principle-centered mechanisms to facilitate aligning group as well as individual missions with organizational missions.

Groups

IS professionals must interact with diverse user groups in team and project activities. IS professionals must possess communication and facilitation skills within team meetings and other related activities. IS professionals must understand the concept of empathetic listening and utilize it proactively to solicit synergistic solutions in which all parties to an agreement can benefit. IS professionals must be able to communicate effectively with a changing work force.

Competency Survey

A survey of IS professionals currently working on software development projects was conducted to determine their perceived needs in some of the above competencies. This survey asked participants to rate their perception of their current capability for each of 20 items on a scale of 1-5 and also asked for their rating of how important they regarded that item in their current work environment, again on a scale of 1-5. Respondents were working on various projects in a large application development contracting organization.

The results of these surveys indicate that IS professionals recognize the importance of factors associated with the organizational and software development environments characterized by complexity and change. The results also indicate that IS professionals perceive their individual competencies in these areas to be relatively low thus hindering their ability to be effective change agents in these environments.

These survey results support the view that the software development environment is changing and that additional and/or enhanced competencies are required for IS professionals to effectively operate as change agents in in this environment. Organizations need to address these needs to effectively prepare their current workforce to be successful in the complex and changing development environments that are already common and may well become the norm within a few years.

Conclusion

Successfully implementing process improvement efforts requires atten-

n = 114
Group Decision Making — 2.3
Conflict Resolution — 2.1
Business Domain Knowledge — 3.6
Risk Analysis — 2.4
Process Control Tools — 1.5
Intergroup Coordination — 3.7
Negotiating — 2.2
Change Management — 2.8
Teamwork Behaviors — 3.8
Metrics and Measurement — 2.3
Customer Focus — 2.6
Process Definition — 2.1
Process Focus — 2.3
Quality Focus — 3.9
Project Management — 4.1
Interpersonal Communication — 3.8
Organizational Learning — 2.4
Technology Transfer — 2.5
Change Advocacy — 1.7
Strategic Alignment — 1.5

Table 1: Ranking of Current Capabilities

n = 114
Group Decision Making — 4.2
Conflict Resolution — 4.3
Business Domain Knowledge — 4.7
Risk Analysis — 3.6
Process Control Tools — 3.2
Intergroup Coordination — 3.9
Negotiating — 3.8
Change Management — 4.7
Teamwork Behaviors — 4.6
Metrics and Measurement — 4.1
Customer Focus — 4.8
Process Definition — 3.5
Process Focus — 3.7
Quality Focus — 4.8
Project Management — 4.8
Interpersonal Communication — 4.0
Organizational Learning — 3.9
Technology Transfer — 4.3
Change Advocacy — 4.2
Strategic Alignment — 4.1

Table 2: Ranking of Perceived Importance

tion to many organizational, people, process, quality, and methodological issues. The factors discussed in this chapter are directly applicable to technical environments where software professionals are facing increasing demands for higher quality with reduced cycle time to meet global competition. The skills and competencies required of IS professionals to successfully operate as change agents in these environments are constantly expanding. This chapter presented the foundations of this environment and the results of a survey of IS professionals operating in this environment. The survey results indicate that IS professionals believe the identified areas to be important (table 2) but also believe that their own competencies in many of these areas are relatively low (table 1). The implications of these results for organizational management are significant. IS professionals are aware of their changing and complex environment and of the new demands to adopt change agent roles that are being placed upon them. They are also aware that their current competency levels need to be improved. Organizational management can use the results of this survey as guidelines to implement improvement programs to enhance the competency levels of their IS professionals.

References

Constantine, L.L. (1993). "Work organization: Paradigms for project management and organization," *Communications of the ACM*, Vol. 36, No. 10, October 1993, pp. 35-43.

Crosby, P.B. (1979). *Quality is free*, McGraw-Hill, New York, NY.

DeMarco, T. & Lister, T. (1987) *Peopleware: Productive Projects and Teams.*

Deming, W.E. (1986). *Out of the crisis*, MIT Center for Advanced Engineering Study, Cambridge, MA.

Feigenbaum, A.V. (1983). *Total quality control*, Third Edition, (first edition in 1951), McGraw-Hill, New York, NY.

Goldstein, J. (1994). *The Unshackled Organization*, Portland, OR: Productivity Press.

Humphrey, W. (1997). *Managing Technical People: Innovation, Teamwork, and the Software Process*, Reading, MA: Addison-Wesley Publishing.

Juran, J. (1979). *Quality control handbook*, Third Edition, The Free Press, New York, NY.

Leonard-Barton, D. (1995). *Wellsprings of Knowledge: Building and Sustaining the Sources of Innovation*, Boston: Harvard Business School Press.

Markus, M.L. & Benjamin, R.I. (1996). Change Agentry — the Next IS Frontier, *MIS Quarterly*, December 1996, pp. 385-407.

McIntyre, S.C. (1992). Overcoming ad hoc development: Enabling/Disabling factors in software quality maturation, *Proceedings of the 25th Hawaii International Conference on Systems Sciences*, IEEE Computer Society Press, Vol IV, January 1992, pp. 624-633.

McIntyre, S.C. (1994). Organizational issues underlie software quality, *Proceedings of the 27th Annual Hawaii International Conference on System Sciences*, IEEE Computer.

McGuire, E.G. (1996a). Factors Affecting the Quality of Software Project

Management: An Empirical Study Based on the Capability Maturity Model, *Software Quality Journal* (5), (1996) pp. 305-317.

McGuire, E.G. (1996b) Maturity Model Linkages Between Software Development Teams, Users, and Quality, *Journal of International Information Management*, Special Issue: End-User Quality, November 1996.

McGuire, E.G. (1997). Responsibilities Under the Capability Maturity Model, *The Responsible Software Engineer: Selected Readings in IT Professionalism*, Springer Verlag, London, pp. 220-228.

McIntyre, S.C. (1992). Overcoming ad hoc development: Enabling/Disabling factors in software quality maturation, *Proceedings of the 25th Hawaii International Conference on Systems Sciences*, IEEE Computer Society Press, Vol IV, January 1992, pp. 624-633.

McIntyre, S.C. (1994). Organizational issues underlie software quality, *Proceedings of the 27th Annual Hawaii International Conference on System Sciences*, IEEE Computer.

Paulk, M., Curtis, B., Chrisis, M.B., & Weber, C.V. (1993). Capability Maturity Model, Version 1.1, *IEEE Software*, July 1993, pp. 18-27.

Mohrman, S.A., Cohen, S.G. and Mohrman, Jr., A. M. (1995). *Designing Team-Based Organizations*, San Francisco: Jossey-Bass, 1995.

Nadler, D.A., Gerstein, M.S, & Shaw, R.B. (1992). *Organizational Architecture: Designs for Changing Organizations*, San Francisco: Jossey-Bass Publishers.

Nonaka, I. & Takeuchi, H. (1995). *The Knowledge-Creating Company*, New York: Oxford University Press.

Olson, D. (1993). *Exploiting Chaos: Cashing in on the Realities of Software Development*, New York: Van Nostrand Reinhold.

Orlikowski, W.J. & Hofman, J.D. (1997). "An Improvisational Model for Change Management: The Case of Groupware Technologies," *Sloan Management Review*, Winter 1997, pp. 11-21.

Pool, R. (1989) Is It Chaos, or Is It Just Noise. *Science*. 243 (January) : 25-28.

Rasch, R.A. & Tosi, H.L. (1992). Factors affecting software developers' performance: An integrated approach, *MIS Quarterly*, September 1992, pp. 395-409.

Senge, P.M. (1994). *The Fifth Discipline: The Art and Practice of the Learning Organization*. New York: Doubleday.

Shannon, C. & Weaver, W. (1963). *The Mathematical Theory of Communication*. Urbana: University of Illinois.

Stokes, S.L. (1991). *Controlling the Future: Managing Technology-Driven Change*, QED Information Sciences: Welleslye, Massachusetts.

Taguchi, G. (1989). *Taguchi methods*, American Supplier Institute, Tokyo, Japan.

Waldrop, M. M. (1992). *Complexity: The Emerging Science at the Edge of Order and Chaos*. New York: Touchstone.

Zelkowitz, M. V. (1996). Software Engineering Technology Infusion Within NASA, *IEEE Transactions on Engineering Management*, Vol. 43, No. 3, August 1996.

Chapter 8

Generic Programming, Partial Evaluation, and a New Programming Paradigm

Christopher Landauer
Aerospace Integration Science Center, USA

Kirstie Bellman
Aerospace Integration Science Center, USA

We describe in this chapter a new approach to generic programming that uses our integration results together with recent progress in partial evaluation methods for adaptation. Our approach to partial evaluation provides an adaptation mechanism by having much more information than is usually available, including explicit meta-knowledge about the program fragments and their intended execution environments. We make some ambitious claims here, so we tried to provide enough detail about our methods to justify our interest in them and our expectations of them. We are not claiming to have solved the problem; only that our methods circumvent some of the known difficulties that were previously identified or encountered in approaches to Generic Programming.

We describe in this chapter a new approach to Generic Programming that uses our integration results together with recent progress in Partial Evaluation methods for adaptation. Our approach to partial evaluation provides an adaptation mechanism by having much more information than usual, including explicit meta-knowledge about the programs and their intended execution environments.

Generic Programming is an attempt to get the right level of abstraction in algorithms, so that the essential parts of the algorithm are displayed, and the details that make it conform to an execution environment are added during pre-compile time by a kind of specialization. Of course, it has been a goal of computer programming since the beginning to get the right level of abstraction in algorithms. The long-anticipated result would be that the program as written would contain all and only the essential parts of the algorithm. All of the characteristics of the execution environment that affect the map from the algorithm to the program would then have to be made explicit, but they could be deferred from program construction time to pre-compile time: the algorithm would then be instantiated or adapted to make the program conform to the specific environmental characteristics before (or during) compilation. Even after many years of progress in this direction, we still have a distance to go (Shaw & Wulf, 1992).

We have a new approach to this problem that we think is very promising.

Problem Posing is a new declarative programming style that unifies all major classes of programming. Programs interpreted in this style do not "call functions", "issue commands", "assert constraints", or "send messages"; they "pose problems". Program fragments are not defined as "functions", "modules", "clauses", or "objects" that do things; they are written as "resources" that can be "applied" to problems.

The Problem Posing Interpretation uses *Knowledge-Based* Polymorphism to map from a problem specification in the ambient context to the computational resources that will provide or coordinate the solution. Any programming language can be interpreted in this new way.

This interpretation is particularly effective in combination with *wrappings* (Landauer and Bellman, 1996c), our computationally reflective knowledge-based approach to integration infrastructure, since wrappings provide the Knowledge-Based Polymorphism that mediates between the posed problems and the applicable resources.

Our approach to Generic Programming is to write programs using *wrex*, the wrapping expression notation, since it explicitly leaves the posed problems in the program, and relies on the selection of computational resources to address the problems. The flexibility of run-time choices may be carried to as much detail as desired, from large-scale "legacy" components to individual arithmetic calculations. Finally, we use Partial Evaluation to make early decisions when possible, in effect "compiling out" the constant decisions, so that there is no run-time cost for decisions that will be made in the same way every time. We describe this new approach to generic programming, especially our integration technology that underlies and powers it.

Constructed Complex Systems

We have defined *Constructed Complex Systems* [Landauer and Bellman, 1996c] to be computer-mediated systems that are too complex for a single model to describe (Landauer et al., 1993). They tend to be software and hardware systems that have heterogeneous processing requirements or that have to function in complex environments. We believe that designing, building and managing such a system requires explicit attention to the infrastructure, including explicit models of the system, its architecture, and the environment in which it is expected to operate [Bellman, 1990], and suitably flexible computer-based design support [Bellman and Gillam, 1990]. Design support systems for constructed complex systems are complex themselves, since they must accommodate many different kinds of model and problem domain. In general, global design management requires integration of multiple criteria, which means that multiplicity is unavoidable because complex tradeoff calculations must be made.

We have developed a particular approach to coordination among systems called "wrapping" (Landauer and Bellman, 1995a; 1995b; 1996a; 1996b), which uses explicit meta-knowledge about every computational resource in a constructed complex system. In our view, sufficiently complex systems cannot be modeled with just one model [Bellman and Brock, 1960] [Bellman, 1990], so we need to consider model integration as one specific technical area (Walter and Bellman, 1990).

In this chapter, we extend our application of the wrapping theory to software development (Landauer and Bellman, 1995a; 1995b) by showing how the meta-knowledge that wrappings contain, and the expressive uniformities that result from stepping up to a meta-level, lead to much simpler ways of dealing with the complexity of constructed complex systems, not because the local complexities are changed, but because the global interactions are represented explicitly, and because the individual models of components and interactions are placed in a coherent computational environment in which their behavior can be organized and monitored.

Our original motivation was very large space systems (Bellman and Gillam, 1988; 1990; Bellman et al., 1993; Landauer et al., 1993), but the results have become much more generally applicable: in our "Integration Science" (Landauer and Bellman, 1996b), we study better integration methods, which are both more permissive, flexible, and semantically powerful, and more supportive of formality in the analyses of the processes and products of integration.

Structure of Paper

In this subsection, we describe the organization of the rest of the chapter. Then we begin a circular journey through some interesting new research areas in Computer Science. Actually, some of them are not really new, but there is new hope that significant progress can be made.

In the rest of this section, we introduce Generic Programming and Partial Evaluation. We first describe the current goals and progress in Generic Programming, and discuss a few example Generic Programs. We then describe the basic approach of Partial Evaluation, a bit of seeming magic called the Futamura Projections, and discuss some performance issues in using Partial Evaluation on real programs.

Later, we introduce the *Problem Posing* programming paradigm, which is a new interpretation of any programming language that uses Knowledge-Based Polymorphism to make programs much more flexible. We describe the basic notions and give some examples.

Then, we proceed to the underlying theory. Problem Posing is particularly effective in combination with "wrappings", our knowledge-based approach to integration infrastructure in constructed complex systems, and explain how it provides a reflective system architecture (Landauer and Bellman, 1995a). Reflection is important because it supports adaptation and customization (Buschmann, 1996). We describe the Problem Managers and the Wrapping Knowledge Base Semantics.

In the "Wrapping and Problem Posing" section, we show how the Problem Posing interpretation works with wrappings, and define the corresponding notation *wrex*. We claim that the meta-knowledge that wrappings contain, and the expressive uniformities that result from stepping up to a meta-level, lead to much cleaner descriptions of any software process, and much easier methods for organizing and understanding the different architectures that are presumed or enforced by those processes. We also describe two interesting applications of wrapping, one to Coordination Languages for distributed systems, and the other to system Reuse without modification of code.

Finally, we describe our conclusions and claims for Generic Programming, Partial Evaluation, and Problem Posing.

Generic Programming

In the most general sense, generic programming is about making programs more flexible, often using more interesting kinds of polymorphism, more interesting kinds of parameters (e.g., programs, types, constructors, etc.), and more interesting kinds of program analysis than compilation. There have been gradual improvements over the last 50 years:

Machine language ➡ assemblers ➡ compilers ➡ interpreters,

but we are still looking for more effective techniques, since we still have some distance to go (Shaw and Wulf, 1992). Partial Evaluation, to be described next, looks like a good way to go, because it makes explicit our choices about when to evaluate expressions and when to instantiate program fragments.

We see examples of generic programs in almost every book that describes a computational technique. The algorithms are often written descriptively for explanation, using some kind of pseudo-code. We want those descriptions to **be** the actual generic programs.

Generic genetic programming algorithm:

```
generate initial population
loop until done
        compute offspring
        retain only the ones with best fitness
```

Generic simulated annealing algorithm:

> set initial temperature and position
> loop until done
>> generate potential new position
>> check movement criterion
>> reduce temperature

Generic k-means clustering algorithm:

> generate initial cluster centers
> loop until done
>> partition data into nearest-center clusters
>> recompute cluster centers

Note that each algorithm has a "loop until done" statement, which means very different things in different contexts.

The use of context to assist in the specialization process is very important to our approach. For example, "sanity checks" in computational design models (Bellman and Gillam, 1988; 1990) are constraints determined by context. In fact, context provides and organizes **all** interpretation of symbols and symbol structures; we use it to collect and organize the symbol structure interpreters. Context determines what representations are important or useful, because it determines what each symbolic expression means or does. In addition, as we try to imbue our symbolic systems with more semantics, we bridge the gap by taking semantics to **be** the interpretation of syntax, and the interpreters to be provided by the context.

Partial Evaluation

The basic approach of Partial Evaluation is very simple (Sterling-Shapiro, 1986; Jones, 1996): if you know a program and some of the parameters, then you can specialize the program, and the resulting specialized program should be (and often is) faster. This is another old dream of computing, from the original high-level languages through extensible languages, very high-level languages, domain-specific languages, and executable specification languages. We particularly want completely automatic techniques, so that we can write our programs in the generic languages and leave the details to the compilation and execution environment. The problem has been that it is very difficult to make it work, though there are some encouraging recent signs (Consel and Danvy, 1993; Hudak and Jones, 1993; Jones et al., 1993; Jones, 1996).

Our wrappings contain much more semantic information about the program components than is usually provided with a program, and therefore much more than can be extracted from a program by itself. It is this extra information that we intend to use in our partial evaluations.

There are also some methods, originally developed for use in optimizing compilers, that are very useful here, such as symbolic execution, unfolding function calls, partly unrolling iterations and recursions, and "program point specializations" (which means replicating parts of the program with different specializations), definition creation, folding, and a kind of memoization of function calls and other program fragments. Replication particularly needs care to avoid exponential blowup.

As we describe some of the promise of partial evaluation, we will imagine a program "mix" that can do partial evaluation (our notation, borrowed from Jones (1996) takes [p] as an executable form of the program p):

for all programs p, and all inputs in1 and in2,
[[mix] (p, in1)] in2 = [p] (in1, in2),

so mix specializes p to the inputs in1 (such programs do exist for some languages [Jones, 1996]). Partial evaluation provides an adaptation mechanism for generic programs (we can easily imagine that in1 is the specialization information for a particular execution environment).

We turn to some formal reasoning that lies at the heart of the promise of partial evaluation: called the Futamura Projections (Jones, 1996), these are ways to use partial evaluation to produce compilers and compiler generators automatically.

We start with a definition: an *interpreter* is a program interp for which:

for all inputs in, and all source programs s,
[interp] (s, in) = [s] in

We claim that a kind of "compilation target" t for source program s can be computed:

t = [mix] (interp, s).

We call it a compilation target because it has the same computational effect as the original program s, since for any input in,

out = [s] in
     = [interp] (s, in)
     = [[mix] (interp, s)] in
     = [t] in,

so mix specializes the interpreter via part of its input (the source program s). This is the *first* Futamura projection.

Now

comp = [mix] (mix, interp)

turns out to be a compiler for the language interpreted by interp:

> for any source program s,
> the compilation target t has
>
> | | |
> |-----|-----|
> | t | = [mix] (interp, s) |
> | | = [[mix] (mix, interp)] s |
> | | = [comp] s. |

This is the *second* Futamura projection.

So far,

> t = [mix] (interp, s)

is a compiled form of s,

> comp = [mix] (mix, interp)

is a compiler for the language interp interprets. Finally,

> cogen = [mix] (mix, mix)

is a compiler generator for the language interp is written in:

> for any interpreter interp,
> source program s, and input in,
>
> | | |
> |-----|-----|
> | [s] in | = [interp] (s, in) |
> | | = [[mix] (interp, s)] in |
> | | = [[[mix] (mix, interp)] s] in |
> | | = [[[[mix] (mix, mix)] interp] s] in, |
> | | = [[[cogen] interp] s] in, |

so

> [cogen] interp = [comp]

is a compiler for the language of s. This is the *third* Futamura projection.

The use of these formal projections is intriguing, but the performance of the programs is important. There is good news here, too. We have shown two ways to produce output with these notions:

> | | |
> |-----|-----|
> | out | = [interp] (s, in) |
> | | = [s] in |
>
> | | |
> |-----|-----|
> | t | = [mix] (interp, s) |

$$= [comp] \ s$$

$$comp \ \ = [mix] \ (mix, \ interp)$$
$$= [cogen] \ interp$$

$$cogen \ = [mix] \ (mix, \ mix)$$
$$= [cogen] \ mix$$

The second way is often something like 10 times faster (this is well-known for the first pair above, in which interpreters in general are slower than compilers). The first way is usually much easier to write (once the program mix is written). We want to use this fact to write faster programs more easily. The hard part here, pretty clearly, is writing the program mix in the first place. In the next part of the chapter, we describe our knowledge-based integration infrastructure, which we believe will lead to much better understanding of some of the issues required for effective partial evaluation.

Problem Posing

In this section, we describe our Problem Posing Programming Paradigm (Landauer and Bellman, 1995a; 1996a; 1996b; 1996c), which underlies our approach to generic programming. We have defined *Problem Posing* as a new declarative interpretation of programs that unifies all major classes of programming. It uses what we have called *Knowledge-Based Polymorphism* to map from problem specifications to the computational resources that will provide or coordinate the solution. Any programming language can be interpreted in this new way. Problem Posing can therefore be viewed as a new programming paradigm that changes the semantics, not the syntax, of any programming language.

In any programming language, whether imperative, functional, object-oriented, or relational, there is a notion of service providers (e.g., functions to be called, state to change, messages to be fielded and acted upon, and assertions to be satisfied), and a corresponding notion of service requests (the function calls, assignments and branches, messages to send, and assertions that cause those service providers to be used). In almost all of those programming languages, we connect the service requests to the service providers by using the same names, i.e., the connections are static and permanent, defined at program construction time.

The Problem Posing interpretation breaks this connection and generally moves it to run-time, recognizing that all of the language processors can tell the difference between the service provider and the service request (this is less straightforward in relational languages such as Prolog, but there are very few programs that actually *use* the supposed reversibility of clause satisfaction). Then the language processors take the service requests and turn them into *posed problems* (hence the name), and use the wrapping processes described below (or any other mapping process) to allow a context-dependent resource selection process to select an appropriate resource for the problem in the problem context. The selection process is guided by knowledge bases that define the resources, the kinds of problems they can address, and the specific requirements for applying the resource to the problem in the context. This is what we mean by "Knowledge-Based" Polymorphism.

Problem Posing

The basic expressive notion of this interpretation is the "posed problem", and the basic computational component is the "resource". They can be connected by the "wrappings" as defined in the next section, or by any other method that uses processes and associated knowledge bases that convert a posed problem into coordinated collections of resources that can address the problem.

We have demonstrated the conceptual utility of "problem posing" in our own descriptions of systems (Landauer and Bellman, 1995a; 1996c). The "Problem posing" interpretation unifies all major classes of programming. Programs interpreted in this style do not "call functions", "issue commands", "assert constraints", or "send messages"; they "pose problems" (these are information service requests). Program fragments are not written as "functions", "modules", "clauses", or "objects" that do things; they are written as "resources" that can be "applied" to problems (these are information service providers). Any programming language can be interpreted in this new way.

Problem posing is a declarative style of programming, in which the problem to be studied (the service request) is separated from the resources that might do the studying (the service providers). It not only separates proposed solutions (the "how" of programs) from local implementation problems (the "what") in the program code, but also keeps the problems in the code explicitly, so that the proposed solutions can be related to the reasons they are there, and so that many such solutions can be made available for each problem. It therefore makes a program an organized collection of posed problems, instead of an organized collection of solutions without problems. That should make programs easier to understand, because the problems at all levels of detail remain in it.

This interpretation is particularly effective in combination with wrappings, since they provide a knowledge-based mapping from problems to resources.

Some Language Examples

The recognition of service requests and service providers in programming languages is very easy: compilers and interpreters always know the difference anyway, and so do we when we write the programs.

Here, we provide examples of the use of the Problem Posing interpretation in imperative, functional, object-oriented, and relational languages.

In C, functions are resources, so are data structures (we make no assumption that the computational resources are *active*: they can be repositories of data that are interpreted by other resources in the same way that executable files in UNIX specify which program is to interpret them). Function calls and data accesses are posed problems (converting complex data accesses to function calls is a common technique for generalization). Each function relates a posed problem to an algorithm that poses other problems (that is the code in the function definition). Data structures are used by other resources to retain and provide data (via their structure declaration).

In Lisp, S-expressions are resources (some are applicable, others not). Applications are posed problems (as in, "apply *this* function to *that* data"). Each applicable S-expression relates a posed problem to an algorithm that poses other problems (all Lisp computation is function application). Other S-expressions are used by other resources to retain and provide data.

In Smalltalk, methods are resources, so are other object components (the objects themselves are only grouping constructs). Messages are posed problems. Each method relates a posed problem, with some constraints on parameters (including which object receives the message), to other posed problems. Other object components are used by other resources to retain and provide data.

In Prolog, clauses are resources, so are tuples. Goals are posed problems. Each clause relates a posed problem, with some constraints on parameters, to other posed problems. Tuples are used by other resources to retain and provide data.

In each case, the usual program constructs are either posed problems or resources, and our interpretation differs from the usual one in the same way: the usual interpretation associates a resource with a problem when they have the same name, whereas our interpretation requires an external connection, through a knowledge base or via some other means. The simplest form of our interpretation is a one-to-one map from problems to resources; this is the same as the usual one. Clearly, then, we can keep as much of the usual interpretation of a programming language as we like, from none of it to all of it, by adjusting the mapping process from problems to resources.

Some Code Examples

We illustrate some of these notions with some small programs written in several different styles of programming language. The languages chosen are only illustrative; many others could have been used, such as Goedel (Hill and Lloyd, 1994), Leda (Budd, 1995), ML (Paulson, 1991; Ullman, 1994), Scheme (Abelson et al., 1985; Dybvig, 1987), SETL (Schwartz et al., 1986), or any of the others mentioned above.

C Code Example

Our first code example is a relentlessly imperative C program, a function for matrix multiplication:

```
int mult(matrix a, matrix b, matrix c)
    {
    int row, col, sub;
    element sum;
    if (a.cols != b.rows)
            return(0);
    if (c.rows != a.rows)
            return(0);
    if (c.cols != b.cols)
            return(0);
    for (row = 0; row < a.rows; row++)
    for (col = 0; col < b.cols; col++)
        {
        sum = 0;
        for (sub = 0; sub < b.cols; sub++)
                sum += a.vals[row][sub] * b.vals[sub][col];
        c.vals[row][col] = sum;
        }
    return(1);
    }
```

This program assumes the existence of datatypes "element" for the individual entries in the matrix, and "matrix," which is a structure that contains the matrix size and elements. It also completely ignores the space allocation question, requiring the caller to make a matrix of the proper size. It first checks for compatibility of the three matrices, and computes the product.

For the usual C interpretations, the type "element" must be one for which the addition and multiplication operator "+" and "*" are defined, and one for which zero is the additive identity. In our new interpretation, the assignments and computations become posed problems, for which other computational resources can be selected for application. So by providing a different problem to resource mapping, we can use the same code for different kinds of matrix multiplication, such as rational or big number arithmetic, or even "and-or" multiplication instead of "times-plus".

Similarly, the outer two for loops can be made completely parallel, since no execution of the inner loop depends on any other (this may be hard to detect in general, of course, but it is pretty easy in this case).

Haskell Code Example

Our next code example is in the functional programming language

Haskell (Thompson, 1996): a sequence filter (from p. 163)

```
filter :: (t -> Bool) -> [t] -> [t]

filter p [ ] = [ ]
filter p (a:x)
      | p a = a : filter p x
      | otherwise = filter p x
```

We first describe the purpose of the code, then examine its interpretation.

The first line here is a type definition: the object "filter" is a function that takes a "criterion" function (of type t -> Bool for some unspecified type t), and a list of elements of type t, and produces a list of elements of type t, by allowing only those that pass the criterion function test to get into the new list.

The second line defines the result of applying "filter" with criterion function "p" to the empty list. The rest of the lines define the result for non-empty lists (using a very common pattern-matching style: a non-empty list has a first element "a" and a rest of the list "x"). So if the expression "p a" succeeds, that is, if the element "a" passes the criterion, then the filter is recursively passed down the list, and the result is appended to the resulting list element "a". If the element "a" does not pass the criterion (the "otherwise" line), it is ignored as the filter passes on to the rest of the original list. Similar programs can easily be found in ML, Lisp, Scheme, and other languages with functional expressions.

In this case, the nature of a list as a sequential structure seems to limit the choices we might have for alternative interpretations, but we can, for example, consider the list to be generated by our filtering of it, using a very lazy evaluation. We regard a list as being defined by a first element and a generator of subsequent elements. Then the evaluation of the expressions "filter p x" might notice that "x" is a generator, and use it to produce a new first element (or not, if the generator returns an empty list). Similarly, the first element "a" might be an element generator, not evaluated until the criterion function "p" is applied to it, or only partially evaluated until "p a" can be computed. In each case, though the definition of the function has not changed, the new interpretation of expressions makes the definition much more flexible.

Declarative Programming

One of the great strengths of any declarative programming style is also its greatest weakness. For many problems, not having to specify a solution method can be terrifically liberating in conceptual clarity. However, not being able to specify a solution method can be a terrible limitation when a good one is known. Since it is one of our underlying philosophical principles [Bellman, 1990; Walter and Bellman, 1990] that **no** one method suffices for all problems, we would rather be able to use an alternative method when we know a good one, and we would rather not have to program it in a backtracking style, or indeed according to any style chosen a priori, since the difficulty of fitting the method to that style is part of why we have a different method in the first place.

We concentrate in the rest of this section on Prolog (Clocksin and Mellish, 1984; Sterling and Shapiro, 1986) to illustrate some of the advantages that the Problem Posing Interpretation brings, rather than, say, Constraint Logic Programming (Jaffar and Lassez, 1987) or Concurrent Constraint Programming (Saraswat, 1993)] styles, because Prolog is complex enough to demonstrate the main point, and because we believe that the design of other more complicated styles would be different if they had been developed using this different viewpoint. We are not singling Prolog out here; all declarative programming styles have this same problem.

Extended Example: Prolog

In this subsection, we describe how the problem posing interpretation applies to Prolog programs. We start with the way it changes the interpretation of Prolog, and then go on to show how several fundamental issues in the evaluation of Prolog programs can be studied using this framework.

Note that many Prolog implementations allow "reaching out" to other programming languages ("foreign function" interface), but few are written to allow other programming languages to "reach in". The Problem Posing Paradigm allows essentially arbitrary mixing of programming notations at the level of individual statements or even expressions. While it is true that most problems do not need that level of heterogeneity, we believe that sufficiently complex or intricate interactions will be much more easily defined using a multiplicity of styles.

The idea is to allow small versions of languages to be used directly, without the overhead required to use a full programming language. A simple extension of this idea is to build the little languages from smaller components, such as a particular expression syntax or control mechanism syntax. Prolog particularly suffers from having an awkward set of equality, comparison, and arithmetic operators, and a fairly strange notion of input and output operations (because of their side effects). The use of more appropriate mechanisms for these aspects of computing would greatly simplify and clarify the use of Prolog.

Most of the discussion of evaluation of Prolog expressions concentrates on arguments for or against one particular algorithm. We believe that no one algorithm *can* suffice for all problems, so we would rather see arguments that relate problem style to choice of algorithm. That would allow us to select an algorithm according to the kind of problem being studied.

Problem Posing Interpretation of Prolog

We view Prolog from a problem posing perspective in the following simple way, using as a first example the simple list membership predicate "member(X, Y)" from (Clocksin and Mellish, 1984) (p. 54 and p. 153), which means that list Y contains element X. The fully general predicate,

member(X, Y)

is the problem statement, and the various rule heads

member(X, [X | _])

and

member(X, [_ | Y])

distinguish the resources that can study the problem when it has the corresponding form. The rules themselves

member(X, [X | _]).

and

member(X, [_ | Y]) :- member(X, Y).

are the resource definitions as plans that decompose the resource behavior into a sequence of (zero or more) posed problems. Finally, the rule ordering is important; matching is considered (at least conceptually) for each rule in turn. Because the interpretation is driven by the problems posed in the program, we can be much more flexible in studying different approaches.

The way that Prolog allows known list structure in the head of a rule to help select the rule is one of the important features that allow programs to be succinct, since the matching process is implicit. It is also a very weak form of our selection criteria for resources, and we will show that our approach allows some other flexibilities in addition.

An example that illustrates this feature is "intersection(X, Y, Z)", which means that list Z is the intersection of lists X and Y [Clocksin and Mellish, 1984] (p. 154):

```
intersection([], X, []).
intersection([X | R], Y, [X | Z]) :- member(X, Y), !, intersection(R, Y, Z).
intersection([X | R], Y, Z) :- intersection(R, Y, Z).
```

The next example is "quicksort(L, S)", which means that the list S of integers is the sorted version of the list L, using C. A. R. Hoare's quicksort algorithm (Clocksin and Mellish, 1984, p. 157):

```
quicksort(L, S) :- quisortx(L, S, []).
```

This example uses two auxiliary relations "quisortx(L, S, X)", which also means that S is the sorted list L, and that X is some auxiliary list:

```
quisortx([H | T], S, X) :- split(H, T, A, B),
                           quisortx(A, S, [H | Y]),
                           quisortx(B, Y, X).
quisortx([], X, X).
```

and "split(H, T, L, M)", which means that the list [H | T] is partitioned into two lists L and M, with the elements of L all at most H, and the elements of M all more than H:

```
split(H, [A | X], [A | Y], Z) :- A =< H,
                                 split(H, X, Y, Z).
split(H, [A | X], Y, [A | Z]) :- A > H,
                                 split(H, X, Y, Z).
split(_, [], [], []).
```

In this example, we get an immediate win from considering the comparisons to be posed problems, namely, generality of application. If A and H are integers, then we can use the usual comparison operations. If they are not, then we can have other resources defined that can make a comparison between two items of the same or compatible types, regardless of what type that is. With that change, the same quicksort procedure applies to a list of any mutually comparable data types.

Basic Algorithms of Prolog

There is much recent work on the study of scheduling methods for logic programs (Marriott et al., 1994), which is the order in which the terms on the right-hand side of rules are considered, on search strategies for complex constraint sets (Saraswat, 1993), which is the more general problem including order of constraints (i.e., rules in Prolog), and on abstract domains for compilers (Cortesi et al., 1994), which are used for generic interpreters for Prolog (LeCharlier and Hentenryck, 1992). We provide an alternative interpretation that allows a rather different kind of flexibility of behavior of Prolog programs.

There are several aspects of the usual conceptual interpreter for Prolog that are good candidates for generalization or at least explicit study: rule set groupings and ordering, scheduling, cut and negation, and perhaps more, but we will consider only these ones in this chapter.

We know that no one method suffices for all problems, so we need to allow problem-specific methods. We believe that we will need to select methods for particular parts of the process at compile time or maybe even run time, according to the particular problem.

We first describe the general shape of the evaluation algorithm, in order to describe the places at which it can be usefully made variable. This particular version implements the usual backtracking method. It would be the default resource for this problem, but in special cases, we want to use some other methods.

We assume that there is a problem state structure, which contains nodes for all of the partially evaluated problems. The node for a problem has all of the bindings found so far, and some state information about where to resume the search (and likely other things, but this is all we need for this discussion). These nodes represent checkpoints to which the backtracking may have to return. Each time we begin to evaluate a problem, we add a problem node to the structure. Each time we begin to examine a rule whose LHS has matched the problem, we add a rule node to the structure. Each time we begin to evaluate a term on the RHS of a rule, we add a term node to the structure. We assume that initially, the structure is empty.

Given a posed problem in the form of a term

symbol(... args ...),

the basic evaluation algorithm is invoked by the ProLog interpreter as a Prolog evaluation resource.

At the time a new problem is considered, the rules that have the same predicate symbol as the problem does are extracted from the complete set (we can only do this statically if the rules are not changed during execution). The rule ordering mechanism is defined by the problem "rule set", which can present the rules in different orders in different contexts. In particular, here is where the careful coordination of concurrency of rules ("OR-parallelism") would be.

When a rule is first matched (i.e., unified) with the problem currently under consideration, the terms in the rule must be checked, accumulating bindings as they succeed. The scheduling mechanism for term ordering in rules is defined by the problem "RHS-body", which can easily produce different orderings in different contexts. In particular, here is where the careful coordination of concurrency of terms ("AND-parallelism") would be.

One of the trickiest operators in Prolog is the 'cut' operator. In order to evaluate a cut, we only have to prevent any of the terms to the left of the cut operator from being restarted, by popping away the backtracking restart points until we get back to the parent node 'fail' rule (this clearly depends on maintaining the presentation order of terms in the rule).

Any other aspect of Prolog interpretation may be made variable by making a resource and defining the context conditions under which it will be connected to a particular posed problem. This style of analysis should make studies of different choices much easier, since different choices depend on context conditions, and the conditions and their implied re-sources are all accessible. Moreover, since the original default methods are all still available, programs that do not satisfy the requisite context conditions do not invoke the new methods and therefore need not be changed at all.

ReUse without Modification

Software ReUse is one of the major practical problems facing most organizations that have or use software. It turns out that the Problem Posing interpretation offers a new way to deal with the problem: reuse without modification.

Since language processors for most programming languages can easily distinguish between symbol definitions and symbol uses, *any* such language may be interpreted differently via the Problem Posing Interpretation. That means we can use same programming languages as now, just different compilers, which are looking at the same syntax with a completely new interpretation. This changed interpretation has tremendous implications for the problem of reusing programs (Landauer and Bellman, 1996a). We can use same source code as we already do, with no changes *at all*, and still add and replace functions because we can intercept the function calls (using code fragments generated by the new compilers) to mediate the connections between function calls and function definitions. We automatically get an enormous increase in flexibility, before we have to change any part of the system's application code.

This is done by identifying and separating the posed problems from the computational resources. For example, we can intercept the function calls and separate them from the called functions. Once we have the separation, we can then insert almost any kind of integration infrastructure, for instrumentation, monitoring, using different functions under different conditions, and using completely new functions for previously difficult situations.

Thus we can gradually wean ourselves from the old code and increase our use of whatever new code is written (for example, when we must migrate the system to a new hardware base, we can do it gradually). Old code is kept only as long as it is still useful.

As we propose many different new interpreters here, we believe that we can rely on the fact that over the last few decades, we have learned how to write them easily and well (Kaplan, 1994), and that the changes we propose to them are very small.

Integration Infrastructure: Wrapping

The Problem Posing interpretation is particularly effective in combination with "wrappings," our computationally reflective knowledge-based approach to integration infrastructure. Wrappings are an approach to the development, integration, and management of heterogeneous computing systems.

In this section, we give an overview of the wrapping approach; many more details are elsewhere (Landauer and Bellman, 1996a; 1996b; 1997f) (and references therein). We have developed a new approach to the development, integration, and management of heterogeneous computing systems, based on two kinds of software entities: *Wrapping Knowledge Bases* (WKBs) and *Problem Managers* (PMs) (Landauer, 1990a; Bellman, 1991b). The WKBs contain explicit, machine-processable, qualitative information (called *wrappings*) about the system components, architecture, and all the computational or information processing elements (called *resources*) in the system: not just how to use them, but also whether and when and why and in what kinds of combinations they should or can be used. The PMs are algorithms that use the wrapping descriptions to determine which resources to use and how to combine them to apply to problems.

These ideas have proven to be useful, even when implemented and applied in informal, *ad hoc* ways in some of the applications that have made or are making use of wrappings even at this preliminary stage of development (Miller and Quilici, 1992; Bellman and Reinhardt, 1993).

The wrappings provide an example of our notion of a coordination system (Landauer and Bellman, 1996b), since the scaffolding (which we have called infrastructure) remains with the program at run-time.

In a similar vein, there has recently been a strong call for retaining the scaffolding used to build theorem proving and other deductive systems (Talcott, 1994; Giunchiglia et al., 1994), to combat the difficulties with their construction and (especially) modification. We believe that these systems are also amenable to our methods, even though they are not usually described as collections of resources that share context and other information to effect a common purpose.

Wrapping Overview

The advantages of our knowledge-based integration technology are (1) a simplifying uniformity of description, using the meta-knowledge organized into *Wrapping Knowledge Bases*, and (2) a corresponding simplifying uniformity of processing that meta-knowledge using algorithms called *Problem Managers*, which are active integration processes that use the meta-knowledge to organize the system's computational resources in response to problems posed to it by users (who can be either computing systems or humans). We have shown its wide applicability in software and system development (Landauer and Bellman, 1996a; 1997a; 1997e) (and references therein). In particular, since the entire process is recursive (Landauer and Bellman, 1993a), wrappings provide a general way to allow specialized methods to participate, in contexts for which they are appropriate.

The wrapping theory has four basic features.

1. ALL parts of a system architecture are *resources* that provide an information service, including programs, data, user interfaces, architecture and interconnection models, and everything else.
2. ALL activities in the system are *problem study*, (i.e., all activities *apply* a resource to a *posed problem*), including user interactions, information requests and announcements within the system, service or processing

requests, etc.. We therefore specifically separate the problem to be studied from the resources that might study it.

3. *Wrapping Knowledge Bases* contain *wrappings*, which are explicit machine-processable descriptions of all of the resources and how they can be applied to problems to support what we have called the *Intelligent User Support* (IUS) functions [Bellman, 1991b]:

- *Selection* (which resources to apply to a problem),
- *Assembly* (how to let them work together),
- *Integration* (when and why they should work together),
- *Adaptation* (how to adjust them to work on the problem), and
- *Explanation* (why certain resources were or will be used).

Wrappings contain much more than "how" to use a resource. They also help decide "when" it is appropriate, "why" you might want to use it, and "whether" it can be used in this current problem and context.

4. *Problem Managers (PMs)*, including the *Study Managers(SMs)*, and the *Coordination Managers (CM)*, are algorithms that use the wrapping descriptions to collect and select resources to apply to problems. They use implicit invocation, both context and problem dependent, to choose and organize resources. The PMs are also resources, and they are also wrapped.

The wrapping information and processes form expert interfaces to all of the different ways to use the resources in a heterogeneous system that are known to the system (Bellman and Gillam, 1988; 1990; Landauer, 1990a). The most important conceptual simplifications that the wrapping approach brings to integration are the uniformities of the first two features: the uniformity of treating everything in the system as resources, and the uniformity of treating everything that happens in the system as problem study. The most important algorithmic simplification is the Computational Reflection (Smith, 1984; Abelson et al., 1985; Smith, 1986; Kiczales et al., 1991; Landauer-Bellman, 1996a) provided by treating the PMs as resources themselves: we explicitly make the entire system reflective by considering these programs that process the wrappings to be resources also, and wrapping them, so that all of our integration support processes apply to themselves, too. It is this ability of the system to analyze and modify its own behavior that provides the power and flexibility of resource use.

Resources

First, every part of the system is a *resource* that provides some kind of *information service*. So a resource is any part of the system that does or represents anything, including tools, functions, ordinary files, databases, programs, data, user interfaces, other communication interfaces, interconnection architectures, symbolic formula manipulation systems, scripts that refer to other resources (e.g., scenarios, event records, plans), analysis tools that refer to other resources (e.g., comparison, parametric study), and everything else (Everything!). We think about *applying resources* instead of "invoking tools" because the resource being applied might not be the active part of that process.

We view any program as an integrated collection of resources, each with its own role or purpose in the collection. The resources communicate through a conceptual message-passing bus, which is responsible for distributing information or service requests and announcements. This viewpoint expects the old programs to be disintegrated into separate resources with information exchanges among them. This explicit decomposition of monolithic programs (which we term "Software Disintegration") does have a slight execution performance impact. But computer hardware is still becoming faster, so we can afford to spend a little time on the run-time integration to get the required flexibility, as we have accepted the slight (and continually decreasing) inefficiencies of using compilers to get more programming flexibility and comprehensibility.

A resource need not be an entire program or tool. Certain uses of a complicated program may be considered separately. Different styles of use of a complex resource can be wrapped separately (i.e., there may be many wrappings for one resource). Combinations of resources that commonly apply together can be wrapped together (i.e., there may be many resources described by one wrapping). In addition, we view the user as a resource also. The user screens define what the system expects to show and tell the user, and what the system expects to get from the user (in the way of selections and input data). These resources are a way of describing the expected interactions. The descriptions are tailored to expected uses, so that the same software may have many different descriptions. A program may have many partial descriptions; complete descriptions are not needed (they are often much too complicated anyway, especially for most of the useful "legacy software" that we might want to retain and use).

Problems

Second, everything that happens in the system is the response to a *posed problem.* Since we know that not all problems can be solved, we think of *studying* problems rather than *solving* them. Moreover, that allows the system to do more or less undirected explorations as it studies certain kinds of problems, so it can treat some problems as suggestions for study when appropriate, not as strict goals. Our notion of problems deals with context as an explicit part of the problem study process: there must be a problem context before posing a problem even makes sense. Therefore, problem study always occurs after a context is chosen and a problem is posed (we allow these choices to be made either by human users or by other programs or program components as users). Therefore, instead of thinking about "issuing commands" to the system, we think about *posing problems* for the system. Then the wrapping processes find resources that can deal with the problems by studying them directly or decomposing them into collections of simpler problems. This *problem posing* interpretation of programs and systems allows the wrapping processes to mediate all problem study using the Wrapping Knowledge Bases. Instead of having direct calls between resources, we have the resources pose problems that correspond to service requests. Other resources announce information services that they provide and the interactions are all mediated through the Wrapping Knowledge Bases. This mediation process can be viewed as a kind of Knowledge-Based Polymorphism.

Wrappings

Third, every resource has one or more *wrappings*, which are explicit machine-processable descriptions of the different ways to use the resource, including the different roles in their use played by the Intelligent User Support functions we described earlier: *Selection, Assembly, Integration, Adaptation,* and *Explanation.* A wrapping is not simply an interface "to" a resource; it is an interface to the "use" of a resource. In any environment, even if it is clear exactly which resource to apply, help may be needed to apply it (getting the appropriate parameter values for a computational tool, for example). We wrap "uses" of resources instead of resources in and of themselves, since many analysis tools have grown by accretion over the years, and common ways to use them have developed their own style. We gain conceptual simplicity by separating the styles of use into different descriptions. Similarly, combinations of resources that often work together may have a single wrapping for the combination, in addition to separate wrappings for separate ways to use the resources by themselves. It follows that there is not a one-to-one correspondence (bijection, to use the proper mathematical term) between wrappings and the resources they describe. This non-bijection is one of the important normalizing features of wrapping, since it allows the uses of resources to be much more simply described.

The wrappings are not actually surrounding a given software resource, as one might imagine various intelligent front-end programs are. Instead, the wrappings are collected into potentially several knowledge bases, which allows us to test this metaknowledge with known static methods for evaluation of knowledge bases (Bellman, 1990; Landauer, 1990c; Bellman and Landauer, 1995a; 1996a).

Eventually, as we learn more about the kinds of information that are important to different users or uses of a resource, there may be a family of wrappings that will differ in what subset of knowledge about a resource's computational process and status they contain. For example, although wrappings are machine-processable in order that the system can help the user select, integrate, and adapt resources, nonetheless a human user will most likely always have a richer understanding of what the wrapping information implies. Hence, we want to keep some information in the wrappings that is meaningful to a human user and not yet (or maybe ever) processable by the system. All knowledge in the wrapping will be accessible, including the purpose of the program, its applicability (e.g., when this program is appropriate), its limitations, assumptions, prerequisites and any default values (i.e., the knowledge to support integration); how to invoke this resource, its different interfaces, and the type and format of both the data it requires and the data it produces, including the domain of inputs and any other constraints on the input values (i.e., the knowledge to support assembly). The wrappings may include knowledge of how, if a given input data set does not fit the program assumptions, it can be altered to fit those assumptions. The wrappings will eventually include such overall characteristics as how long the resource takes to apply and how much it usually costs to use it. It will include any error handling mechanisms or explanations of errors. Lastly, it includes information on the type of algorithms, and other information that may be needed for deciding whether to use the program or for explaining its use.

Problem Managers

Fourth, the *Problem Managers* (PMs) are algorithms that use the wrapping descriptions to collect and select resources to apply to problems. There is a distinguished class of PMs called *Study Managers* (SMs) that coordinate the basic problem study process, and a specialized PM called the *Coordination Manager* (CM), which is a kind of basic "heartbeat" that drives all of the processing. This process is described in more detail in the next subsection. The SMs mediate between the problem at hand and the wrappings to select and apply resources to the problem, and the CM cycles between posing problems and using the SM to study them.

Finally, and perhaps most importantly, we explicitly make the entire system reflective by considering these programs that process the wrappings to be resources also, and wrapping them, so that all of our integration support processes apply to themselves, too. The entire system is therefore Computationally Reflective [Maes and Nardi, 1988; Kiczales et al., 1991; Landauer-Bellman, 1993a; 1996a; Buschmann, 1996]. It is this ability of the system to analyze and modify its own behavior that provides the power and flexibility of resource use.

Wrapping Processes

The processes that use the wrapping information are as important to us as the information itself [Landauer and Bellman, 1992; 1993a]. The wrapping processes are active coordination processes that use the wrappings for the Intelligent User Support functions. They also provide overview via perspective and navigation tools, context maintenance functions, monitors, and other explicit infrastructure activities.

Coordination Manager

The alternation between problem definition and problem study is organized by the *Coordination Manager* (CM), which is a special resource that coordinates the wrapping processes. The basic problem study sequence is monitored by a resource called the *Study Manager* (SM), which organizes problem solving into a sequence of basic steps that we believe represent a fundamental part of problem study and solution.

The CM runs a sequence of steps shown in Figure 1, and later in Figure 3 (written in the *wrex* notation, which we describe in detail later), that manages the overall system behavior.

To "Find context" means to establish a context for problem study, possibly by requesting a selection from a user, but more often getting it explicitly or implicitly from the system invocation. It is our placeholder for conversions from that part of the system's invocation environment that is necessary for the system to represent to whatever internal context structures are used by the system. To "Pose problem" means to get a problem to study from the problem poser (a user or the system), which includes a problem name and some problem data, and to convert it into whatever kind of problem structure is used by the system (we expect this is mainly by parsing of some kind). To "Study problem" means to use an SM and the wrappings to study the given problem in the given context, and to "Present results" means to tell the poser what happened. Each step is a problem posed to the system by the CM, which then uses the default SM to manage the system's response to the problem. The first problem, "Find context", is posed by the CM in the initial context of "no context yet", or in some default context determined by the invocation style of the program.

The main purpose of the CM is cycling through the other three problems, which are posed by the CM in the context found by the first step. This way of providing context and tasking for the SM is familiar from many interactive programming environments: the "Find context" part is usually left implicit, and the rest is exactly analogous to LISP's "read-eval-print" loop, though with very different processing at each step, mediated by one of the SMs. In this sense, the CM is a kind of "heartbeat" that keeps the system moving.

Study Manager

The Study Manager is the central algorithm of our problem study strategy. It is the default resource for the problem "Study problem". It assumes that it is given a context, problem poser, problem, and some associated data (usually by the CM). Its purpose is to organize the resources

```
Find context: determine containing context from user or by invocation
indefinite loop:
        Pose problem: determine current problem and problem data
        Study problem: use an SM to do something about problem
        Present results: to user
```

Figure 1: Coordination Manager (CM) Step Sequence

that process the wrappings, and to cause and monitor the behaviors the wrappings describe. There may be other resources that are intended for this same problem, but the SM is the one that is chosen if no other resource applies. This overlap of function illustrates a general principle of resource coordination we have used throughout this approach to integration: instead of trying to find one general method for all cases (which we do not believe is possible anyway [Bellman and Brock, 1960; Bellman, 1990]), we combine general methods for certain processes with powerful specialized methods that apply in certain contexts. For example, the "means-end" analysis of GPS [Newell and Simon, 1961; Ernst and Newell, 1969; Newell and Simon, 1972] is a general method for searching through a space, but it needs to be augmented with special searches organized differently for different spaces [Allen et al., 1990].

We have divided the "Study problem" process into three main steps: "Interpret problem", which means to find a resource to apply to the problem; "Apply resource", which means to apply the resource to the problem in the current context; and "Assess results", which means to evaluate the result of applying the resource, and possibly posing new problems. We further subdivide problem interpretation into five steps, which organize it into a sequence of basic steps that we believe represent a fundamental part of problem study and solution. The default SM step sequence is shown in Figure 2, and later in Figure 5 in the *wrex* notation.

To "Match resources" is to find a set of resources that might apply to the current problem in the current context. It is intended to allow a superficial first pass through a possibly large collection of Wrapping Knowledge Bases. To "Resolve resources" is to eliminate those that do not apply. It is intended to allow negotiations between the posed problem and each wrapping of the resource to determine whether or not it can be applied, and make some initial bindings of formal parameters of resources that still apply. To "Select resource" is simply to make a choice of which of the remaining candidate resources (if any) to use. To "Adapt resource" is to set it up for the current problem and problem context, including finishing all required bindings. To "Advise poser" is to tell the problem poser (who could be a user or another part of the system) what is about to happen, i.e., what resource was chosen and how it was set up to be applied. To "Apply resource" is to use the resource for its information service, which either does something, presents something, or makes some information or service available. To "Assess results" is to determine whether the application succeeded or failed, and to help decide what to do next.

SM Recursion

Up to this point in the description, the SM is just a (very) simple type of planning algorithm. The Computational Reflection that makes it a framework for something more comes from several additional design features. First, all of the wrapping processes, including the CM and SM, are themselves wrapped, as we mentioned before. Second, the processing is

---

Interpret problem:

> **Match resources**: get list of candidate resources
> **Resolve resources**: reduce list via negotiation, make some bindings
> **Select resource**: choose one resource to apply
> **Adapt resource**: finish parameter bindings, use defaults
> **Advise poser**: describe resource and bindings chosen

Apply resource: go do it
Assess results: evaluate

Figure 2: Simplest Study Manager (SM) Step Sequence

completely recursive: "Match resources" is itself a problem, and is studied using the same SM steps, as are "Resolve resources", "Select resource", and ALL of the other steps listed above for the SM and for the CM, that is, every step in their definitions is a posed problem. The simple form we described above is the default SM at the bottom of the recursion. Third, there are other SMs that have slightly more interesting algorithms (such as looping through all the candidate resources to find one that succeeds, as described in the next section). These three features mean that every new planning idea that applies to a particular problem domain (which information would be part of the context) can be written as a resource that is selectable according to context; it also means that every new mechanism we find for adaptation or every specialization we have for application can be implemented as a separate resource and selected at an appropriate time. It is this recursion that leads to the power of wrapping, allowing basic problem study algorithms to be dynamically selected and applied according to the problem at hand and the context of its consideration.

The recursion in the SM immediately gives it a more robust and flexible strategy, since the resources that carry out the various steps of the processing can be selected and varied according to context. At every step, the SM has the choice of *posing* a new problem for that step or using a basic function that "bottoms out" the recursion. The choice is generally made to pose new problems, unless (1) there would thereby be a circularity: same problem, same context (the definition of context is such that this condition is relatively easy to check), or (2) there is an explicit indication that posing a problem would not be fruitful (we will show how that case is determined a little later). The important point is that the SM is only our most basic mechanism for controlling these steps; more advanced versions of matching, selecting and so forth will be implemented by resources that are chosen like any others, using the same recursive steps.

This SM recursion is unusual, since it is a recursion in the "meta-" direction, not within the problem domain or within the planning process. The result is that planning the planning process itself is an integral part of the SM behavior, not a separate kind of function. The SM recursion also means that there are many layers of study context, each with its own problem context, problem poser, and problem specification.

In particular, the "study problem" step in the CM means that the SM is chosen in the same way as any other resource: resources that can address a "study problem" problem are selected using the default SM. That means that the SM we described above is only a default that occurs at the bottom of the recursion: others can be used.

The recursive use of the SM to pose problems that are part of its own and the CM processing prevents them from being just another general planner or recursive problem solver. The basic steps and their ordering in the CM and SM form a default case that can be superseded by any more clever mechanisms for particular problem contexts.

Recursion in the meta-direction is another way to view Computational Reflection, and it has some interesting limitations discussed elsewhere (Landauer and Bellman, 1993a; 1995a). Note here that the posed problem approach sidesteps the limitations mentioned, by making everything a resource, as far down as one cares to go into the implementation, and that it is the WKBs that help select whether to further the meta-recursion by invoking the SM, or to stop it by going to a specially coded resource.

We are going to make essential use of this reflection in our partial evaluations: since the system has access to its own computational resources, it has a much better chance to make appropriate simplifications and specializations than if it had no knowledge of its own structure.

Another SM

In this section, we describe the looping SM mentioned in the previous section. Since the basic SM problem study sequence is completely recursive, the bottom of the recursion is very important; it contains the most general (or default) problem study processes. For this set of processes to be adequate for our needs, it must perform enough of the right fundamental activities to allow the extendibility we have briefly described above. We have made one set of such choices; others are likely to be possible. The *basic* SM step functions (our name for the processes at the bottom of the recursion) are very simple processes (matcher, resolver, selector, adaptor, advisor, applier, assessor) that do the most basic form of each step of the process.

For example, the match step in the SM either poses the problem "Match resources," or it calls the basic matcher, which examines the PKB to make its candidate list, and the resolve step either poses a problem "Resolve candidates," or it calls the basic resolver, which examines the WKB to check on other requirements for each candidate resource. Similarly, the select step either poses the recursive problem, or it calls the basic selector, which chooses the first unselected candidate resource, and removes it from the list (the reason we describe the selection in this way will become apparent shortly).

The basic adaptor does nothing at all, since we have decided that there is no *basic* adaptation function. Adaptation is hard, and we have simply decided that there is no fundamental kind of adaptation, and whatever kinds we decide to use will be selected according to problem context and other criteria. The basic advisor tells the problem poser what resource application is to be applied (this includes both the selected resource and any bindings required for invocation parameters). The basic applier reads the WKB to find out how to apply the resource and then does that.

The basic assessor checks for successful application. It interacts with the basic selector to provide a simple way to try each candidate successively. There are three possibilities for each resource application here: application success, application failure, and no application. The resource is expected to notify the Study Manager (or whomever applies it) of application success or failure; the criteria to be used are relevant only to the resource itself, and need not be made available. If the application succeeds, the assessor simply notifies the containing SM step (in the next higher level of the recursion) and terminates. If the application fails, then the assessor goes back to the selection step, so that other candidate resources can be selected (this is the meaning of the use of the term *unselected* in the description of the basic selector). If there are no candidate resources to be applied, certain of the steps above are skipped, and the assessor notifies the SM that whatever problem it was trying to solve has no applicable resources. Then that instance of the recursion is marked to use the basic step function only, since further recursion would not be fruitful.

It is clear from the recursive description above that the looping SM is collecting the alternative possibilities (candidate resources) and trying them all (with the assessor and selector). This seems to make the SM into a very simple-minded kind of planner, which in this context is any resource that transforms a problem into an organized set of resource applications.

However, the recursive use of the SM to pose problems that are part of its own processing prevents the SM from being just another general planner or recursive problem solver. The basic steps and their ordering in the SM form a default case that can be superseded by any more clever mechanisms for particular problem contexts. The recursion means that if there is a better matcher, then there will be a PKB entry for the problem "Match resources" that refers to it, and it may get selected, depending on context, instead of the basic matcher described above. Similarly, if there is an adaptation mechanism implemented as a resource, then there will be a PKB entry for the problem "Adapt resource" that refers to this new resource, and it may get selected, depending on context, instead of the basic "do-nothing" adaptor described above.

The original SM we described has a simpler basic selector and assessor. The selector chooses the first candidate, and does not retain or adjust the candidate list, and the assessor treats application failure by notifying the containing SM step of the failure, without trying anything else.

We can also change the original SM in a different way, by reconsidering the resources that apply to the steps. The SM above is a one-step-at-a-time planner, with immediate application of resources when selected. Instead, we can apply a resource by placing an invocation command into a configuration script for later execution, or setting it into a UNIX 'make'file, or even analyzing it and placing the result in a structure (e.g., Verification and Validation studies). Other SMs can plan more complex combinations (e.g., the Planning Parser).

An Application

The SM recursion has profound implications in other applications of wrapping [Landauer and Bellman, 1995a], but for its application to software development, the fact that the SM can be selected is a key. Since the SM steps above that interact with the Wrapping Knowledge Base (WKB) are themselves posed problems, we can use completely different syntax and semantics for different parts of the WKB in different contexts, as long as they support the SM steps above, and select the appropriate processing algorithms according to context. In particular, whether one writes about one WKB or several is a matter of taste and viewpoint. Finally, the SM is only one of a family of processes called *Problem Managers* (PMs), each of which is wrapped and selectable according to context, and each of which can pose problems and organize their study in different ways. Other PMs we have written include a Planning Parser that decomposes problems into smaller ones, and another that implements the "means-ends" analysis mentioned above. For example, the original context and problem are problems posed by the CM, since all of the CM steps are problems posed to the system and studied by the SM. The kinds of resources that might be chosen by the SM to apply to the first two problems would be menus or other requests to the human user to make a choice of context and problem, and the SM is itself the main resource that applies to the "Study problem" problem.

The recurrence of posing and studying problems is managed by the CM. The pose problem resource (i.e., any of the resources applied by the SM to the "Pose problem" problem) reads expressions from somewhere, as determined by context, and the SM interprets them. The pose problem resources usually have a parser (different ones may have different parsers), which reads text and makes symbol structures, within a particular context defined by the "Find context" step of the CM.

The wrapping approach provides a very straightforward place to perform studies of different kinds of resources needed for application system development. It also makes a very good approach to the problem of software infrastructure for large system integration (nothing requires all of the resources to be software).

For the application of all this to software development, this approach offers the following intriguing property: you can change the fundamental nature of the programming language (or architecture), not by replacing the old one with a new one, but by adding a new one to work side by side with the old one, with context information used to disambiguate if the expressions (or applications) themselves do not. There are "little languages" with little parsers (Kaplan, 1994) to make the connection between language expressions and activity in other servers or databases and ALL of those choices are variable (these can be more dynamic than those in [Wile, 1991;

Pepper and Wile, 1992]). Compatibility is not the issue; NO one language can express all the things we might want to express, so there cannot be one comprehensive compatible organization; we have to accept the notion that there will be multiple partially incompatible languages.

Wrapping Knowledge Bases

The Wrapping Knowledge Base (WKB) information is not just about how to use the resource, but also why, when, and whether to use it. It contains information about assumptions, limitations, applicability, scope, and styles of use. Since the SM steps are selected, the syntax and semantics can be heterogeneous, as long as there are some common entries that support the SM steps above.

The information contained in the wrappings is organized into two KBs. The *Wrapping* KB (or WKB) holds the main information about each resource, and the *Planner* KB (or PKB) holds information that lets it act as a preliminary filter for the WKB. The PKB has entries that direct a problem study to a set of resources, and will be described later on in this section.

The Wrapping Knowledge Base (WKB) has an entry for each style of use of each resource. It describes how to use a resource, when and whether to use it and in which particular contexts, but does not necessarily define what the resource is or does (i.e., it is not expected to be a formal specification of the effects of using the resource).

The Study Manager uses the current problem context to help make selections. The basic idea is to treat each resource as being appropriate only in certain problem contexts, providing certain services, and having certain service requirements. Then these service units are combined into a configuration that provides the service needed to solve the problem.

The wrapping semantics that support this combination of resources include both local interpretation of problem language in resource-specific terms and explicit scope restrictions that describe appropriate constraints on the individual resources. Our approach to wrapping semantics assumes that resources will be examined in a context that contains goals (i.e., problems), available information, and services to be provided or constructed.

The WKB is designed to be used by the SM for both choosing and using resources, and the PKBs are explicitly organized as a preliminary filter for the choice process:

• Match step uses PKB to help with the Select function,
• Resolve step uses WKB to help with the Assemble and Integrate functions,
• Select step is for the Select function,
• Adapt step uses WKB to help with the Adapt and Assemble functions,
• Advise step helps with the Explanation function,
• Apply step uses WKB to help with the Assemble function,
• Assess step helps with the Explanation function.

The "Integrate" IUS function primarily shows up as choosing what to apply, and the "Assembly" IUS function is about deciding how to apply it. We have taken "Select" as the fundamental IUS function, and will build the others using resources selected for those tasks.

WKB Semantics

The information in a wrapping is organized into several sections, all of which contain resource-centered descriptions:

- Identification Section (Who and what am I?),
- Problem Section (What problem is this?), including an interpretation part (What does this problem mean to me?),
- Context Section (What problem and context conditions allow me to be considered?),
- Requirements Section (What information services do I need from my environment in order to be applied?), including specialization and application parts (How can I be adapted? How can I be applied?), and
- Products Section (What new information services do I produce when applied?).

The viewpoint in an individual wrapping is completely local; it describes only this style of use of this resource: whether and how it can be used, how to convert a more problem-domain type of problem into resource-local terminology, and what sort of conditions there on the style of use of the resource.

First, the Identification Section names and describes the style of resource use. It gives the resource use style a reference name for use by the system, and the generic type of the style of use of the resource (e.g., simulation, text file, user interface, etc.).

The Problem Section describes whether and how the resource applies to particular problems. For each problem that can be interpreted by this style of use of this resource, there is a *Problem Application Description*, which describes whether and how the resource applies to the particular problem. The Problem Application Description has a Problem Statement and contains the other sections. The Problem Statement is currently a structured problem specification with a name and (zero or more) qualifier keywords (so that the problems may be grouped into major classes, and distinguished within the classes by qualifiers). We expect that eventually Problem Statement notations will be devised that are interpreted to understand what problem is being addressed. This Problem Statement is actually a partial problem specification, which can be more or less specific. If it is very specific, then there are likely to be many problem statements for any given class of problem, and thus the search for a particular wrapping will be time-consuming, but each one can be very simple. Conversely, if it is not specific, there will only be a few problem statements for each class of problem, the search for an appropriate wrapping will be faster, but each one will have more complicated conditions and behavior descriptions.

The Problem Application Description divides the rest of its information into several parts: Interpretation, Context, Requirements, Application, and Products. The parts divide up the selection criteria and application instructions for this resource. They are used in the process of planning the use of the resource or its combination with others.

The Interpretation part of the Problem Section maps the external problem language, which is suited to the problem, into an internal language, which is more suited to the resource. It tells what the problem means to the resource, and what role the resource plays in the problem. This separation means that new applications and application areas can use their own problem language, and the wrappings will have to be provided or arranged to interpret that language in their own terms.

The Context Section describes the conditions under which it is appropriate to consider the resource, including properties of the problem specification, the existing context, and the expectations for availability (or non) of other resources, services, and goals. Different contexts may place different constraints on the use of a resource, and cause it to provide different products.

The Requirements Section describes what requirements the resource needs from the environment in order to be applied, including availability or not of input data, supporting processes and services, particular kinds or items of information, or known-to-be-solvable problems. Satisfying these requirements may involve posing further problems before the selected resource may be applied.

The Adaptation part of the Requirements Section defines how the resource is adapted (in this context, for this problem). It defines resource specializations in terms of default bindings, alternative resources for special cases, and sometimes expert interfaces, which are other resources that have expert information about the use of this one.

The Application part of the Requirements Section defines how the resource is used (in this context, for this problem). It defines resource access in terms of data access declarations and protocol access declarations, as described in the discussion of the Assemble IUS function above.

The Products Section of a Problem Application Description in a resource wrapping defines what new information is produced when the resource is applied, or what service is provided. This notion of having the resource itself say what it can do is important for reasons of locality and scaling, locality because the information is local to that resource wrapping, and scaling because there is no need to have the wrapping contain descriptions of all possible uses of a resource. "Locality" as used here allows the system to have distributed knowledge, which is a crucial part of allowing the system to be "open" to new resources with new capabilities. Knowledge of system resources can be added incrementally, instead of having to alter the organization of one central store of that knowledge whenever a new resource is made available.

Planner Knowledge Base

The Planner Knowledge Base (PKB) is used as a quick filter for the WKB for "Match resource" (which is the only IUS function that searches). It has entries of the form

(problem, information, resource),

where "problem" is a partial specification of one of the problems considered in the WKB, "information" is a sequence of context conditions that are prerequisites for considering or applying the resource, and "resource" is a partial specification of the resource being described (i.e., the resource and some of its argument bindings). It is the PKB that is used in the "Match resources" step to find a set of candidate resources for application, and the WKB that is used to "Resolve resources" down to a smaller set that can be applied.

The level of detail one wants in the PKB problem entries is application- and even problem-dependent.

In case the original problem specification is very detailed, the PKB can contain enough information about problems to produce very few matches, and the resource(s) selected for resolve (i.e., the resources that are used to study the "Resolve resource" problem) can reduce that list to a very short one. In this case, the adapt resource may only have to fill in a few more bindings. However, sometimes resolve will go too far (down to nothing), and the assess and associated recovery processes will need to be more cleverly written. If the problem specification is less detailed, then there will be many matches, and the resolve process will be much harder, or at least more time-consuming. Then adapt may have to fill in lots of bindings, and may have to pose many more problems to get help.

Planning Parsers and other PMs

An alternative to the "one step at a time" process of the SMs is a planning PM called the Planning Parser (PP). The PP tries to collect together a complete set of resources that can solve a problem (or a set of problems) before any resources are applied. The PP uses the information in the WKB in a planning process that determines which resources are to be used. It uses a parser for matching and resolving these wrappings, and for building scripts to invoke groups of resources together. It assumes that we have both initial problems and information available. Problems to be studied are treated as goals: information to be found or services to be constructed. Information is context, available data, or available services. The wrapping may mention these either as requirements or as products.

We use a variant of the Cocke-Kasami-Younger parsing algorithm [Aho and Ullman, 1973], as modified by V. Pratt for LINGOL [Pratt, 1975] and extended by C. Landauer for METER [Landauer, 1977; Landauer and Mah, 1981] to use Early algorithm type pre-filtering of the WKB entries as rules (see [Graham et al., 1980] for a description and complexity analysis of a similar combination parser, [Kay, 1980] for a general description of this style of parser, called a *chart* parser, and [Norvig, 1992] for a recent description and example implementation of a similar parser). This parser matches both goals and available information simultaneously (both bottom-up and top-down), which is both forward and backward reasoning in the planning context, and uses a pre-filter of applicable rules to reduce the search effort.

The difference between parsing applied to string patterns and parsing in this planning context is that there is no notion of "position" in the string. The pre-filter in this application uses PKB information instead of location.

We use this parser because it produces all partial parses, which in this application means that it computes all sets of resource applications that satisfy the original goal(s), and also produces all partial sets that satisfy some of the goals. This property is invaluable for diagnosing planning failures, using both what information was missing and what resources could not be applied. Then the rest of the selection process can choose one plan to implement.

Combinatorial explosion in this process is mitigated by having an analog of context-sensitive syntax checking. The WKB entries are used in a "Resolve resources" manner to reduce the number of resources that are applicable, and hence the number of alternative entries in the plan (partial parse tree).

With some restrictions on the allowed resource invocation and definition syntax, we can also use a Prolog-style unification algorithm [Robinson, 1965; Clocksin and Mellish, 1984; Sterling and Shapiro, 1986] for the matching process. In some problem contexts, such as application areas with a well-defined problem specification language, we can also use unifiers as resources for matching or as PMs in their own right. With some slight modifications, a unifier can also keep track of its partial and complete matches.

Problem Decomposition

In this section, we discuss how problem decomposition would work in a wrapping environment. To pose and study a problem (often) means to pose and study a corresponding network of related problems [Forbus and deKleer, 1993]. The CM and SM do not need to coordinate their activities, since the decomposition plan is simply another resource that might apply to the problem. In particular, in some application areas, if other methods have failed, the decomposition is expected to occur. This requires a notion of preference ordering on the candidate resources, which is as simple as another resource that implements the selection criteria.

There are generally no default resources for a problem called "decomposition" that would take problems and decompose them, since the question of how decomposition works is very problem specific. These decomposition resources would be other PMs that have domain-specific knowledge of problem structure, or explicit plans as programs already decomposed and written as problems posed for other resources [Agre and Chapman, 1990] [Payton, 1990]. Many plans will have hard-coded versions in addition to the explicit plan version, so we can gradually get more flexible plans.

The systems will have many SMs, including the monolithic algorithms we have described before and ones built by combining simpler steps: this choice allows multiplicity in problem study. In fact, we use individual resources, plans built from steps, and more detailed plans from smaller steps; we need comparisons, evaluations, monitors, and methods for re-encapsulation. In some application areas, such as autonomous systems, it matters how fast these resources are [Maes, 1990a].

There is a refinement sequence in the sets of resources that can study a problem:

• problem studied by resource (one method),
• problem studied by resource with steps (one method each step),
• problem set studied by separate resources (one resource each method).

This approach requires a notion of refinement, at least de facto, since it involves trying different combinations of basic computational steps for studying problems. In particular, it includes the simplest version of refinement, in which one step is refined into a configuration of steps, but we do not need to solve the hard theoretical problem of partially compatible refinements.

Case-Based Planning and the Meta-Bump

In this section, we consider the use and reuse of plans for case-based reasoning [Alterman, 1986; Hammond, 1986; Hammond, 1989; Kolodner, 1993; Converse, 1994]. We assume a repository of cases for case-based planning: a case includes a problem specification, a resource that was applied to it (the plan is the resource), and the actual behavior during the study. The problem specification language must also include some context conditions and details. A plan includes a pattern of event steps, each of which is a resource application (or a problem statement, with enough context to make the resource selection possible). Plans can also include tests and branches and other control information.

The general problem is "Study problem" with known example cases. The plan is roughly (this is implemented by the SM invoked in the context "case study"):

• find analogous problems (this SM has combined match, resolve, and select

steps);
- adapt corresponding plans to current problem;
- monitor plan behavior (this SM has combined apply and assess steps);
- when plan behavior diverges from analogous case behavior, then the analogy fails.

There is also the problem of what to do with failures: when there is a failure, bump up the analysis to a metalevel (this is the "meta-bump"). We believe that this bumping will eventually converge most of the time, and when it doesn't, it is because there aren't enough resources for the problem.

The phrase "bumping up", using the "meta-bump," means that instead of deciding that our set of resources "does not apply", we use "how to adapt" and "what to adapt" resources and analogies to proceed. This corresponds to "fixing" the plan, using an explicit strategy (Converse, 1994). It is not the same as the usual recursion in planning, in which a new goal is pushed into the goal set. The meta-bump is also not the same as the "abstraction hierarchy" (Sacerdoti,1975a; Sacerdoti, 1975b; Sacerdoti, 1977), which takes more and more abstract representations of the original problem space, and organizes its planning around them. Perhaps the closest work in planning to our meta-bump is the work on meta-planning (Stefik, 1981a; Stefik, 1981; Wilensky, 1981), which explicitly allows the planning algorithm to assist in planning the planning process itself.

So the first plan is (more precisely):

- theory: find analogy (however thin),
- make (adapt) plans accordingly, and
- monitor;
- bump up if the plan diverges;
- then bumping up will eventually converge

.

It can also be given by a sequence of steps as shown in Figure 3.

The information needed to decide "divergence[]" would be maintained in the context. An alternative problem specification for "bump up" is

$$\text{MBSM ["plan", (<problem>, <data>)].}$$

There need to be (one or more) resources corresponding to each of the problems in the above plan:

- find analogy,
- adapt to,
- monitor application,
- divergence, and
- bump up.

When the analogy that led to the plan diverges from the actual behavior (this test is performed by another resource, or even combined with user

```
define
MBSM [ <problem>, <data> ]:
        [
        <oplan> = find analogy [ <problem>, <data> ],
        <plan> = adapt [ <oplan> ] to [ <problem>, <data> ],
        monitor application [ <plan> ],
        if (divergence []): then
                bump up,
        ],
```

Figure 3: Steps in Meta-Plan

observation, as in Oates and Cohen [1994]), then we bump up to the next meta-level. There must also be a resource that prevents an indefinite "bump up."

This PM (or a different one) could also establish shortcut connections and monitor them, comparing them with background connection computations; it can supersede direct connections with connection computations when the monitor chooses to. There are also need to be resources for each of the operations in the above description:

• establish,
• monitor,
• comparing,
• supersede, and
• chooses.

The important issues in this approach are how to find methods to code, retain, and retrieve cases for analogizing.

Wrapping and Problem Posing

In this section, we show how the problem posing interpretation works with wrappings, and describe the *wrex* notation we can use to express problems.

The basic expressive notion of wrapping is the "posed problem", and the basic computational component is the "resource" (this research led directly to the Problem Posing Interpretation). They are connected by the "wrappings," which consist of processes and associated knowledge bases that convert a posed problem into coordinated collections of resources that can address the problem. We have developed this notion into the *wrex* notation, which extends the application of wrapping all the way down to the data access and expression evaluation level of detail. For example, the Meta-Bump Study Manager of Figure 3 was written in *wrex*, and the CM and SM can also be written in *wrex*, as in Figure 4 and Figure 5.

The Wrapping Expression Notation *wrex*

The wrapping expression notation *wrex* [Landauer and Bellman, 1995a] is one possible way to use the Problem Posing paradigm. It is a "Problem Posing" notation intended both for programming "in-the-large", i.e., as an architecture description language for resources written in other more ordinary programming languages, and for programming "in-the-small", i.e., as a language in which to write some of the (perhaps less time-constrained or more experimental) computational resources. We think that both kinds of programming are necessary for building reliable systems because they allow us to make explicit the interconnection between architectural models and the component models (Allen and Garlan, 1994; Garlan and Perry, 1995; Rice and Seidman, 1994; Shaw, 1994; Shaw et al., 1995; Shaw and Garlan, 1996).

The *wrex* notation extends the application of wrapping all the way down to the data access and expression evaluation level of detail. In this notation, a program does not issue commands, impose constraints, assert facts, invoke functions, or even send messages; it *poses problems*. The CM and SM step sequences in Figure 1 and Figure 2 can be written in *wrex*: the SM is in Figure 5, and the CM is in Figure 4.

Object-oriented languages like Smalltalk (Goldberg and Robson, 1983) gain at least part of their impressive conceptual simplicity and power of expression from having implicit notations for sending messages, and interpreting all expression evaluation as sending messages of one kind or another. The expression syntax of *wrex* reflects the central role of problem study even as the syntax for Smalltalk reflects the central role of message passing. We are not nearly as interested as programmers in the selected resource (the analogue of message destination) as in the posed problem (the analogue of message type), since many different resources can satisfy an information service request.

Since the fundamental activity of wrapping is "apply resource to problem", and the Study Manager (SM) is the resource usually applied to study a problem, we make that operation implicit, and use explicit text in the program for problem specifications and plans.

The analogue of message transmission in Smalltalk, in which juxtaposition is the implicit operator for sending messages, is the posing of problems (in some appropriate syntax):

<posed problem> ::= <problem name> '[' <problem specification> ']'
['by' <resource>] ['in' <context>]

(using <resource> = default SM if omitted, which is usually, and <context> = poser context if omitted, which is almost always), in which juxtaposition is the implicit operator for studying problems. The <resource> is the one expected to interpret the problem posed, not the one expected to apply to the problem. The problem data is part of the <problem specification>, and is

```
define
CM [ <user> ]:
        [
        Find context [ <user> ],

        for ever :
                [
                <problem> = Pose problem [ <user> ],
                <result> = Study problem [ <user>, <problem>, <context> ],
                Present results [ <user>, <result> ]
                ]
        ],
```

Figure 4: Coordination Manager (CM) Step Sequence, in *wrex*

```
define
SM-simple [ <poser>, <probname>, <data>, <context> ]:
        [
        <candidates> = Match resources [ <probname>, <data>, <context> ],
        if ( <candidates> == empty): then return FAIL_NO_CANDS,

        <candidate applications> = Resolve resources [ <candidates>,
                                <probname>,
                                <data>, <context> ],
        if ( <candidate applications> == empty): then return FAIL_NO_APPLS,

        /* choose one of the remaining candidate resources */
        <selection> = Select resource [ <candidate applications> ],

        <resource application> = Adapt resource [ <selection>, <probname>,
                                <data>, <context> ],

        <resp> = Advise poser [ <poser>, <resource application>, <probname>,
                                <data>, <context> ],
        if (not <resp>): then return FAIL_NO_APPLS,

        <result> = Apply resource [ <poser>, <resource application>, <con
                text> ],

        <success flag> = Assess results [ <result>, <probname>, <data>,
                                <context> ],
        return <result>
        ],
```

Figure 5: Study Manager (SM) Step Sequence, in *wrex*

usually considered to be the same as the specification. The differences are unimportant for the purposes of this chapter. In general, we can pass the values that specify the problem either as problem data or in the context. The former is more useful in case the data is problem specific or transient, and the latter when it might also be useful later on in the program.

Every problem has some amount of problem data (possibly empty). Every resource application has a success or failure result (which is made available to other problem specifications). All control issues are problem grouping and ordering issues. Control statements in *wrex* look almost the same as they do in current programming languages: sequencing with ',', grouping with blocks and procedures, and even grouping with loops and conditionals.

Nearer the low end in granularity, expression evaluations are also posed problems. We can use any usual syntax here, too, if we change the interpretation, so that, for example,

 a + b

is the problem '+', with data 'a' and 'b'. It is easy to make compilers convert the infix notation properly.

Finally, the innermost part of expression evaluation is read-style data access, and the last part of assignment evaluation is write-style data access. The basic access mechanisms are reading and writing values, and the only real question is what kinds of value structures (i.e., data types) we want to allow. This question is application specific, and not part of the generic notation.

Syntax of *wrex*

We describe the syntax of *wrex* briefly in this subsection; most of the details should be clear from the examples. The syntactic items of *wrex* are Variables, Constants, and three kinds of grouping structures. Variables consist of multiple words, delimited by '<' and '>'. Constants are words, other symbols (such as operator symbols and delimiters), numbers (integers and otherwise), or strings (both single and double quoted).

The three Constructors for grouping items into structures are List, Set, and Group. A List contains multiple items, separated by commas, and delimited by '[' and ']'. A Set contains multiple items, separated by commas, and delimited by '{' and '}'. Finally, a Group also contains multiple items, separated by commas, and delimited by '(' and ')', but Groups not in other Groups can omit the parentheses. Syntax recognition of these structures is extremely easy.

To facilitate readability, we allow separated problem names, such as

 find [...] in [...] using [...],

which has 'find ... in ... using' as a problem name. Programs are sequences of these syntactic items (i.e., Groups without parentheses). The simple posed problem is a Group whose last element is a List.

We describe these syntactic items using the features of the CM in Figure 4. The entire resource is one group (with a comma at the end to separate it from the following ones):

'define' 'CM' '[...]' ':' '[...]'.

'Find context'

is a separated problem name. So is

'define' ... ':' '[...]'.

Then

'for every ':' [...]'

is a posed problem with *wrex* statements as data, and

'<problem> = Pose problem [<user>]'

is also a group without parentheses. It is also a posed problem with problem name '='. Finally, 'if' and 'for' expressions are defined concepts, not primitive. So is '='.

Decision Times and Performance

Finally, we want to make a point about performance issues, and claim that the flexibility of *wrex* need not cost too much. Here we rely on the fact that partial evaluation has much more information to use than is usually the case.

Decisions about program structure are made at many different times

- Language Design time
- Compiler Generation time
- Program Generation time
- Compile time
- Link time
- Load time (for operating systems, this is boot time)
- Run time (for operating systems, this is multi-user time)

Requiring too many decisions to be made at Run time is as rigid as restricting them to any other times, and it also costs greatly in performance. If it is provided, a program can use knowledge of the execution environment with partial evaluation to reduce the time considerably (Kiczales et al., 1991). When it has available the context and collection of available resources, it can reason about which resource selections are made. If it can deduce that a posed problem is only addressed by one resource, it can avoid the full search and the SM recursion entirely.

In particular, in considering the partial evaluation of *wrex*, there are many more kinds of input available than for programs in most other programming languages:

- Program and input data (as usual),
- Wrappings and other semantic information as context data, and
- Collection of available resources.

Much greater specialization will result, and we hope much better programs: both faster AND more easily changed.

Conclusions and Other Claims

We have now come full circle, back to the implications of these results to Generic Programming. The common theme of this paper has been to make the times at which design decisions must be made more flexible, without costing too much in performance. For Generic Programming, we can defer many decisions from Program Generation, Compile, and even Link time, to Run time. Actually, with Domain-Specific Languages and Architectures [Hayes and Roth et al., 1995], we can make those decisions earlier as well as later. Because of Partial Evaluation, we can defer many decisions from Language Design and Compiler Generation time to Run time.

Our main claim for this research is that the perennial goal of programming, to make programs easier to write and more reliable, will be easier to achieve this way than others.

Using Partial Evaluation, the Problem Posing interpretation can produce regular compiler code, instead of leaving the decisions all to Run time. We don't know how fast it will be, but we're very hopeful about it. We want programs that are BOTH easier to write AND faster to run. Of course, before this can happen, we need to write some partial evaluators like "mix" for *wrex*, which we expect to be hard.

The Knowledge-Based Polymorphism with wrappings that we get with Problem Posing has interesting reuse and system re-engineering implications, such as Reuse without modification, and the Problem Posing interpretation also provides a kind of interoperability for systems written in (almost) any programming language. To use *wrex* as a coordination language, the various components need to be written in languages that can accept unsolicited information from outside the program, which is hard for some.

Finally, none of this solves the hard modeling problems in any particular domain (they are still hard). However, it does allow them to be solved more separately, and the integration of even partial solutions to be more automatic or at least better supported by the system.

References

Abelson,Harold, Gerald Sussman, with Julie Sussman (1985). *The Structure and Interpretation of Computer Programs*, Bradford Books, now MIT.

Agre, Philip E. & David Chapman (1990). "What Are Plans for?", 17-34 in Maes, 1990b.

Aho, Alfred V. & Jeffrey D. Ullman,(1973). *The Theory of Parsing, Translation, and Compiling, Volume I: Parsing*, Prentice-Hall.

Allen, James, James Hendler & Austin Tate (eds.) (1990). *Planning*, Morgan Kaufmann.

Allen, Robert & David Garlan (1994). "Formal Connectors", CMU-CS-94-115, CS Department, CMU (March).

Alterman,Richard (1986). "An Adaptive Planner", 65-69 in *Proceedings AAAI'86: The Fifth National Conference on Artificial Intelligence*, 11-15 August 1986, Philadelphia, Pennsylvania, AAAI (1986); reprinted in pp. 660-664 in Allen et al., 1990].

Bellman,Kirstie L. (1990). "The Modelling Issues Inherent in Testing and Evaluating Knowledge-based Systems", 199-215 in Chris Culbert (ed.), Special Issue: *Verification and Validation of Knowledge Based Systems, Expert Systems With Applications Journal,*1(3).

Bellman,Kirstie L. (1991b). "An Approach to Integrating and Creating Flexible Software Environments Supporting the Design of Complex Systems", 1101-1105 in *Proceedings of WSC'91: The 1991 Winter Simulation Conference*, 8-11 December 1991, Phoenix, Arizona (1991); revised version in Kirstie L. Bellman, Christopher Landauer, "Flexible Software Environments Supporting the Design of Complex Systems", *Proceedings of the Artificial Intelligence in Logistics Meeting*, 8-10 March 1993, Williamsburg, Va., American Defense Preparedness Association (1993).

Bellman, Kirstie L. and April Gillam (1988). "A knowledge-based approach to the conceptual design of space systems", 23-27 in *Proceedings of the 1988 SCS Eastern MultiConference*, March 1988, The Society for Computer Simulation.

Bellman, Kirstie L. & April Gillam (1990). "Achieving Openness and Flexibility in *VEHICLES* ", 255-260 in *Proceedings of the SCS Eastern MultiConference*, 23-26 April 1990, Nashville, Tennessee, Simulation Series, Volume 22, No. 3, SCS.

Bellman Kirstie L., April Gillam & Christopher Landauer (1993)."Challenges for Conceptual Design Environments: The VEHICLES Experience", *Revue Internationale de CFAO et d'Infographie*, Hermes, Paris (September).

Bellman,Kirstie L. & Christopher Landauer (1995a). "Designing Testable, Heterogeneous Software Environments", pp. 199-217 in Robert Plant (ed.), *Special Issue: Software Quality in Knowledge-Based Systems, Journal of Systems and Software*, Volume 29, No. 3.

Bellman, Kirstie L. & Al Reinhardt (1993). "Debris Analysis Workstation: A Modelling Environment for Studies on Space Debris", *Proceedings of the First European Conference on Space Debris*, 5-7 April 1993, Darmstadt, Germany.

Bellman,Richard & P. Brock (1960). "On the concepts of a problem and problem-solving", *American Mathematical Monthly*, Volume 67, pp. 119-134.

Budd,Timothy A. (1995). *Multiparadigm Programming in Leda*, Addison-Wesley (1995).

Burstein, Mark H. (ed.) (1994). *Proceedings ARPA / Rome Laboratory Workshop on Knowledge-Based Planning and Scheduling Initiative*, 21-24 February 1994, Tucson.

Buschmann,Frank (1996). "Reflection", Chapter 17, pp. 271-294 in [Vlissides-et-al.96].

Clocksin,W.F. & C. S. Mellish (1984). *Programming in Prolog*, Springer (1981); second edition.

Consel,C. & O. Danvy (1993). "Tutorial Notes on Partial Evaluation", *Proceedings 20th PoPL: The 1993 ACM Symposium on Principles of Programming Languages*, Charleston, SC.

Converse, Timothy M. (1994)."Plan Reuse in the Long Term", pp. 27-33 in [Burstein, 1994].

Coplien, James O. (1995). Douglas C. Schmidt (eds.), "Pattern Languages of Program Design", *Proceedings PLoP'94: First Annual Conference on Pattern Languages of Programs*, August 1994, Monticello, Illinois.

Cortesi,Agostino, Baudoin Le Charlier & Pascal van Hentenryck (1994). "Combinations of Abstract Domains for Logic Programs", pp. 227-239 in *Proceedings of PoPL'94: The 21st ACM SIGACT-SIGPLAN Symposium on Principles of Programming Languages*, 17-21 January, Portland, Oregon.

Davis,Paul K. & Richard Hillestad (eds.) (1992). *Proceedings of DARPA Variable-Resolution Modeling Conference*, 5-6 May 1992, Herndon, Virginia, Conference Proceedings CF-103-DARPA, RAND Corp.

Dybvig,R. Kent (1987). *The Scheme Programming Language*, Prentice-Hall

Ernst, G. & A. Newell (1969). *GPS: A Case Study in Generality and Problem Solving*, ACM Monograph Series, Academic Press.

Feigenbaum,E.A. & J. Feldman (eds.) (1963). *Computers and Thought*, McGraw-Hill.

Forbus, Kenneth D. & Johann de Kleer (1993). *Building Problem Solvers*, A Bradford Book, MIT Press.

Garlan,David & Dewayne E. Perry (eds.) (1995). "Special Issue on Software Architecture", *IEEE Transactions on Software Engineering*, Volume SE-21, No. 4 (April).

Giunchiglia, F., P. Pecchiari & C. L. Talcott (1994). "Reasoning Theories: Towards An Architecture for Open Mechanized Reasoning Systems", IRST Technical Report 9409-15 and Stanford University Technical Note STAN-CS-TN-94-15 (December 1994); also available via anonymous ftp from host "steam.stanford.edu", file "/pub/MT/94omrs.ps.Z", 227Kb (availability last checked 20 October 1998); revised version pp. 157-174 in *Proceedings of FroCoS'96: The First International Workshop on Frontiers of Combining Systems*, 26-29 March 1995, Munich, Germany (March 1996); also available via anonymous ftp from host "steam.stanford.edu", file "/pub/MT/96frocos.ps.Z", 77Kb (availability last checked 20 October 1998).

Goldberg, Adele & David Robson (1983).*Smalltalk-80: The Language and its Implementation*, Addison-Wesley.

Graham, Susan L., Michael A. Harrison & Walter L. Ruzzo (1980). "An Improved Context-Free Recognizer", *ACM Transactions on Programming Languages and Systems*, Volume 2, No. 3, pp. 415-462 (July).

Hammond, Kristian (1986). "CHEF: A Model of Case-Based Planning", pp. 267-271 in *Proceedings AAAI'86: The Fifth National Conference on Artificial Intelligence*, 11-15 August 1986, Philadelphia, Pennsylvania, AAAI; reprinted in pp. 655-659 in [Allen et al, 1990].

Hammond,Kristian (1989). *Case-Based Planning: Viewing Planning as a Memory Task*, Volume 1 of *Perspectives in Artificial Intelligence*, Academic Press.

Harrison, William & Harold Ossher (1993). "Subject-Oriented Programming (A Critique of Pure Objects)", pp. 411-428 in Andreas Paepke (ed.), *Proceedings of OOPSLA'93: The Eighth Conference on Object-Oriented Programming, Systems,*

Languages and Applications, 28-30 September 1993, Washington, D.C.

Hayes-Roth,Barbara, Karl Pfleger, Philippe Lalanda, Philippe Morignot, & Marka Balabanovic (1995). "A Domain-Specific Software Architecture for Adaptive Intelligent Systems", *IEEE Transactions on Software Engineering*], Volume SE-21, No. 4, pp. 288-301 (April 1995).

Hill, Patricia & John Lloyd (1994). *The Goedel Programming Language*, MIT.

Hudak, P. & N. D. Jones (eds.) (1993). "Partial Evaluation and Semantics-Based Program Manipulation", *SIGPLAN Notices*, Volume 26, No. 9.

Jaffar, Joxan & Jean-Louis Lassez (1987). "Constraint Logic Programming", pp. 111-119 in *Proceedings PoPL'87: 1997 ACM SIGACT-SIGPLAN Symposium on Principles of Programming Languages*, January 1987, ACM (1987).

Jones,N.D. (1996). "Partial Evaluation", *Computing Surveys*, Volume 28, No. 3 (September).

Jones,N.D, C. K. Gomard & P. Sestoft (1993). *Partial Evaluation and Automatic Program Generation*, Prentice-Hall.

Kaplan,Randy M. (1994). *Constructing Language Processors for Little Languages* (includes PC disk), John Wiley.

Kay,Martin (1980). "Algorithm schemata and data structures in syntactic processing", Report CSL-80-12, Xerox PARC; reprinted in Barbara Grosz, Karen Sparck-Jones, Bonnie Lynn Webber (eds.) (1986). *Readings in Natural Language Processing*, Morgan Kauffman.

Kiczales, Gregor, Jim des Rivieres & Daniel G. Bobrow (1991). *The Art of the Meta-Object Protocol*, MIT Press.

Kolodner, Janet (1993). Case-Based Reasoning, Morgan Kaufmann.

Lakoff, George (1987). *Women, Fire, and Dangerous Things*, U. Chicago Press.

Landauer, Christopher (1977). "Table Parser Description", informal report (available from the author), Pattern Analysis and Recognition Corp.

Landauer, Christopher (1990a). "Wrapping Mathematical Tools", pp. 261-266 in *Proceedings of the 1990 SCS Eastern MultiConference*, 23-26 April 1990, Nashville, Tennessee, Simulation Series, Volume 22, No. 3, SCS (1990); also pp. 415-419 in *Proceedings of Interface'90: The 22nd Symposium on the Interface (between Computer Science and Statistics)*, 17-19 May 1990, East Lansing, Michigan.

Landauer, Christopher (1990c). "Correctness Principles for Rule-Based Expert Systems", pp. 291-316 in Chris Culbert (ed.), *Special Issue: Verification and Validation of Knowledge Based Systems, Expert Systems With Applications Journal*, Volume 1, No. 3.

Landauer, Christopher & Kirstie L. Bellman (1992). "Integrated Simulation Environments" (invited paper), pp. 409-431 in [Davis-Hillestad92]; shortened version in Christopher Landauer, Kirstie Bellman, "Integrated Simulation Environments", *Proceedings of the Artificial Intelligence in Logistics Meeting*, 8-10 March 1993, Williamsburg, Va., American Defense Preparedness Association.

Landauer, Christopher & Kirstie L. Bellman (1993a). "The Role of Self-Referential Logics in a Software Architecture Using Wrappings", *Proceedings of ISS '93: the 3rd Irvine Software Symposium*, 30 April 1993, U. C. Irvine, California.

Landauer, Christopher & Kirstie L. Bellman (1995a). "The Organization and Active Processing of Meta-Knowledge for Large-Scale Dynamic Integration", pp. 149-160 in *Proceedings 10th IEEE International Symposium on Intelligent Control, Workshop on Architectures for Semiotic Modeling and Situation Analysis in Large Complex Systems*, 27-30 August 1995, Monterey.

Landauer, Christopher & Kirstie L. Bellman (1995b). "Active Integration Frameworks", *Proceedings IEEE International Conference on Engineering of Complex*

Computing Systems, 6-10 November 1995, Ft. Lauderdale.

Landauer, Christopher & Kirstie L. Bellman (1996a). "Knowledge-Based Integration Infrastructure for Complex Systems", *International Journal of Intelligent Control and Systems*, Volume 1, No. 1, pp. 133-153.

Landauer, Christopher & Kirstie L. Bellman (1996b). "Integration Systems and Interaction Spaces", pp. 161-178 in *Proceedings of FroCoS'96: The First International Workshop on Frontiers of Combining Systems*, 26-29 March 1996, Munich.

Landauer, Christopher & Kirstie L. Bellman (1996c). "Constructed Complex Systems: Issues, Architectures and Wrappings", pp. 233-238 in *Proceedings EMCSR 96: Thirteenth European Meeting on Cybernetics and Systems Research, Symposium on Complex Systems Analysis and Design*, 9-12 April 1996, Vienna .

Landauer, Christopher & Kirstie L. Bellman (1997a). "Model-Based Simulation Design with Wrappings", pp. 169-174 in *Proceedings of OOS'97: Object Oriented Simulation Conference, WMC'97: 1997 SCS Western Multi-Conference*, 12-15 January, Phoenix, SCS International (1997).

Landauer, Christopher & Kirstie L. Bellman (1997e). "MUDs, Integration Spaces, and Learning Environments", *31st Hawaii Conference on System Sciences, Volume I: Collaboration Technologies*, 6-9 January 1998, Kona, Hawaii.

Landauer, Christopher & Kirstie L. Bellman (1997f). "Wrappings for Software Development", pp. 420-429 in *31st Hawaii Conference on System Sciences, Volume III: Emerging Technologies*, 6-9 January 1998, Kona, Hawaii.

Landauer, Chrisopher, Kirstie L. Bellman & April Gillam (1993). "Software Infrastructure for System Engineering Support", *Proceedings AAAI '93 Workshop on Artificial Intelligence for Software Engineering*, 12 July 1993, Washington, D.C.

Landauer, Christopher & Clinton Mah (1981). "Message Extraction Through Estimation of Relevance", Chapter 8, in Oddy et al., 1981.

Le Charlier, Baudoin & Pascal van Hentenryck (1992). "A Generic Abstract Interpretation Algorithm for Prolog", pp. 137-146 in *Proceedings of ICCL'92: the 1992 International Conference on Computer Languages*, 20-23 April 1992, Oakland, California.

Luger (ed.),George F. (1995). *Computation and Intelligence Collected Readings*, AAAI, MIT.

Maes, Pattie (1990a). "Situated Agents can have Goals", pp. 49-70 in [Maes, 1990b].

Maes, Pattie (ed.), (1990b). Special Issues of *Robotics and Autonomous Systems*, Volume 6, Nos. 1 and 2 (June); reprinted as Pattie Maes (ed.), *Designing Autonomous Agents: Theory and Practice from Biology to Engineering and Back*, MIT / Elsevier (1993).

Maes,Pattie & D. Nardi (eds.) (1988). *Meta-Level Architectures and Reflection, Proceedings of the Workshop on Meta-Level Architectures and Reflection*, 27-30 October 1986, Alghero, Italy, North-Holland.

Marriott, Kim, Maria Jose Garcia de la Banda & Manuel Hermenegildo (1994). "Analyzing Logic Programs with Dynamic Scheduling", pp. 240-253 in *Proceedings of PoPL'94: The 21st ACM SIGACT-SIGPLAN Symposium on Principles of Programming Languages*, 17-21 January, Portland, Oregon.

Miller,Lawrence H. and Alex Quilici (1992). "A Knowledge-Based Approach to Encouraging Reuse of Simulation and Modeling Programs", in *Proceedings of SEKE'92: The Fourth International Conference on Software Engineering and Knowledge Engineering*, IEEE Press.

Newell, Allen & H. A. Simon (1961). "GPS, A Program that Simulates Human Thought", in *Lernende Automaten*, R. Oldenbourg KG; reprinted in pp. 279-293 in [Feigenbaum & Feldman, 1963]; reprinted in pp. 59-66 in [Allen et al., 1990];

reprinted in pp. 415-428 in [Luger, 1995].

Newell, Allen & H. A. Simon (1972). *Human Problem Solving*, Prentice-Hall.

Norvig,Peter (1992). *Artificial Intelligence Programming: Case Studies in Common Lisp*, Morgan Kauffman.

Oates,Tim & Paul R. Cohen (1994)."Mixed-Initiative Schedule Maintenance: a First Step Toward Plan Steering", pp. 133-143 in [Burstein, 1994].

Oddy,R.N., S. E. Robertson, C. J. van Rijsbergen & P. Williams (eds.) (1981). *Information Retrieval Research], Proceedings of the Joint ACM and BCS Symposium on Research and Development in Information Retrieval*, June, 1980, Cambridge University, Butterworths, London.

Paulson, Lawrence C. (1991). *ML for the Working Programmer*, Cambridge U. Press.

Payton, David W. (1990). "Internalized Plans: A Representation for Action Resources", pp. 89-104 in [Maes, 1990b].

Pepper, Peter & David Wile (1992)."Local Formalisms: An Algebraic View", Technical Report, Information Sciences Institute, USC (28 June 1992).

Pratt, Vaughan (1975)."LINGOL - A Progress Report", working paper 89, MIT; also available via World-Wide Web at URL "http://boole.stanford.edu/pub/lingol75.ps.gz", 26kb (availability last checked 20 October 1998).

Rice, M.D. & S. B. Seidman (1994). "A Formal Model for Module Interconnection Languages", *IEEE Transactions on Software Engineering*, Volume SE-20, No. 1, pp. 88-101.

Robinson,J.A. (1965). "A Machine-Oriented Logic based on the Resolution Principle", *Journal of the ACM*, Volume 12, No. 1, pp. 23-41.

Sacerdoti, Earl D. (1975a). "Planning in a Hierarchy of Abstraction Spaces", *Artificial Intelligence*, Volume 5, No. 2 (1975); reprinted in pp. 98-108 in [Allen-et-al.90].

Sacerdoti, Earl (1975b). "The Nonlinear Nature of Plans", pp. 206-214 in *Proceedings IJCAI'75: The 4th International Joint Conference on Artificial Intelligence*, Morgan Kaufmann; reprinted in pp. 162-170 in [Allen et al., 1990].

Sacerdoti,Earl D. (1977). *A Structure for Plans and Behavior*, Elsevier North-Holland.

Saraswat,Vijay A. (1993). *Concurrent Constraint Programming*, MIT.

Schwartz,J.T., R. B. K. Dewar, E. Dubinsky, E. Schonberg (1986). *Programming with Sets: An Introduction to SETL*, Springer.

Shaw, Mary (1994). "Procedure Calls Are the Assembly Language of Software Interconnection: *Connectors Deserve First-Class Status*", CMU-CS-94-107, CS Department, CMU (January).

Shaw,Mary, Robert DeLine, Daniel V. Klein, Theodore L. Ross, David M. Young, and Gregory Zelesik (1995). "Abstractions for Software Architecture and Tools to Support Them", pp. 314-335 in [Garlan & Perry, 1995].

Shaw, Mary & David Garlan (1996). *Software Architecture: Perspectives on an Emerging Discipline*, Prentice-Hall (1996).

Shaw, Mary & William A. Wulf (1992)."Tyrannical Languages *still* Preempt System Design", pp. 200-211 in *Proceedings ICCL'92: The 1992 International Conference on Computer Languages*, 20-23 April 1992, Oakland, California; includes and comments on Mary Shaw, William A. Wulf, "Toward Relaxing Assumptions in Languages and their Implementations", *ACM SIGPLAN Notices*, Volume 15, No. 3, pp. 45-51 (March 1980).

Smith, Brian Cantwell (1984). "Reflection and Semantics in LISP", *Proceedings of PoPL'84: The Eleventh Annual ACM Symposium on Principles of Programming*

Languages, 15-18 January, Salt Lake City.

Smith, Brian Cantwell (1986). "Varieties of Self-Reference", in Joseph Y. Halpern (ed.), *Proceedings of TARK '86: Theoretical Aspects of Reasoning about Knowledge*, 19-22 March 1986, Monterey, California.

Stefik, Mark J. (1981a). "Planning with Constraints", *Artificial Intelligence Journal*, Volume 16, pp. 111-140.

Stefik, Mark J. (1981b). "Planning and Meta-Planning", *Artificial Intelligence Journal*, Volume 16, pp. 141-169.

Sterling, Leon & Ehud Shapiro (1986). *The Art of Prolog*, MIT.

Talcott, Carolyn L. (1994). "Reasoning Specialists Should Be Logical Services, Not Black Boxes", pp. 1-6 in *Proceedings of CADE-12: Conference on Automated Deduction, Workshop on Theory Reasoning in Automated Deduction*, 26 June - 1 July, Nancy, France (1994); also available via anonymous ftp from host "steam.stanford.edu", in file "/pub/MT/94cade-tr-work.ps.Z", 33Kb (availability last checked 20 October 1998).

Thompson, Simon (1996). *Haskell: The Craft of Functional Programming*, Addison-Wesley.

Ullman, Jeffrey D. (1994). *Elements of ML Programming*, Prentice-Hall.

Vlissides,John M., James O. Coplien, Norman L. Kerth (eds.) (1996). "Pattern Languages of Program Design 2", *Proceedings PLoP'95: Second Annual Conference on Pattern Languages of Programs*, August 1995, Monticello, Illinois.

Walter, Donald O. & Kirstie L. Bellman (1990). "Some Issues in Model Integration", pp. 249-254 in *Proceedings of the SCS Eastern MultiConference*, 23-26 April 1990, Nashville, Tennessee, Simulation Series, Volume 22, No. 3, SCS.

Wile, David (1991). "Integrating Syntaxes and their Associated Semantics", Technical Report, Information Sciences Institute, USC.

Wilensky, Robert (1981). "A Model for Planning in Complex Situations", *Cognition and Brain Theory*, Volume IV, No. 4; reprinted on pp. 263-274 in Allen et al, 1990].

Chapter 9

Communicating Project Drift Through Cost/Benefit Scenarios

David McComb
First Principles, Inc., USA

Jill Smith Slater
University of Denver, USA

Software risk-management practices acknowledge the vital, albeit difficult imperative of communicating the status of project risk to stakeholders while attempting to mitigate and/or control risk manifestations. The problem is that risks are typically dynamic, unpredictable, and may be outside the purview and control of the project manager. This chapter presents a communication mechanism to explain the phenomenon of "project drift" through a series of abstract cost/benefit scenarios. The scenarios may be used either separately or in various combinations to continually reassess risk both at project inception and in light of project history to date. Three important aspects of the cost/benefit scenarios are that they are (1) conceptually simple, (2) useful in assessing and validating some decisions that might not be apparent in the absence of this type of evaluative model, and (3) politically neutral in that they are may be used to explain project drift without affixing blame.

Change is perceived as difference, and difference is sometimes unnoticeable when it is continuous and fluid.
— Gilbreath (1986), *Winning at Project Management*

Like the growth of one's own children, change in the status of a software project may occur so slowly as to go undetected on a day-to-day basis. Yet it is clear that something is astir in most major software undertakings. Late schedules, excessive costs, unacceptable performance, and user dissatisfaction are often cited ailments. Difficulty of specifying initial requirements, commercial pressures with accompanying tight deadlines, and/or the expansion of requirements after project initiation often drive change requests (Joch & Sharp, 1995).

Distributed computing intensifies problems. For example, distributed computing may lead to (1) duplication of resources, (2) decrease in standardization, (3) difficulty in meshing user needs with those of the overall organization, and (4) minimal transfer of learning from one project to another (Jenkins, 1994). Because distributed computing projects are more widespread, emergent risk problems become exposed to increased managerial scrutiny.

Software process improvement (SPI) efforts in general, and a subset of SPI, risk management, in particular, attempt to improve the software development process in the face of these obstacles. This paper addresses risk management issues and offers a series of conceptual cost/benefit scenarios useful in understanding risk dynamics and in conversing with external management about the cause and consequence of unfolding risks.

Risk Management and Communication.

The Risk Management Program sponsored by Carnegie Mellon's Software Engineering Institute (SEI) affirms three objectives: risk prevention, risk mitigation and correction, and ensuring safe system failure if the project aborts. Recognizing the difficulty of predicting all risks in advance, the overriding objective of SEI is risk mitigation and correction (Higuera & Haimes, 1996):

> The goal of SEI Risk Program is to enable engineers, managers, and other decision makers to identify, sufficiently early, the risks associated with software acquisition, development, integration, and deployment so that appropriate management and mitigation strategies can be developed on a timely basis. Time is critical and the goal is to act early before a source of risk evolves into a major crisis. *In other words, being mainly reactive in risk mitigation and control rather than proactive in risk prevention and control is at the heart of good risk management* [italics in the original] (p. 2).

The uncertainties associated with software development require effective communication.This means speaking openly and sharing concerns on the part of everyone involved both within the domain of the project and with external stakeholders including user management and end users (if different). The SEI Risk Program recognizes the pervasiveness and importance of internal and external communication of risk management by placing communication as an integral component of every risk activity rather than as a supplemental action (Higuera & Haimes, 1996):

... In order to be analyzed and managed correctly, risks must be communicated to and between the appropriate organizational levels. This includes levels within the development project and organization, within the customer organization, and most especially, across that threshold between the developer, the customer, and where different, the user (p. 20).

However, speaking openly with stakeholders outside the project team is often a significant problem because of disparate goals. Understandably, these stakeholders (particularly line managers) are subject to pressures of a different kind than quality software processes. Practitioner literature stresses the difficulty of convincing mangers outside the project that time spent improving the development process (including acting promptly on risk mitigation) is important (Strehlo 1996, August 5, 19, 26); Jenkins, 1994; Joch & Sharp, 1995). Used to basing corporate direction on financial arguments, some managers disregard software process improvement efforts because it is difficult to forecast costs (Computer Finance, 1995).

More effective communication structures are needed to meet objectives of risk management and control. One structure is introduced here. The structure offers a generic set of abstract systems diagrams based on cost/benefit analysis diagramming conventions.

Communication by Abstraction

High-level abstraction permits a project manager to convey general risk direction based on archetypes, or generalized stories. Peter Senge modeled the use of archetype diagrams in the *Fifth Discipline* to portray organizational events in terms of broader system implications (Senge, 1990). Archetype diagrams serve as a template to describe events specific to an organization.

The motivation for high-level abstraction is that one may present arguments with less chance of political repercussions. An example from another field is a recent practice in organizational development called the Search Conference. This is a forum for all organizational stakeholders (or a deep, representative slice) to create a common vision and action plans based on that vision. Facilitators suggest that if a diverse group can address issues at a high level, removed from political agendas, they are more likely to achieve agreement on principles (Emery, 1995; Emery & Purser, 1996). The cost/benefit diagrams adhere to this reasoning.

Cost/benefit Diagrams

Cost/benefit analysis is common business language. The diagrams remove the quantification of costs and benefits to provide a conceptual method to explain and manage project drift. Project drift is the tendency of a project to move across its predetermined cost/benefit zone due to changes

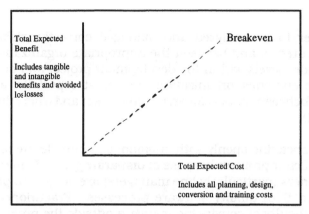

Figure 1: Simplified Project Economics

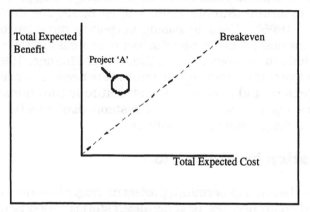

Figure 2: Typical Project at Inception

occurring during the process of project management. Three important aspects of the cost/benefit scenarios are that they are (1) conceptually simple, (2) useful in assessing and validating some decisions that might not be apparent in the absence of this type of evaluative model, and (3) politically neutral in that they are may be used to explain project drift without affixing blame.

The following diagrams provide a lens through which project drift may be explained and managed. The fundamental principle is to reduce the entire project funding decision (or continuation of funding) to a simple cost/benefit equation. Simply defined, a successful project is one that is worth more than it costs.

A very real issue is that many systems being developed or contemplated currently rely extensively on intangible benefits or tangible benefits that are difficult to quantify. Nevertheless, management has the job of determining the overall value and benefit of systems projects and weighing the benefits against their total expected cost. Thus the diagrams assume that any strategic or non-quantified reasons for proceeding with the project are included in the benefit equation. Total expected costs include all planning, design, implementation, conversion, and training costs. Figure 1 is a very simple abstract representation of the context against which to mark changes in a project's economics. The figure illustrates the total expected benefit of a project, total expected cost, and a diagonal line representing possible break-even points.

Each project has a position within this decision space. Figure 2 positions a typical project. In this case Project A has some moderate cost and some benefit in excess of its cost, giving it a favorable cost/benefit ratio. In the typical justification section of a project plan, the cost/benefit analysis would eventually boil down to being the vertical distance that this project is above the break-even line. In other words, to what extent or in what ratio do the benefits exceed the level of expenditures.

Few projects are economically initiated in the region under the dotted line as with Project B in Figure 3. Presumably, management would not proceed with projects identified that would cost more than all of the total expected benefit. However, there are two reasons to consider the projects in this region. One reason is that many projects are initiated without going through even the most informal cost/benefit analysis. Second, due to the nature of some costs (illustrated later), many projects will drift into the unfeasible area. However, there may still be good business reasons to continue the projects at that juncture. The major point is that it is rare that a project would be knowingly initiated in its unfeasible zone.

Within the feasible zone, there tends to be three main types of projects (Figure 4). This breakdown is similar to McFarlan's (1981) applications portfolio mix which would include projects from each category. Those with the highest benefit-to-cost ratio which represent little risk in terms of outlay of cash are opportunistic projects. Almost every company has projects such as these. These are the easiest projects to justify and complete. However, often these projects are made possible only through some significant previous oversight, or they rely on short-term fixes to pressing problems. If fact, over the longer term, these projects cause significant additional problems especially as the number of the opportunistic solutions increase. Over reliance strictly on quantifiable benefits tends to push many companies almost entirely into the opportunistic project mode which can actually be counterproductive or lead to systems discontinuity.

The typical project replacement of a major application subsystem such as billing, inventory control or purchasing falls in the middle zone and if well-scoped and controlled, the benefits should outweigh the total expected costs. In the third category are strategic systems which represent the highest total corporate cost exposure, but will often also be the projects of sweeping strategic importance. These are projects that define systems that will help restructure a given industry such as the early airline reservation systems, the systems of Federal Express, or, currently, the pioneer systems in electronic commerce.

For the remainder of this discussion the following diagramming con-

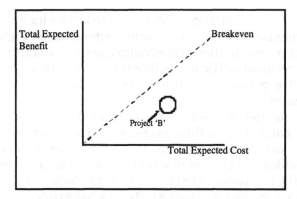

Figure 3: Infeasible Projects

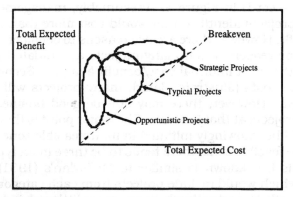

Figure 4: Generic Types of Feasible Projects

vention recognizes that the project and its expectations are not static, and that the knowledge about both the benefit and final cost will continue to drift until the project is completed in one fashion or another. To simplify presentation, three symbols indicate the project manager's belief about the total expected costs and benefits of the project at three points. Illustrated in Figure 5, a circle represents conception, a triangle indicates software completion, and an modified circle signifies final implementation. Final implementation denotes system conversion, system roll out to all applicable sites, and completion of user training.

Figure 6 shows a not untypical drift of a project over its lifetime. This pattern has been observed over and over again. The project when conceived had a very high benefit to cost ratio. The drift to the right represents that through the design and development process the project ran over budget and additionally, may represent further overruns on roll-out costs. However, very often with troubled projects there is less and less inclination to estimate further down-stream costs. The reduction of benefits represented by the arrow pointing down is very often caused because the project management,

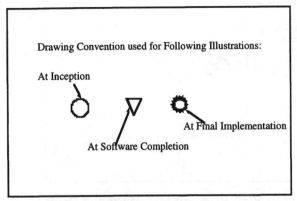

Figure 5: Drifting Expectations

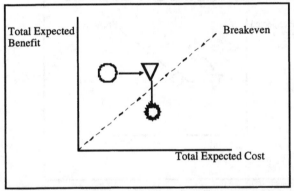

**Figure 6: Project Over-run with Compromised
Implementation Benefits**

once running over budget, began consciously or unconsciously scaling back on features to be delivered.

In many cases the implementation team, different from the planning and design team, may not have fully understood the detailed parts of the system that were going to deliver the full benefit, or they may have understood and for cost considerations chosen to exclude them. In any event, it is not unusual at that point to deliver the system to the field and have it implemented only to discover that the benefits realized not only were less than expected, but were low enough that the project would not have been justified had this information been known at its inception. Yet this type of project, while somewhat compromised, is not a complete failure. Indeed, a certain level of fairly substantial benefits has been achieved and the only shortfall has been whether the level of benefit could have been achieved with less expenditure, or whether the originally projected benefits could have been achieved within the costs that were expended.

In contrast, Figure 7 shows an illustration of the drift of a well-planned, well-managed project. The system finally delivered very closely matches up

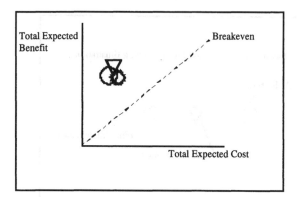

Figure 7: Well Planned and Managed Project

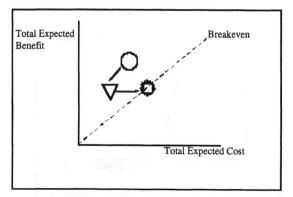

Figure 8: De-Scoped Project

with the expectations of the user and the project team. It is worth noting that with this level of abstraction it is impossible to determine what restricted the drift for this project. The explanation may be either a very stable project environment, or the result of a project manager who anticipated environmental and internal changes and made appropriate mid-course corrections.

In Figure 8, we show the pattern for a typically de-scoped project. The project, for whatever reason, discovers a potential for cost overrun and takes proactive action to reduce the scope usually eliminating some of the "less important features." This is occasionally effective and often is the right move when the alternative would have been to escalate costs drastically. However, initially a de-scoped project reduces its costs at the expense of benefits. It is rarely possible to reduce cost without a commensurate reduction in benefits. It is more common for the once-cut features to move back into the system as it moves into implementation and further into its life cycle. Alternatively, the lack of planned features hampers the users' ability to extract all benefits from the system.

In Figure 9 we have a diagram of constructive change. In the course of

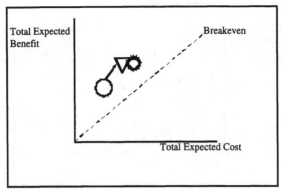

Figure 9: Constructive Changes

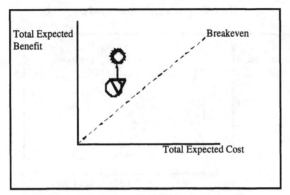

Figure 10: Unanticipated Benefits

the development of the system either the project management team or the users discover some changes that need to be made in the system that will increase benefits. Very often just the examination of the problem over a period of time will suggest new approaches and this illustration shows that if well-managed, the system can move onto a higher plateau. However, while the total amount of benefit has increased, it is rare that the ratio of benefit to cost is increased through these type of changes.

Figure 10 illustrates a very unusual but occasional case of benefits that were not expected from the system but came about as a by-product once the system was implemented. In many cases systems modernization has made it far easier to respond to competitive threats even though no one anticipated these threats when approving the project.

The next set of illustrations shows the impact of abandoning a system after incurring costs. Figure 11, a very common case, occurs when a system runs considerably over budget once the software development is complete. The system is then canceled. As can be seen, once the project is abandoned the expected benefits are zero and the total loss to the project and to the company is the horizontal displacement of the cost.

In Figure 12 we see the relatively constructive use of the early

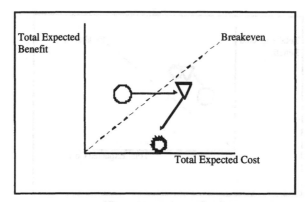

**Figure 11: Abandonment After Software
Development Complete**

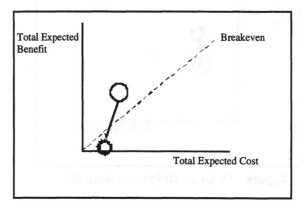

Figure 12: Early Abandonment

abandonment of a project. If sufficient foresight can be put to a project to realize that a Figure 12 style abandonment is likely, the earlier the project can be terminated the more money can be saved. Relatively speaking, this is a successful outcome compared to Figure 11.

However (Figure 13), it may well be that once the funds are expended, and once it is realized that the total cost may exceed the total benefit, there is still a greater pay back in continuing the system. In this scenario, users could at least realize the majority of the benefits. This is a classic sunk-cost analysis. Note that it is the horizontal distance from the dotted line that indicates the "net loss" of the project. Completing a project as in Figure 13 may result in a net loss, but far less than abandoning the project as in Figure 11.

Finally, Figure 14 shows the relationship of project risk to the possibility of the outcome drifting once the project has been conceived. This Figure may facilitate discussion of risk at the project's initiation. Project size, the newness of the technology, and/or organizational factors competing for resources are some of the main reasons it may drift. Also, the more

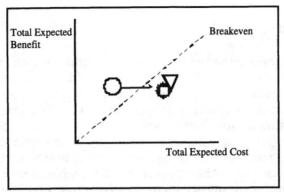

Figure 13: Implementation Despite "Sunk Costs"

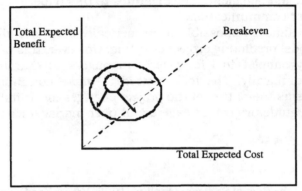

Figure 14: Project Risk—Probability of Outcome Drifting

unstructured the project and the less experienced the team is with the technology, the greater likelihood of project drift.

Discussion

The preceding 14 cost/benefit diagrams may be useful either separately or in various combinations to communicate the ramifications of project drift. A project manager may employ the diagrams at different points in the project life cycle to illustrate potential risk, "as is" uncertainty, or explain a past project's success or failure. Further, the abstractness inherent in the diagramming conventions permit discussion of what is happening and foreseeable or transpired impact(s) while bypassing blame. For example, faced with rising costs, a project manager could recommend either a de-scoped project (Figure 8) or an early abandonment (Figure 12). Also, the diagrams would be useful in portraying the impact of sunk costs (Figure 13) versus abandonment once software is complete (Figure 11). Of course, these diagrams could be used in conjunction with a more-detailed quantitative assessment of costs and benefits if time permits and quantitative figures are available.

Conclusion

Risks manifest themselves through changes over the course of a software project's life. The reason the risk profile changes is because many of the fundamental assumptions about the project change as the project executes. The assumptions may be wrong in project planning (e.g. a low man-hour estimate) and then show up as a schedule slip during project execution. Or, risks may occur dynamically as the project unfolds (e.g. a change in user requirements or in sponsor commitment). The basic problem is that many of these changes are subtle and project managers fail to recognize negative ramifications in time to adjust management strategies. Or, they may recognize danger but experience difficulty in communicating the danger to management. The diagrams in this paper represent an effort toward better communication.

It would be almost impossible to numerically correlate all changes to a dynamic model predicting project outcome. However, this paper presents a conceptually simpler tool for project managers to examine risk consequences dynamically. The tool is used to make continual cost/benefit assessments as the nature of the project changes (or drifts) during execution, and to guide project managers and user management in mid-course corrections.

References

Counting the Cost of Software Quality. (1995, November 1). *Computer Finance, 6*(6).

Emery, F. (1995, January/February). Participative design: Effective, flexible and successful, now! *Journal for Quality & Participation, 18*(1), 6-9.

Emery, M., & Purser, R. (1996). *The Search Conference.* San Franscisco: Jossey-Bass.

Gilbreath, R. (1986). *Winning at Project Management.* New York, N.Y.: John Wiley & Sons.

Higuera, Ronald P. & Yacov Y. Haimes. (1996). *Software Risk Management* [CMU/SEI-96-TR-012; ESC-TR-96-012].

Jenkins, R. L. (1994, December 2). Growing User Dominance Has Strategic Implications. *Credit Union News, 14*(23), 10-21.

Joch, Alan & Oliver Sharp. (1995, December). How Software Doesn't Work. *Byte,* p. 48.

McFarlan, F. W. (1981, September-October). Portfolio Approach to Information Systems. *Harvard Business Review,* pp. 142-159.

Putting a Financial Value on Software: Part 2. (1996, March 1). *Computer Finance, 10*(6).

Senge, P. (1990). *The Fifth Discipline: The Art and Practice of the Learning Organization.* New York, N.Y.: Currency Doubleday.

Strehlo, Kevin. (1996, August 26). Developer's Advocate:; Don't tinker with new toys, improve the process. *InfoWorld,* p. 77.

Strehlo, Kevin. (1996, August 5). Developer's Advocate: Process control expensive? Consider buggy code costs. *InfoWorld,* p. 63.

Strehlo, Kevin. (1996, August 19). Developer's Advocate: Processes need people to make good connections. *InfoWorld,* p. 61.

Chapter 10

Group-Enabled
Software Inspections

Thomas L. Rodgers, University of Arizona, USA
Conan C. Albrecht, University of Arizona, USA
Douglas D. Dean, University of Arizona, USA

To be counted in the ranks of world-class software engineering firms is very difficult. There are relatively few deserving such distinction and those that do are continually raising the stakes at an ever increasing rate. The challenge is to not only match their rate of productivity improvement but to catch up to their performance levels. A widely-accepted process practice used by world-class software engineering firms is inspections This chapter explores group-enabled software inspections as a software process improvement activity. Past and present of software inspections are first explored as a basis for discussing several research concepts and their applications to future software inspections. The concepts addressed include primary collaborative process, feedback, distributed inspections, and knowledge management. The chapter concludes with a discussion of current research agendas and rationalization of why software inspection is a software improvement activity.

Software Inspection - Past and Present

During the past twenty-two years, much has been written about inspections and various types of formal technical reviews. In a 1976 article in the *IBM Systems Journal*, Michael E. Fagan described formal inspections of design and of code that are now referred to as Fagan inspections. Fagan asserted "substantial net improvements in programming quality and productivity" (Fagan, 1976b). In subsequent years, over four hundred academic and practitioner articles have addressed various aspects of inspections, and for the most part have supported inspections as a productive means to identify and remove defects.

Fagan inspections are well scripted and when done formally, produce consistent results. Participants in a Fagan inspection include the following (Fagan, 1976a):

Author   is assumed by the individual responsible for effecting changes to the document (usually, but not necessarily, the same person who wrote it). The author's role at the inspection meeting is to address specific questions that the reviewer is not able to answer, and to detect defects based on their special understanding of the product.

Moderator   is responsible for organization and management of the inspection. The moderator ensures that the inspection procedures are followed, and that the other reviewers perform their responsibilities for each step of the inspection process.

Reviewer   is a problem finder during the inspection. All of the inspection team members are reviewers, including the author, regardless of their other procedural roles. It is the reviewer's role to detect defects, and not to offer solutions.

SEPG staff   supports the inspection process (as a member of the software engineering process group).

Editor   is responsible for recording the logging meeting and preparing the final report (possibly the moderator or a SEPG staff). The editor is also referred to as the recorder or scribe. The role is to record and classify all defects detected and to assist the moderator in preparing other inspection meeting reports.

Reader   leads the team through the work in a complete and logical fashion at the inspection meeting. The reader is prepared to describe various parts and functions of the work, paraphrasing the material, in detail, at a moderate pace suitable for thorough examination.

Although variations exist between recognized inspection experts and practitioners, Fagan inspections follow a six-step process that is described below.

Step 1. Planning the inspection includes the following tasks:
• Establish a schedule for completion of the inspection.
• Choose inspectors and invite them to participate.
• Define one or more specialist defect checking roles for each reviewer.
• Divide material into chunks that can be reviewed in less than a couple of hours.
• Determine optimum review rates for material to be reviewed.
• Obtain and distribute all necessary supporting documents (sources, rules, checklists).
• Prepare suggestions for improvement objectives and strategies for meeting them.

- Ensure that selected documents are clearly marked, lines numbered, and copied.
- Ensure that inspection team members get copies, or access to electronic copies of all relevant documents.
- Agree on meeting times and book meeting space.
- Log time spent in phase for moderator and author.

Step 2. *Overview (kickoff) meeting* includes the following tasks:
- Describe materials to be inspected (author or moderator describes to participants).
- Familiarize inspectors with their tasks.
- Agree on individual special defect-searching 'role assignments.'
- Hand out recently produced materials as well as source materials, relevant rules and checklists.
- Ask any general questions about the documents being checked.
- Obtain group or individual instruction on how to do the inspection work.
- Obtain group or individual instruction from moderator on how to interpret any document.
- Inform team about current logging rates and effectiveness.
- Attempt to set numeric team improvement targets (e.g. "more than 70% of issues logged to be majors").
- Identify and agree on suitable new tactics for meeting their improvement targets (for example "slow down from last time to achieve the optimal rate of checking").
- Log time spent in overview meeting by all participants.

Step 3. *Individual preparation (issue identification)* includes the following tasks:
- Individually study inspection material.
- Complete preparation before time agreed to hold a logging meeting.
- Make use of the recommended optimum review rate.
- Perform assigned specialist roles.
- Contact the moderator early if reviewer encounters difficulties, or suspect that the team's time might somehow be wasted.
- Make every effort to follow the defined checking procedure during individual preparation.
- Focus efforts on major defect issues.
- Log time spent in individual preparation phase.

Step 4. *Logging meeting* includes the following detailed tasks:
- Moderator leads a formal sequential examination of the inspection material.
- Record all potential defects identified during preparation as issues in the issue log.
- Perform a checking process in a group environment to determine that the potential defects are in fact actual defects and possibly determine whether the severity is major or minor.
- Identify additional issues found during the group process that were not

found during individual preparation.
- Record improvement suggestions and questions of intent to the author. Note that this task was not included in the original Fagan inspection but is advocated by various inspection experts.
- Log time spent in meeting by all participants.

Step 5. Rework (check) includes the following detailed tasks:
- Revise product.
- Assign final severity (major, minor) defect classification whenever in the moderator judgement the initially logged classification was incorrect.
- For minor and major issues, classify defect by type.
- For major issues, possibly classify defect by review trigger, test trigger, impact, source, qualifier, and activity. This is an integral part of orthogonal defect classification.
- Correct the product document (according to sources and rules).
- Send a change request to the source document owner when an issue has been raised in the source that cannot be resolved by the editor directly.
- Note in the issue log that an appropriate change has in fact been made earlier in this edit or elsewhere.
- Send a request for improvement to the owner of rules or checklists. This may result from a direct improvement logged by a reviewer or by a decision of the editor as to how to treat anything logged, or by a new initiative by the editor during editing.
- Voluntarily improve any of the documents, rules, or checklists.
- Log time spent and number of issues discovered by defect classifications.

Step 6. Follow-up includes the following detailed tasks:
- Verify satisfactory resolution of identified defects.
- Check that all listed issues are acted on in writing.
- Check that improvement suggestions are sent to appropriate process owners.
- Report final inspection metrics for defects by severity and hours used for all six inspection steps.

Some of the detailed tasks include recommendation based on practical experience by widely recognized "how-to" experts including the following: (1) Tom Gilb and Dorothy Graham (1993), (2) Robert Ebenau and Susan Strauss (1994), (3) Charles P. Hollocker (1990), and (4) Daniel P. Freedman and Gerald M. Weinberg (1993). Although similar to Fagan inspections, Gilb inspections add defect prevention and process improvement objectives (Gilb & Graham, 1993). Within IBM, Fagan inspections were the basis for defect prevention efforts (Jones, 1985) and subsequently for orthogonal defect classification (Chillarege et.al., 1992).

Inspections are now integrated into many software engineering practices including the Capability Maturity Model (Humphrey, 1989, Paulk, 1995) and Personal Software Processes (Humphrey, 1995). Inspections have been widely adopted by world class organizations including AT&T

(Fowler, 1986) and Hewlett Packard (Grady & Van Slack, 1994). In short, inspections are widely recognized as a means for increasing software quality.

During recent years, inspections remain a topic of continued research interest. Lawrence Votta, from AT&T, suggests that the value of an inspection comes from preparation and that need for face-to-face meetings might be diminishing (Votta, 1993). Adam Porter, from the University of Maryland, finds that people-input factors are most important (Porter, et.al., 1998) and that traditional checklist and ad hoc review approaches are ineffective (Porter & Votta, May 1994). Based on industrial experience in Europe, Michiel van Genuchten finds that inspection defect yields improve significantly when using an electronic meeting system (van Genuchten, et.al., 1997).

The number of software inspection tools have been developed include the following based in part on reviews by (Harjumaa & Tervonen, 1997) and Philip Johnson (at http:// www.ics.hawaii.edu/~johnson/FTR/tools):

- *ASSIST* (Asynchronous/Scnchronous Software Inspection Support Tool) includes a generic special-purpose language for describing inspection phases including both synchronous and asynchronous tasks. Details are available on the ASSIST homepage: http://www.cs.strath.ac.uk/CS/research/efocs/assist.html (Macdonald, 1996).
- *CheckMate* automatically checks C and C++ source code against a predetermined coding policy. Details can be found at http://www.sybernet.ie.
- *Collaborative Software Inspection* (CSI) is an electronic meeting tool that supports a wide range of inspection tasks. CSI was developed at the University of Minnesota and details can be obtained from John Riedl (riedl@cs.umn.edu) (Mashyekhi, 1993).
- *CSRS* (Collaborative Software Review System) is a comprehensive system that requires adoption of a defined process and that captures a complete set of defect and inspection process metrics. CSRS was developed at the University of Hawaii under the direction of Philip Johnson (johnson@hawaii.edu) (Johnson, 1993).
- *ICICLE* (Intelligent Code Inspection Environment in a C Language Environment) is one of the first groupware tools designed for software inspections. It automatically detects some routine types of defects; however it only supports face-to-face meeting. ICICLE was developed at Bellcore (Brothers, 1990).
- *INSPEQ* supports "phased inspections" and was developed at the University of Virginia by John Knight (knight@virginia.edu).
- *LEAP* is a second-generation effort by the University of Hawaii designed to support individual software developers and satisfy four major criteria: (1) "Light-weight" implies easy to learn, easy to integrate with existing methods, and tools, and above all, not impose significant new overhead on the developer unless that investment of overhead will provide a direct return-on-investment to that same developer. (2) Empirical implies emphasis on quantitative as well as qualitative metrics. Software developer improvement should be able to be shown through measurements of effort,

defects, size, and so forth. (3) Automated to support light-weight support for empirically-based developer improvement. (4) Portability recognizes that software developers change jobs and companies on a regular basis. Useful support cannot be locked into a particular organization such that the developer must "give up" the data and tools when they leave the organization. LEAP is web enabled and accessible at http:// csdl.ics.hawaii.edu/Tools/LEAP/LEAP.html.

- *Reasoning/2000* automates Y2K compliance audits of COBOL applications. Details are found at: http://www.reasoning.com/.
- *Remote Inspection* is a commercial system that uses the review features of Microsft Word97 as the workgroup system. Details are found via email to vertical@nolan.com or at http://www.nolan.com/~pnolan/rem_insp.html.
- *ReviewPro* is a commercial tool developed by Software Development Technologies Corporation. It runs on Windows and Unix platforms.
- *Scrutiny* is an automated asynchronous inspection tool that compares favorably with traditional face-to-face inspection. Scrutiny was developed by Bull HN Information Systems in conjunction with the University of Illinois. For additional information contact John Gintell (gintell@shore.net) or Simon Kaplan (kaplan@cs.uiuc.edu). (Gintell, 1993)
- *TAMMi* supports the individual checking phase; however it lacks collaborative capabilities (Putaala, 1996).
- *Web inspection Prototype* (WiP) was the first Web-based inspection tool and was developed at the University of Oulu (Harjumaa & Tervonen, 1997).
- *CodeReview* is a Web-based collaborative inspection tool and is being developed at the University of Arizona in part by the authors of this chapter. Following is a description of CodeReview version 1.1.

CodeReview Version 1.1 Description

CodeReview is a distributed, platform-independent tool that supports inspections. The user interface has been designed to flatten any learning curve; in fact, the goal is to allow reviewers to be productive with the tool with less than a minute of instruction. CodeReview can be accessed via the World-Wide Web at http://128.196.205.213/codereview.html (logonid = "guest" and password = "guest").

CodeReview applet is written in Java. This means that it can be run in any environment that supports Java applets, such as Windows NT, Windows 95/98, Unix, or Macintosh. Note that although all popular browsers support Java, not all of them support the more current version 1.1. Therefore, you must be sure that the browser you are using supports the Java Development Kit (JDK) 1.1. The browsers in the following list support this version of Java and run the CodeReview applet (all of the listed browsers were free at the writing of this chapter):

- Netscape Navigator 4.5 and higher;
- Microsoft Internet Explorer 4.0 and higher. Due to bugs in the first release of IE 4, please install IE 4.0 with Service Pack 1;
- Netscape Navigator 4.0. This version of Navigator must have the JDK 1.1

patch installed to run the applet. This patch is available from Netscape's download site.
• Sun HotJava 1.1.

Reviewing Code
Once a session is set up, reviewers can log into a session from any Java 1.1-enabled web browser. The session administrator should give the applet's URL to all reviewers participating in the session.

Login Procedure
To begin reviewing the code in a session, enter the proper URL into the browser's location box; the CodeReview applet will then be loaded. It may take a few minutes based upon the speed of your Internet connection (the applet is currently about 300K). The applet will load directly within the browser window.

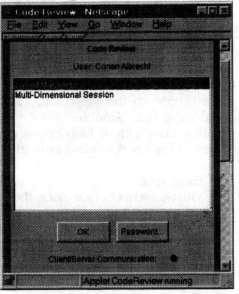

Code Review Login Screen

Click on the Login window and enter your username and password in the dialog box that appears. After your password is verified on the server, the applet will show the sessions you have been included in. The Login button will change to an OK button to allow you to open sessions.

This login screen is the applet's home screen. Due to the behavior of Java applets, it is very important that you do not close this browser window or navigate to other web pages while session windows are open. If you do, open sessions will become unstable and/or crash. When closing the application, close any open session windows before closing the browser window.

Note also that once you have logged in, browsers will save the web page and applet state until you close them. Therefore, even if you close all sessions and navigate to other web pages, without first closing the entire browser application, the applet will continue to run. If you are on a publicly-accessible browser, other users will be able to press the browser's "back" button and open sessions under your username. To prevent this, be sure to close all browser windows (i.e. exit the application) when you are finished reviewing.

CodeReview Main Window
After you have successfully logged in, the browser window will show the sessions you have been included in; select a session and press OK to open

it. The Client/Server communication circle will blink as data is loaded from the server. The session will open into a new window. The screen is divided into two areas: the document area and the user area.

Main Session Window

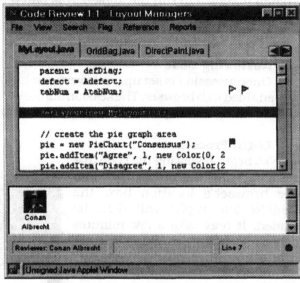

Document Area
Each document file is loaded into its own tab on the screen. The lines of the document are listed on the left and flags are listed on the right. Double-clicking (or pressing Enter on) a line with pre-existing flags brings up the View Flag dialog box. Double-clicking a line with no flags brings up the Add Flag dialog box. Both of these dialog boxes are described later in this document.

User Area
The user area shows along the bottom of the window. This area shows all users currently logged into the system. You can either click a user icon or hold your mouse over an icon to view the user's information, such as name, phone number, or e-mail address. In synchronous (distributed or same-place) meetings, these icons give you a sense of the other reviewers in the session.

Navigating
You can navigate the session window with either the keyboard or the mouse. Different Java implementations produce unwanted keyboard behavior at times, so click with your mouse if the keyboard focus is lost.

Viewing Reference Documents
Reference documents are HTML pages that support a session. They can be defined to open at the beginning or end of the session, or they can just show under the "Reference" menu. Beginning forms display whenever reviewers log into the session and usually take the form of scripts, checklists, instructions, or directions for the reviewer. Ending forms are often used to gather session metrics via CGI forms. If beginning or ending forms have been defined by your session's administrator, they will open automatically. Other types of reference documents are available for your information and include checklists, session guidelines, rules, or other documents. Be sure to check

the "Reference" menu for supporting documents the first time you open a session so you are aware of the documentation available to you.

When you (or the session) opens a reference document, a new browser window will open to show the document. You can then read, print, and save the document using the regular browser menus. Due to quirks of Java's behavior in some browsers, the new browser window may show up in the background—behind the main document window. You may be required to bring them to the top of the screen manually by clicking them with your mouse.

For security reasons, the applet may make a copy of original reference documents before displaying them in your browser window. When the session is closed, these files are deleted and can no longer be referenced from outside the session.

Adding Flags

Flags are the heart of the CodeReview tool. They are markers in the document that represent defects, issues, questions, comments, or other ideas. Double-click (or press Enter on) an empty line to bring up the Add Flag dialog box. Each line of the document can have up to four different flags on it.

Selecting Attribute Values

Each flag is made up of a set of attribute values. The number and type of attributes that show in this dialog box is set by your session administrator; therefore, the dialog box displayed on your screen might differ slightly from the one displayed in this manual. Select the value in each attribute that best describes the issue you are flagging.

Although some attributes might be mandatory as defined by your session administrator, many attributes do not require you to make a selection. Therefore, do not force values when they are not required and do not fit the flag you are creating.

As you choose different values for attributes, the flag image will change to reflect your selections. Some attributes affect the flag color and others affect the flag shape or inclusion of other objects in the image.

Add Flag Dialog Box

Comments

As the author of a flag, you can record its first comment. Type in a representative and concise statement of the flag into the "Comments" edit box. Other user will then be able to make additional comments on your flag. When you submit the flag, the applet will save the flag data on the server and also relay a message to all other connected clients. After one or two seconds, the flag will show in your main document window as well as all other reviewer's document windows.

Reviewing Flags

The main document window will show all flags submitted by session reviewers. Double-clicking (or pressing Enter on) on a line with flag(s) will bring up the Display Flag dialog box. A tab is created for each flag on the line showing the flag image, the reviewer who submitted the flag, the flag attribute information, and comments reviewers have made about the flag. If less than four flags have been submitted for a line, you can press the "New Flag" button to submit a new flag on the line. Depending upon your flag rights, you can also delete the currently selected flag by pressing the "Delete Flag" button. The flag image will then disappear from all reviewers' screens and the tab will be removed.

Display Flag Dialog Box

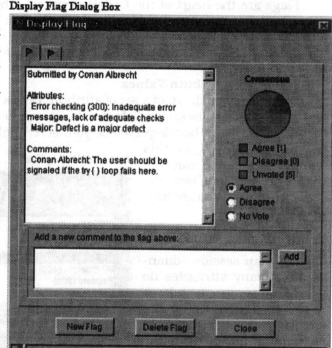

Voting on Flags

You are allowed to vote your agreement or disagreement on flags. A pie graph shows the current voting tally and gives the percentage of consensus among the team. Flag votes show which flags need further discussion from team members.

Commenting on Flags

You are allowed to make comments in the Display Flag dialog box on any existing flag. These comments are recorded in order of submission and are very important to the dialog of the session. The comments area is the forum for discussion of flag issues, whether they be agreement, disagreement, or explanation. Make comments that are informative and concise and that apply specifically to the flag you are submitting them for.

Multi-User

The CodeReview applet is fully multi-user in the sense that all changes recorded by one reviewer are reflected in all other reviewers' document windows. The applet also provides a separate chat-style forum for discussion of each flag. In addition, the following general multi-user options are supported:

Session-Wide Chat Window

A session-wide chat window is provided to allow reviewers to have a general discussion about the session. This is the forum for review process concerns, suggestions, and dialog. The window allows you to view either all messages or only today's messages to allow you to stay up-to-date on the session specifics. The chat window is opened from the "View" menu.

Synchronize Views

When meetings are held synchronously, facilitators may want to lead reviewers through the code in a systematic way. This activity is supported through the "Synchronize" function available on the "View" menu. When this option is selected, each reviewer logged into the session is asked if they want to be synchronized with your screen. If they select "Yes", their screen positions will be changed to match yours.

View User Information

The user information panel at the bottom of the screen shows all reviewers currently logged into the session. This display gives reviewers a sense of who is also working on the document and supports distributed meeting dynamics. You can either click a user icon or hold your mouse over an icon to view the user's information, such as name, phone number, or e-mail address.

Reports

CodeReview is currently geared toward inspection facilitation rather than after-the-fact inspection analysis. Given this fact, the applet does produce basic reports to assist reviewers in basic analyses. It currently produces three reports: a code listing, a summary report, and a session-wide chat log.

Code Listing

The code listing report shows basic session information followed by the attribute sets for the session. It then lists the entire source code of each file in the session. Lines with flags are shown in red and are followed by each flag's attributes and reviewer comments.

The code listing report is useful for session editors that want to review flags in written form and also for authors/editors who need to make revisions to the source documents.

Summary Report
The summary report shows basic session information. It is divided into three sections: defect list attributes, defect listing, and basic defect statistics. The defect list attributes section shows the attributes sets for the session. The defect listing section gives a tabular summary of all flags recorded for the session, including the line number, the contributor, and the defect attribute values. The basic defect statistics section gives a summary of each attribute value, including the number found and its percentage of the total.

Session-Wide Chat Log
The session chat report displays all chat comments that have been submitted in tabular format. The report is sorted by date and grouped by each day. This report provides valuable information for process and session improvements.

Export
The tool provides export capabilities to the CSV (comma-separated values) format so other analysis-geared applications can be used. Many applications exist that are specialized and advanced in the analysis of inspection metrics.

The CSV format is a specialized format of delimited text files. Each field in the export is bounded by quotes (") and separated from other fields by commas. Quotes that appear within fields are converted to double quotes (""). This format is common to many analysis applications and to standard spreadsheet and database programs such as Microsoft Access and Microsoft Excel.

Software Inspection - A Primary Collaborative Process

The concept of primary collaborative process was introduced by Michiel van Genuchten and is based loosely on an analogy to Alvin Tofler's book, The Third Wave (Tofler, 1980). Toffler posited three waves of societal development. The first wave is based on agrarian development and has virtually disappeared. The second wave is the industrial revolution and for which we are living in the waning days of its influence. The third wave is a post-industrial, information-based society. The analogy carries into the realm of collaborative technology. Starting in the 1980s, the first wave was driven primarily from a scientific perspective and focused on innovation and basic research. Results of the first wave include understandings about anonymity, process gains, and process losses. The second wave, which is currently peaking, is consultant and facilitator driven. Most international consulting firms have collaborative experts that used electronic meeting systems and advise Fortune 500 clients in the used of collaborative technologies. To a great extent the second wave is constrained by the ability of facilitators and capability of technology to enable large groups of people to work productively together. The third wave focuses on application of collaborative technologies to primary process of organizations. In this chapter, the third wave is referred to as "primary collaborative processes" (van Genuchten, Vogel, & Nunamaker, 1998).

Although primary collaborative process is not precisely defined by van Genuchten, examples include education of students in a school, treating of patients in a hospital, and developing software by a software company. Another rich example is crisis response in a military setting. Imagine a collaboratively-enabled series of war rooms on a Naval command ship, and you are describing primary collaborative processes. More to the point of this chapter, envision software inspections as a primary collaborative process. Collaboration is a natural by-product of the process and not a facilitator or research driven activity.

Primary Collaborative Process Scenario
Using CodeReview Version 1.1

In the following narrative, a software inspection is described as a primary collaborative process using CodeReview version 1.1. The scenario described can be contrasted with traditional, formal inspections, such as Fagan inspections. While the core concepts of inspection are still found in a group-enabled inspection, much of the overhead is reduced or even eliminated.

Step 1. Setup
The instigator of the inspection usually sets up the reviewing session. This role can be filled by the author, the moderator, the team leader, or the SEPG (Software Engineering Process Group) member assigned to the project. Setup involves the following two tasks:

Task 1.1. Define session protocol
A time schedule is first created giving the target exit dates for the phases of the inspection. The schedule must be specific to the project at hand and must allow participants to successfully complete each phase of the inspection. Depending upon the nature of the inspection, the time schedule can be rigid or flexible in its deadlines.

Inspection is a team process. This fact is the main reason tool support is so vital to its success and its efficiency. The "team" as defined for this document are the different players in the inspection process. Roles must also be assigned to each member of the team. Scribe and defect summarization tasks are not assigned to any roles, but are automated by the tool.

Task 1.2. Create supporting documentation
Most inspections have supporting documentation in the form of checklists, reference documents, instructional sheets, or directions. These forms

should be accessible to the reviewers at all times during the issue discovery phase. The tool supports the following types of supporting documentation: beginning forms, reference documents, and ending forms. All of these forms show in a browser window and as such, can be any type of HTML document. The reviewer can also print or save these forms locally. A beginning form displays whenever a reviewer logs into the session on the tool. These forms are usually checklists, instructions, or directions for the reviewer. Reference documents are available via menu option to the reviewer and are usually supporting documents for the source documents. Ending forms displays when the reviewer logs off of a session on the tool. These forms provide an excellent place for the gathering of session metrics via CGI scripts. They typically gather logging times and other metrics to be analyzed after the issue discovery phase.

Task 1.3. Create a session
The session must be created within the review tool. The following tasks are required:

• Chunk source documents: The source documents should be chunked into the small, and reviewable pieces. These files are then copied into the tool and assigned to the session.
• Add users: Team members will have been added as users by the system administrator with their information and individual passwords. The team members are assigned to this review session.
• Assign flag attribute lists: Attribute lists are the heart of any inspection. They define the assignable attributes of any issue. Examples of attribute lists are defect type (logic error, interface issue, comment, etc.), severity (major, minor), injection point, find phase, etc. The applicable attribute lists are assigned to the session. For example, a Fagan inspection would require defect type and severity. An ODC inspection would require additional attribute lists.

Note that the entire setup phase can be accomplished by one person in a relatively short time (especially if many of the tasks were already completed in prior inspections). The phase does not require meetings or any other team member's time.

Step 2. Kickoff Meeting
Once the inspection session is setup, a kickoff meeting is held to introduce the team members to the session protocols, source documents, and deadlines. The meeting can take different forms depending upon the nature of the inspection and the document being reviewed. The following list outlines a few of the possible forms the meeting might take:

• Traditional: The team members meet at a designed location and time. This type of meeting is appropriate for teams that are geographically close and who need a synchronous meeting.

- Tool-supported: The tool provides chat features and a screen-synchronization feature to allow the moderator to lead team members through the session windows online. This type of meeting is appropriate for teams who cannot meet in the same place but still want a synchronous meeting.
- E-mail: Some teams may not need an explicit kickoff meeting. These teams are usually knowledgeable with the inspection process as well as the source documents. A simple e-mail might suffice for these teams.

Task 2.1. Team building

One goal of the kickoff meeting is to orient the team to the inspection process itself. Inexperienced teams may need training about the different roles and protocols involved in the inspection. Kickoff activities should motivate team members to perform their roles at peak performance. Team members should leave the meeting feeling part of a successful team, excited about their roles in the inspection, and informed about the tasks to be completed. The schedule is also presented, and team members should feel comfortable with the deadlines they must meet.

Task 2.2. Description of source document

The second goal of the kickoff meeting is to familiarize team members with the source documents. The author leads team members through the documents and their sections. Any concerns or issues team members have are raised at this point.

Step 3. Issue Discovery

A traditional inspection first gives reviewers time to individually inspect the source documents and to flag issues. Then the reviewers meet to compile and log their issues and to find more issues. These preparation and meeting times are converted to an online reviewing session in the tool-supported inspection. The online reviewing session can take place in traditional format, with a meeting in an EMS-capable room. However, the tool adds additional possibilities of asynchronous and/or different-place reviewing sessions. Since the tools runs within an Internet browser, reviewers can log in from any location at any time.

Task 3.1. Record defects

The source documents show in a tab-style window with each source document in its own tab. Issues are flagged by selecting an attribute from the available attribute list (included in the session during setup above). For example, in a Fagan inspection, an issue might be a logic error with major severity. A flag image shows on the screen representing the issue. Different flag colors, and shapes represent the attributes of each specific issue.

Task 3.2. Review other's defects

The tool is fully group-enabled. Flags that are logged by one reviewer show up simultaneously on all reviewer's screens. The traditional logging meeting is not needed because the tool already shows every flag recorded by every user - the issues are already logged and compiled. In addition, reviewers do not duplicate work because all issues are compiled and shown in real time.

Reviewers will soon become familiar with the flag shapes and colors that represent issue attributes. Therefore, reviewers can quickly discern what issues have been logged by other team members. Reviewers can vote their agreement or disagreement of issues. This gives a measurable consensus number showing which issues need to be discussed further; issues that the team agrees upon usually need very little additional discussion, while issues that the team disagrees upon need further exploration. The tool shows a pie graph displaying the summary of team votes.

Each issue also contains its own chat session. Reviewers can make comments on the issue that describe the problem or concern, and can then have an ongoing discussion about the defect. These comments provide valuable information to the editor as he or she makes corrections to the source documents in the editing phase.

Task 3.3. Make process suggestions

Teams using traditional inspection processes usually hold follow-up meetings to discuss the inspection process itself. The tool provides a session-specific chat window that allows users to make suggestions, have discussions, and express concerns about the inspection process. The dialog from this chat session can be used as a basis for teams who still hold the traditional follow-up meeting.

The chat window is important because it allows reviewers to make comments while they are still in the inspection process, rather than having to keep notes for a later meeting. They can make the comments while the issue is being encountered and is still fresh in their minds.

Task 3.4. When to exit

Ultimately, the inspection leader decides when the issue discovery phase is completed. He or she logs in and observes the session in real time and tracks its progress. The following list gives some suggestions for exit triggers:

- Schedule: The schedule may dictate when the inspection process is completed.
- Team reporting: The team members may report to the inspection leader when they have accomplished their individual tasks. The leader gives the exit signal when all team members have reported in.
- Number of issues: Some formal inspection processes set issue discovery goals during the kickoff meeting. The discovery phase is complete when these goals are reached.
- Observation: All discovery sessions run a similar course, whether they be inspections, brainstorm sessions, etc. By observing the status of the inspection from time to time, the leader can decide when issue detection rates decline enough to signal exit.

Step 4. Editing

The tool provides annotated source document reports including the issues flagged, attributes given, and comments made during the session. The editor takes this document and resolves the issues in the original source document. The editor consults with the author or the reviewer who recorded the issue as necessary while editing the document. Any unresolved issues are also resolved at this point.

In most formal inspections, another team member compares the revised source document with the annotated source document (or issue log) to verify that correct changes were made. The document is then given the "inspected" stamp of approval and exited from the inspection.

Step 5. Analysis

Although the document itself has exited the inspection, the issue data and inspection metrics should be analyzed. This analysis provide insights into improvements that will drive issues out of the process itself. The ultimate goal of most inspections is to decrease major issues in future projects.

Task 5.1. Analysis of defect log

The tool is geared toward inspection facilitation rather than inspection analysis. However, the tool does provide basic reports to aid inspection analysis. One report provides an issue summary for both historical and analysis reasons. It is divided into three sections: issue list attributes, issue listing, and basic issue statistics. The issue list attributes section shows the attributes sets for the session. The issue listing section gives a tabular summary of all flags recorded for the session, including the line number, the contributor, and the issue attribute values. The basic issue statistics section gives a summary of each attribute value, including the number found and its percentage of the total.

The tool also provides an export capability to the common CSV (comma separated values) format. This format is used by many commercial and research-based inspection analysis tools. These tools excel at their analysis techniques and methods. In addition, the CSV format is supported in most database and spreadsheet applications like Microsoft Access and Excel.

Task 5.2. Analysis of session chat log

The session chat log should also be analyzed in this phase. It provides valuable information about the inspection process itself and gives potential efficiency gains for future inspections.

Task 5.3. Create measures to improve process and prevent issues in future

After a complete analysis of the issues found and the inspection process itself, the team leader or SEPG member should create measures to implement the findings in future projects and in future inspections. These measures will be tailored to the specific findings of each analysis.

Software Inspection - Feedback

Software inspections can involve feedback mechanisms. Feedback mechanisms are widely recognized within engineering literature and to a lesser extent within the inspection literature. Defect prevention efforts are based on casual analysis which is considered a feedback mechanism (Jones, 1985). Similar causal analysis forms the basis for the second level of Personal Software Processes (Humphrey, 1995). Analyzing prior defect patterns helps focus inspections and remove recurring errors.

The focus of our interest is on two feedback mechanisms that have not been considered in prior research. They were initially recognized in a conference paper and shown in the causal model on the following page (Rodgers, et.al., 1998). The model suggested that inspection processes are cognitive processes in which people (players) are allocated along with causes in order to identify defects. The two feedback mechanisms both cause and affect the cognitive processes. The cited conference paper posits that feedback mechanisms help explain sources of variation in inspection processes. We now explore the assertion by surveying experienced inspectors.

Research Objectives

As a beginning to a study of feedback mechanisms, this section explores process maturity and inspector proficiency. The primary issues are how to

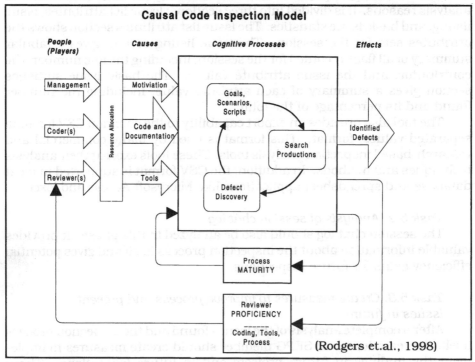

Causal Code Inspection Model

(Rodgers et.al., 1998)

define and measure both constructs. Two specific research objectives are considered.

Research Objective #1: Does process maturity significantly affect results of software inspections?

Maturity is the condition of being fully-grown or developed. Inspection processes can be considered more mature as they become established, predictable, and ultimately managed. Process maturity does not necessarily imply formality or predictability. Formality is unnecessary if participants understand their roles and expectations. A process can be mature in the sense of being well established, yet ineffective and lack predictable outcomes. For example, a mature process would be one in which the participants know exactly how many defects they are expected to find and are given opportunity to manipulate the results.

Three distinct over-lapping phases of process maturity are shown in the following graph. The first is a process definition phase in which a team forms a consensus about how and what to do during the process. During this first phase, the team is learning and establishing the process. The second phases focuses on productivity and doing the process effectively. The third phase focuses on proficiency and process efficiency. During this later phase, the team realizes that the process must be more selective because the issues are more complex.

An alternative method of representing process maturity is using a framework similar to the Capability Maturity Model. (Humphrey, 1989) which posits five progressive levels: ad hoc, repeatable, defined, managed, and optimized. Although intended for organizational assessment of key process areas, CMM levels can be adopted to inspection processes. Level one, ad hoc, applies to new or infrequent use of inspections within a professional business environment. Level two, repeatable, refers to inspec-

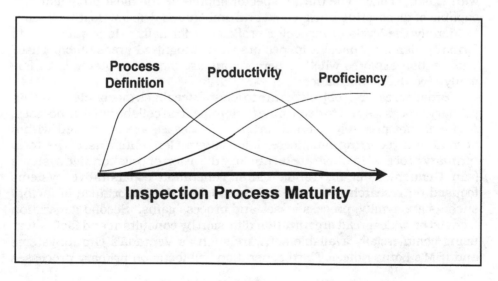

tions conducted on a somewhat regular basis. Level three, defined, refers to repeatable inspections in which the process, standards and defect types are well understood. Level four, managed, refers to defined inspections in which the number of major issues to be found is anticipated based on experience. Level five, optimized, refers to managed inspections which is or can be tailored to find specific types of defects— the results of which can be manipulated by the reviewers. In part, this chapter explores whether such a classification can be intuitively perceived or predicted based on inspection practices.

Research Objective #2: Does inspector proficiency significantly affect results of software inspections? If so, should inspector proficiency be assessed formally or informally?

Proficiency refers to the ability to do something well. Inspector proficiency refers to the ability to find defects in another person's work. This section explores perceptions concerning whether inspector proficiency is important and how acceptable it is to formally record proficiency information.

Prior knowledge of inspector proficiency has value when inspection teams are formed. For example, assume use of a scenario based code inspection in which three inspectors are assigned different roles as suggested by Porter, Votta, and Basili (1995). The first reviewer focuses on data type consistencies including coding and documentation standards; the second focuses on incorrect functionality; and the third focuses on ambiguity or missing functionality. Each assignment is progressively more difficult and may suggest assigning individuals with different skill levels to each role. The first inspector might be a junior programmer for which the review process serves as a learning experience. The second inspector might be a programmer or analyst with proficiency in matching required functionality with existing code. The third inspector should be the most proficient and capable of discovering unexpected and ambiguous defects. Is it necessary to identify the levels of inspector proficiency formally? Is it sufficient to formally identify proficient inspectors with recognized areas of expertise? This section explores whether perceptions are more acceptable than formally recorded performance.

Broader research objectives are to identify feedback mechanisms within primary processes and to determine their impact on collaborative processes. Although not precisely defined, primary processes are integrated within normal and recurring practices. Michiel van Genuchten used the term "primary process" to illustrate technology diffusion of collaborative systems (van Genuchten, et.al., 1998). First generation collaborative systems focused on research interests and established the importance of factors such as anonymity, process losses and process gains. Second generation focused on widespread organization diffusion by consultant and facilitators using commercially available software such as Ventana's GroupSystems and IBM's Lotus Notes. Third generation will focus on primary processes that support workgroups engaged in recurring activities. Genuchten identified software inspections as a primary process and a rich area for exploring collaborative issues. This chapter explores whether two feedback mechanisms are important within the inspection process. If significance is established, a broader question is whether feedback mechanisms have importance for other collaborative primary processes.

Method

This investigation is based on observation of experienced inspectors through survey and qualitative interviews. The findings also help develop a theoretical foundation for the study of collaboratively enabled software inspections.

The three-part survey is contained in Appendix 1. The first section covers background information including years of relevant experience and number of inspections during the last year and over the career. The second section covers process maturity related issues. The third section covers inspector proficiency related issues.

Three experienced inspectors reviewed a preliminary version of the survey. Based on their suggestions, changes were made, including replacing the term "reviewer" with "inspector" and adding question choices such as an expectation to "learn the inspection practice of the company".

This survey is primarily an exploratory devise. Most questions are open-ended or contain open-ended answer choices. Only one question (#10) measures a single construct (process maturity using a CMM framework). All other questions explore perceptions about aspects of the two primary constructs, process maturity and inspector proficiency.

The process maturity section contains twelve questions. Question #8 solicits the type and team composition of the participant's last inspection. Question #10 solicits an assessment of the process maturity using a CMM framework. Questions #18 and #19 solicit open-ended discussion about the impact and variability of process maturity. The remaining eight questions cover nine different aspects: (1) expected accomplishments, (2) type of inspection, (3) inspector roles, (4) process formality, (5) volume inspected, (6) team composition, (7) type of defects, (8) number of anticipated defects originally expected to be found, and (9) number of defects actually found. For question #17 (number of defects) choices are given to indicate that the quantities are unknown.

The inspector proficiency section contains five questions. Questions #23 and #24 solicit open-ended discussion about past performance and formal recording of proficiency information. The other three questions use seven point Likert scales to assess perceptions. Question #20 asks how important various factors are to the inspection proficiency construct. Question #21 asks whether specific metrics indicate proficiency. Question #22 asks whether perceptions about proficiency should be considered when inspectors are selected and assigned to inspections. Most question choices are closely associated and labeled with similar wordings between the three questions. The choices are loosely categorized into (1) experience, (2) productivity, (3) review rate, and (4) efficiency.

Results

This section summarizes survey results. First, it establishes that experienced inspectors participated in the survey. Second, quantitative survey responses are summarized. Last, factor analysis is used to identify underlying dimensions of the two primary constructs.

Survey Participation

Thirty-one experienced software developers were surveyed. Two participants were interviewed concerning survey contents and specific issues suggested by the tabulated results. Survey participants represent eleven organizations ranging from small software development teams to large international firms.

- Thirteen represent an international hardware and software development firm with a reputation for maturity (CMM level 4).
- Six represent small United State software development firms with international markets.
- Four represent European software development firms most of which have multinational development efforts.
- Eight are graduate students who also work for software development firms. A large international hardware and software development firm employs five of the eight students.

On average, those surveyed have 12.6 years of software development experience and 12.2 years of employment with their current employer. Individuals were asked to participate based on having software inspection experience. On average within the last twelve months, they participated in 19.8 code reviews, 21.6 design reviews and 4.5 other formal technical reviews. Out of sixty individuals asked to participate thirty-one responded (with a 52% return rate). The rate was significantly higher for the twenty-three individuals that were directly asked to participate (with 18 responses and a 78% return rate). This compares to thirty-seven individuals who were asked to participate by a quality/process leader within a single large international firm (with 13 responses and a 35% return rate). In summary, the individuals surveyed have significant relevant experience.

Survey Responses

Detailed survey responses are available upon request. Major results are presented.

Significant process variations exist within mature development organizations. The thirteen individuals from the same international firm stated that inspection practices for their last inspection process ranged the entire spectrum of process maturity (2 ad hoc, 1 repeatable, 4 defined, 3 managed, and 3 optimized). The volume reviewed was bipolar with six reporting that they last inspected less than 50 lines of code or 5 pages and the other seven reporting that they inspected over 4,000 lines of code or 25 pages. Only three had expectations about the number of major issues to be found and only five reported the actual number of issues uncovered. Only one reported a significant number of issues uncovered (141 total issues of which 54 were major and 25 majors were anticipated based on inspection of 5,000 lines of code).

Following are quantitative results for all survey participants. The majority surveyed expect to find general defects (29 of 31) and specific types of defects (19 of 31). Additional expectations include requirement assurance, product usability, and verification of known defect fixes. Similar to the findings reported for the single firm, last inspection process ranged the entire spectrum of process maturity (6 ad hoc, 9 repeatable, 9 defined, 3 managed, and 4 optimized). For most, inspectors came from the same development team (22 of 31) and the same project (20 of 31). Methods for assigning inspector roles varied widely (8 informally, 14 to the same tasks, 8 to different main responsibilities, 2 involved only one inspector, and 1 used a checklist). For most, written standards and guidelines exist (17 of 31); however the formality of the process definition was subject to wide variations (10 informally defined, 11 written processes, 8 defect codes and type

In order to be a proficient inspector, how important are the following?	Average Rank	Standard Deviation
• programming language proficiency (for code inspections)	6.1	1.0
• cognitive ability to find defects	5.9	1.0
• experience as an inspector	5.3	1.5
• development environment proficiency	5.2	1.4
• experience as an author being reviewed	4.1	1.7

Assuming the following information can be record or derived about prior individual performance, how acceptable is it to use the following information to select and assign inspectors to an inspection team?

• experience (number of prior inspections)	5.0	1.4
• efficiency (percent of defects found per defects suggested)	4.5	2.2
• experience (pages or lines of code inspected)	3.9	1.5
• review rate (pages/lines of code reviewed per hour)	3.7	1.9
• productivity (number of defects per page/lines of code)	3.7	2.1
• productivity (defects found per preparation hour)	3.6	1.9
• productivity (defects found per meeting hour)	3.5	1.9

Assume the inspector proficiency information is not formally recorded or available, what factors should be considered when inspectors are selected and assigned to inspections?

• experience with programming language	5.5	1.4
• experience as an inspector	5.1	1.5
• productivity as a person who can find defects	5.1	1.9
• efficiency as a finder of defects	5.0	1.8
• experience with the development environment	4.9	1.8
• review rate as a through and detailed inspector	4.3	2.0
• experience as an author of reviewed materials	4.0	1.7

Table1 - Ranking of Inspector Proficiency Perceptions

classification, 14 checklists, 1 script, and 2 scenarios). Most worked with individual inspection members on similar reviews numerous times previously (28 of 31 with 7 reporting an average of 2.4 times during the last twelve months).

The preceding table summarizes perceptions about whether inspector proficiency can and should be assessed formally, informally, or not at all. Surveyors were asked to use a seven-point Likert scale (with 1 = no importance, 3 = some importance, 5 = important, and 7 = extremely important and expected). The responses are ranked from most important down to least important.

Factor Analysis

Quantitative answers were used to assess underlying dimensions of the two primary constructs. Five different types of quantitative answers are included or derived from the survey. Multiple choice answers are treated as qualitative variables and coded with a nominal value (true="1" or false="0"). Likert scale answers are coded with the corresponding ordinal value (from 1 to 7). Numeric counts (such as the number of inspections or defects expected) are coded with ratio scales; however these counts have little value within the following analysis other than to indicate whether the quantity is known or equal to zero. Instead, aggregated ordinal scales (unknown = "(1)", zero value = "0", and positive value = "1") are used to characterize numeric count questions. Finally, aggregated counts of nominal values are used for several questions with similar answer choices and for which a count of similar choices is presumed to infer a stronger relationship (such as within question #11 to distinguish whether the reviewer comes from the same project, company, division, or development team).

Given thirty-one participants and seventy-one quantitative answers, it is difficult to make statistical inferences or generalize findings. A larger sample size would provide greater statistical power; however, given selective participation in the survey, large sample sizes might not enhance the ability to generalize findings. For statistical analysis, the number of factors to be analyzed is limited by the sample size of thirty-one participants. In addition, using a number of factors approaching the sample size prevents obtaining some standardized statistical metrics such as Cronbach's alpha. Nevertheless, given the exploratory nature of the survey, some insight can be gained by exploring latent factors.

Process maturity construct measurement is more complex than participant perceptions. Attempts to use regression to predict the process maturity level (from question #10) resulted in models with very low statistical significance (adjusted $R^2 < .15$) and the only factor having some significance is the number of defects expected (probability value = .032). As previously stated, participants within relatively mature organizations perceive wide variations in inspection process maturity. During a follow-up interview, it was suggested that the classification wording might imply "goodness" of personal practices and thus is difficult to assess. Inspector proficiency is even more difficult to measure and subject to measurement dysfunction

(Austin, 1996) as illustrated in the following participant quotes. "Yes, although this is difficult to quantify." "People will be less open about the inspections and their results." "People will not log if they think management will base performance evaluation of author on the results." "Counting is ridiculous especially if you have to justify what you find is over or under an expected amount."

Using heuristics based on inspection practices might be more stable than using perceptions of maturity level. A heuristic was adopted based on the CMM assessment method. The heuristic requires demonstration of competence in all key process areas at the current and lower levels before being designated at that current level. For analysis purposes, qualitative answers were aggregated by how relevant they were to each process maturity level. Process maturity level was determined based on the presence of at least one indicator within the level and the lower levels (with the exception of level one - ad hoc for which no key process area is assumed). The only apparent difficulty with the heuristic occurred with an indication of a level five (optimized) process and none for level four (managed). In this case, the process was classified as a level five. For the thirteen participants from the single firm, the distribution changed significantly. Ten of the thirteen participants indicate either level four or five (which is more similar to their organization's level 4 CMM designation). Three participants indicated a level two (repeatable). Perhaps, process maturity should be assessed based on inspection practices within key processing areas in a manner similar to CMM.

Exploratory factor analysis reveals significant underlying dimensions. Factor analysis was used for both major constructs. For process maturity, analysis was done at summary and detailed levels. For inspector proficiency, analysis was done at the detailed level. The factors identified might not generalize; however, they give insight into perceptions of those surveyed.

Using summary level analysis, process maturity contains two major dimensions (with Cronback's alpha = .63). The first relates to process formation based on defined roles, process formality, and team interactions. The second relates to anticipated and actual results based on known volumes inspected and number of issues found. However, aggregated coding might cause distortion. Therefore, detailed level analysis was also conducted.

Using detailed level analysis, process maturity contains nine significant dimensions. Each dimension is briefly described along with significant positively and negatively correlated variables with larger than a (.40 correlation. (1) *Immature process* relates to an expectation of establishing standards and unknown numbers of issues expected or actually found. (2) *Informal process* relates to informally defined role, a perception of ad hoc level one maturity level, and working together previously. Informal processes are negatively related to written processes, standards, guidelines, working on similar reviews and working on the same discovery task. (3) *Specific or targeted issues* relate to an expectation of finding specific issues, reviewing an unknown volume, finding an unknown number of issues, and working within the same development team. (4) *Corporate practices* relate to working within the same company or development team, and written standards, defect codes and types. Corporate practices are negatively related to an expectation of establishing standards. (5) *Recurring issues* relate to an expectation of finding general defects, use of checklists, and written standards and guidelines. Recurring issues are negatively related to looking for unknown defect types. (6) *Issue recognition* relates to first-time experiences, use of scenarios, written defect codes and types, and perception of managed level-four maturity level. (7) *Learning expectation* relates to an expectation of learning and assignment to different main tasks. Learning expectation is negatively related to working within the team and assignment of the same task. (8) *Project formality* relates to working together, with reviewers from the same project, using a written process, and not being a first-time experience. (9) *Non-recurring issues* relate to looking for pre-designated issue type and a perception of an optimized level-five process maturity. The first factor (immature process) from the detailed analysis is similar in nature to the second factor (anticipated and actual results) from the summary analysis. Also the remaining eight factors from the detailed analysis appear to be dimensions of the first factor (process formation) from the summary analysis.

Using detailed level analysis, inspector proficiency contains five significant dimensions. (1) *Problem solving skills* relate to the perception of being a finder of defects through productivity, review rate, and efficiency, as well as having a high percentage of defects found per defects suggested. (2) *Inspection productivity* relates to the prior individual performance in terms of the number of defects found in total, in preparation, and during meetings. (3) *Inspection experience* relates to prior inspection experience whether perceived or actually counted and as either an author or inspector. (4) *Programming skills* relate to the importance of programming language proficiency, and perceptions of experience with the programming language or development environment. (5) *Environmental awareness* relates to the importance of development environment proficiency and the cognitive ability to find defects.

Discussion

This section discusses the stated research objective of exploring whether the two feedback mechanisms significantly affect software inspection results. This chapter does not prove the research objectives; rather it explores perceptions of experienced inspectors. Nevertheless, the findings generally support the research objectives and suggest additional avenues of inquiry.

The first objective is to determine whether process maturity significantly affects results of software inspections. Question #18 most directly addresses the stated objective. This open-end question asks what impact, if any, does process maturity have on inspections? More specifically, does the nature of the inspection change as the process matures? Twenty-eight of the thirty-one participants responded to the questions. Only five of the

	Definition Phase	Productivity Phase	Proficiency Phase
Factor Analysis	* Process formation	* Anticipated and actual results	* Specific or targeted issues
	* Immature process * Informal process	* Corporate practice * Recurring issues * Learning experience	* Issue recognition * Non-recurring issues
Qualitative Reponses	* Team ownership * Training	* Inspection rates * Workload * Project commitment	* Problem-solving skills

Table 2 - Categorization of Factors and Responses by Process Maturity Phases

responses suggested minimal or no impact. Most of the remaining comments supported the assertion that process maturity impacts inspections. One of the more interesting lines of reasoning was established in a follow-up interview. The participant asserted that the team composition is a given constraint, and "although people are more important, you must manage the process." Another insightful comment follows, "This is a soft issue; if the organization has experience, culture, and willingness to work along defined routes, inspections are taken seriously and actually carried out and followed-up. In a low maturity organization it is difficult to actually prove the effects of inspections and they tend to get postponed or canceled."

Measuring process maturity presents problems. As previously documented, the use of a CMM framework might provide a more consistent assessment, especially given the establishment of key practice areas. Can process maturity be assessed based on overlapping phases such as definition, productivity, and proficiency? In this alternate phase-related framework, the category is not as important as understanding the support requirements for each phase and identifying how much associated support is required for the current inspection. One quote supports the notion that process mature in a non-linear manner, specifically "Our process matures chaotically." As shown in the preceding table, factor analysis and previous qualitative observations can be categorized within such a framework. Such categorization serves as a foundation for further defining and exploring each phase. Whether three phases is sufficient or necessary remains unresolved.

A potentially important aspect of process maturity is the inspection review rate. Most experts consider review rates as very important. Inspection expert Tom Gilb states, "check at your organization's optimum rates to find major defects" (Gilb, 1998). Michiel van Genuchten finds that review rate must be controlled in order for electronic meeting system inspections to be more effective than traditional Fagan inspections. He also finds that very few defects are found for either method when the review rate is too fast. Survey participants appear to place relatively little emphasis on review rates. Use of review rate is given a relatively low 3.9 ranking with a relatively large 1.9 standard deviation (see Table 1). The observation is similar for the related issue of perceived thoroughness that is given a 4.3 ranking and a 2.0 standard deviation. The only quote related to thoroughness and indirectly to review rates follows. "You want people who spend time and find problems." Apparently, this is an issue that many inspectors either do not remember or have forgotten.

Further, process maturity should focus on how-to support teams. Teams own inspection processes as supported in the following quotes. "Our goal is to find defects ourselves as a development team, not to create professional super-inspectors. Every member should inspect once in a while." "The team typically knows who are the good inspectors. The data about it should be owned by the individual or the team." Follow-up interviews supported this assertion. One participant observed that there are at most ten people in the world who have sufficient expertise to inspect their code. This observation appears to apply for both large and small organizations. In large organizations, inspection responsibility falls on development teams that usually consist of ten or less members. In small organizations, there might only be a few developers in the entire organization.

Process maturity is directly affected by workload and project commitments. This assertion is supported by the following quotes. "We barely have time for reviews, much less all the formalization." "Our environment is changing given shortened time-to-market constraints. We need to tailor processes to fit the life cycle." "Don't include a person that is not motivated to participate." Do not "increase overhead." "Inspection is not a popular pastime. Many of us find it drudgery even though it is of critical importance to quality. People may decide to find fewer defects if they know the more they find, the more review time they must spend."

As processes mature, opportunity must be given for training of new team members and transferring institutional knowledge. This assertion is supported in the following quotes. "Others ought to be included to improve their skills." "Other members can be in training." "Everybody needs to be in the game." For an organization with responsibility for maintaining large amounts of legacy code, the observation was made that inspections provide a significant source for training and knowledge transfer even when few defects are found. Individuals who maintain the code will eventually retire and inspections provide a structured opportunity to transfer knowledge from senior to junior level team members.

The inspector proficiency research objective has two parts. The first is to establish significance and the later addresses whether proficiency should be assessed formally or informally.

There appears to be support for the assertion that inspector proficiency affects results of software inspections. Question #23 most directly addresses the stated objective. This open-end question asks whether a person's past performance should be considered when an inspection review team is formed? If so, how? If not, why not? Only three of the twenty-eight responses suggest that inspector proficiency does not affect the results and one of these merely state concerns about privacy and formal recording of performance information. However, the tenor of the discussion is supportive. Two supportive quotes follow. "The team typically knows who are the good reviewers." "Only certain people can be considered good reviewers, or can learn to be good reviewers."

A significant aspect of inspector proficiency is problem-solving skill. Both quantitative and qualitative supports exist for this assertion. As previously stated and based on factor analysis, problem solving is the most significant proficiency factor. The factor relates to the perception of being a finder of defects through productivity, review rate, and efficiency, as well as having a high percentage of defects found per defects suggested. The qualitative support comes from the following quotes. "Are they good engineers?" Inspectors need the "knack" and ability to "see to the heart of the problem." "At least one person who can find defects is a must to make the review worthwhile." "Only certain people can be considered good reviewers, or can learn to be good reviewers."

The issue of formally recording inspector proficiency information appears to depend on the organizational culture. Question #24 asks, "What concerns, if any, do you have about formally recording inspector proficiency information?" The 30 responses, out a possible total of thirty-one, are divided into ten strongly supportive comments and thirteen strongly opposing comments. Many expressed concerns like "it is valuable information for performance evaluation. But I don't think it needs to be a formal process to record. A close working relationship among the team members would yield better information." The assertion that the response depends on the organizational culture is best stated in the following quote. "As with all data concerning a person, it can be used constructively or destructively. Whether formal recording should be used is a function of the person's organization personality." This finding is also supported by Robert Austin's research (Austin, 1996). Austin recommends that, for difficult-to-measure performance constructs, organizations need to either develop reliable measurement instruments or else rely on the team to do what is right without quantitative measures.

Perceptions about individual performance might be preferable to formal recordings of actual performance. Maintaining formal records adds overhead, forces formally defined metrics and raises privacy concerns. Can perceptions sufficiently measure individual proficiency? Most individuals are painfully aware of their inadequacies. To formally record painful information might not be advantageous. Also, most team members have a sense of who to rely upon within their team. The assertion is supported by the following quotes. "If you can record the original error maker, you can record who can find the error." But recording "can hurt a person's privacy" "Sure, if I know that they are not checking details, I probably won't use them." "It is valuable information for performance evaluation. But I don't think it needs to be a formal process to record. A close working relationship among the team members would yield better information." "Don't waste time doing recording." Although not statistically significant, rankings for the second question (see Table 1 on page 12) related to formal recordings are lower than the other two questions related to perceptions.

Perhaps the focus of inspector proficiency should shift to how-to-best support recognized expertise within an inspection process. Inspectors know when they are beginners or even productive team members who are expected to contribute. What might not be known is how to recognize expertise and constructively use the expertise without burning it out. Thus there might be a need to manage a list of corporate or outside consulting inspection expertise. One of the follow-up interviews bought out the need for a non-team member with expertise in the Windows/NT operating system. What if the inspection was tailored to maximize knowledge transfer for specific questions asked of recognized experts?

The findings of this survey might not generalize to industrial settings; however traditional remedies for threats to internal validity might also restrict the ability to generalize findings. Porter considers selection and maturation as threats to internal validity (Porter, et.al., 1997). Porter recommends randomly assigning team members for each inspection to avoid selection bias and randomly assigning treatments for each inspection to spread any performance improvement across all treatments. Porter's assertions fail to recognize that selection and maturation are normal industrial practices and sources of competitive advantage. The lack of consideration given to selection and maturation might be major reasons that process-related factors are found to be insignificant. Porter's experiments have been conducted either in an inspection-mature organization or in a graduate-level computer science classroom. Random selection from a large mature organization with a history and culture supportive of inspections does not reflect results from smaller less mature development firms. Selection of graduate students presupposes extensive training in industrial practices and establishment of a culture similar to an industrial environment. While this might be possible given an integrated and mandatory curriculum, it is not the norm for most institutions of higher learning. Thus threats to internal validity exist based on randomization of people and treatments. A better experimental approach might be to measure and treat selection and maturation as independent variables that are potential sources of significant variation.

Significance

This survey explores perceptions of two feedback mechanisms, process maturity and inspector proficiency. Some feedback mechanisms might be intuitive and used by teams to enhance their performance. For example, the team might sense who the good inspectors are and assign important inspection task accordingly. As Robert Austin suggests, performance measures are best left unmeasured if the team collectively moves along the best performance path (Austin, 1996). The challenge is to identify the impact of feedback mechanisms or calibrate their effects.

Feedback mechanisms might impact the development of tools. Providing access to easily quantifiable factors such as number of major issues expected and actually found should have a major impact on group performance. For more difficult to quantify factors like process maturity and inspector proficiency, the question is will workgroups recognize and support their integration within a collaborative tool.

Process maturity might impact how inspection tasks are defined and shared among inspectors. Task templates might be used to match process maturity expectations. More specifically, the tool might prompt for inspection type, objectives and anticipated inspectors. The system would then provide a base template of inspection tasks assigned to inspectors. The moderator can modify inspectors and task assignments. The tool would assess the optimum review rates and identify any potential mismatches of task and proficiency.

Inspection processes might be tailored to support expert inspectors. Perhaps the inspection tool should interface with corporate personnel skill databases or to an external cottage industry of expert inspection consultants. If a particular expertise is needed, enable the inspection team with the ability to identify and obtain appropriate expertise.

Recognition of feedback mechanisms should enable better allocation of (people) resources and assignment of (process) tasks. The expected benefits include improved quality, increased productivity, and faster time-to-market. Within distributed contexts, feedback mechanisms should enable different-time, different-place work processes.

Distributed Software Inspections

Software development is rapidly becoming a global activity. In many firms development is parceled to different locations around the world. Firms have development locations in the United States, Europe, India, and the Far East. For the most part, the development has been restricted to non-overlapping functions. However, the shift to joint development is occurring. For example, Microsoft builds a common product testing version from distributed modules every twenty-four hours. Distributed software inspections will become more and more important as this shift toward global development continues. This section explores aspects of distributed inspections and forms a basis for continuing research.

Distributed software inspections will require new concepts and methods. Distributed inspections can be asynchronous or synchronous, same-time or different-time, or a combination of each. In fact, some inspections could be one protocol for some members (for example, same-time, same-place) and another protocol for other members. Providing such flexibility while also fostering productivity is a challenge. The following list explains some of the issues that need further research:

• Presence of other reviewers is an issue in distributed synchronous, same-time inspections. The importance of the "meeting framework" in the productivity of a review session must be researched. Preliminary observation hints that distributed reviewers should know who else is online with them-in a stronger sense than a simple list of names. Should reviewer pictures or other information be shown on flag detail display screens? CodeReview includes user-specific icons to alert participants to the presence of other reviewers.

- Simultaneity of use by reviewers. Distributed users should be able to contribute to a common repository of issues in real time. How important is it for issues logged by one reviewer to appear immediately on other reviewer's screens, rather than in batch mode? If important, simultaneity forces internetworked tool solutions rather than stand-alone products.

- Issue tagging alerts reviewers to the presence of potential issues. Should tags include visual clues that transfer significance? Does color coding of defect types increase productivity? How do participants raise questions, make comments, and record improvement suggestions in an intuitively appealing manner? In CodeReview, there is a presumption that issue tagging is very important because it facilitates cognitive processes. An independent reviewer observed that the visual tags are "cute." However, the aspect that needs to be explored is how to focus attention of reviewers on issues of greatest potential. Perhaps filters are needed to remove minor issues that have been resolved or that have little likelihood of interest to the specific reviewer.

- Issue categorization needs to be incorporated into the inspection process because it is less likely that a synchronous meeting will occur to resolve conflicts. Does issue categorization become more consistent and thus usable when collaboratively enabled? As a result, is there a learning curve and does the inspection process ultimately become more efficient? What distributed mechanisms exist to support dialog and consensus among team members on issues?

- Process maturation needs to be supported. Does the inspection support definition, productivity, and proficiency concerns? Are the supporting metrics a by-product of the process, and do they automate the traditional, significant, independent effort to produce?

- Facilitator needs must be addressed. Traditional meetings allow facilitators and authors to walk through the code, exploring each issue with the team. Current Internet facilities for distributed meetings using multimedia support are still immature.

- Inspection memory issues need to be researched. Distributed inspections do not necessarily have a wrap-up meeting for process discussion. What alternatives exist to meet process needs during an inspection? Distributed tools must support some parallel concept to traditional wrap-up meetings that allow reviewers to improve the inspection process itself.

Few, if any, organizations currently support distributed inspections. However, traditional inspections provide a rich context for speculation and research on the nature of distributed processes because traditional inspections are well understood.

Software Inspection - Knowledge Management

A major obstacle to the evolving information-based society is information over-load. Knowledge management is being herald as a means to address information overload within organizations. In a sense, knowledge management is needed within inspection processes.

As recognized in the LEAP initiative at the University of Hawaii, a need exists for portability of metrics by individual developers. LEAP support is envisioned as a kind of "personal information assistant" for developer's software engineering skill set.

At the organization level, inspections need to feed information at the appropriate level of detail into the Software Engineering Process Group. In an orthogonal defect classification environment, issue categorization is a valuable corporate resource. Doing so without introducing measurement dysfunction is a challenge (Austin, 1996). Perhaps specific defect knowledge needs to be preserved at the individual author level and summary analysis needs to be incorporated in the corporate knowledge bases.

An interesting aspect of inspector proficiency is recognition expertise. Because most development groups are relatively small, the question is not who is the beginner or even the moderately proficient developer; rather, who is an expert in the area in which the that the group needs help. This expertise might be of a temporal nature while members of the group acquire knowledge or of a specific technical nature outside the interests of the development team. As examples, consider knowledge of a relatively new operating systems during a conversion effort or of a specific devise characteristics during development of a device driver. The development team might want to develop internal expertise regarding the new operating system and rely on outside expertise for the specific devise characteristics. The main point being that the inspection process will need to support inclusion of an outside expert within the inspection process.

Support of expert inspectors also creates an opportunity to facilitate knowledge transfer and assess processes. Assume that the inspection team seeks an outside expert. It would be desirable to determine how well the expert worked with other groups in the past and to determine the availability of the expert to participate. Upon completion, the team is also in a position to evaluate how well the expert contributed. On the other hand the expert is uniquely qualified to evaluate the inspection process and the task assigned. Facilitating exchanges between inspection teams and expert inspectors might provide insights into use of inspection agents and more basically knowledge transfer.

Software Inspection - Research Agendas

Philip Johnson, from the University of Hawaii, envisions radical inspection changes on the horizon including method-specific inspections, minimal meetings, defect-correction emphasis, organizational guideline knowledge bases, outsourcing review, computer-mediation, and review mega-groups (Johnson, 1998). Do advances in technology including object-orientation and wider information access call for radical changes in inspections? Technology can enable wider participation in asynchronous settings; however the question remains as to whether the inspection process needs to be reengineered.

Active research agendas are being pursued by various groups including (and by no means limited to) the following: (1) Adam Porter and Vic Basili at the University of Maryland at College Park, (2) Philip Johnson at the University of Hawaii, (3) Lasse Harjumaa and Ilkka Tervonen at the University of Oulu, and (4) Michiel van Genuchten and University of Arizona efforts championed by the authors of this chapter. In general, the first two groups come from a computer science orientation; while the latter two come from a groupware orientation. Hopefully, out of the diversity of these and other perspectives an emerging consensus will develop concerning a new generation of software inspections.

Software Inspection - Software Process Improvement Activity

W. Edwards Deming's point number three in this "Fourteen Points for Managing Never-Ending Improvement" is "cease dependence upon mass inspection." Identifying and correcting the root cause makes more sense than mass inspections that are designed to correct every mistake. Why then are software inspections advocated as a software improvement activity?

The goal of software inspections is both to identify major issues and to eliminate the need for inspections. Because software development is constantly evolving and involves complex human-to-human and human-to-machine interactions, the need for inspections will continue indefinitely. The need for "mass inspections" is probably needed in only very few situations. In less mature organizations in which process definition is the focus it is unwise to advocate 100% inspection; rather selective inspections can accomplish the more important objectives of process definition and knowledge transfer to less experienced developers. In extremely mature organizations, the need might be reduced due to more economical methods related to individual programmer disciplines and mature testing facilities. The idea is to drive out errors and change the inspection process until such time that it is only used to verify quality assurance goals or to focus on specific issues such as capacity constraints or cross-platform performance.

Inspections should be placed at the points of greatest potential return. Several inspection experts advise that inspections should only occur based on previously inspected source documents. The implication is that inspections are best done during design and requirements phases. This argument is intuitively and economically appealing and supports the notion that validation and verification of requirements reduces the number and complexity of implementation related defects. Discovering defects sooner is cheaper and better than later and can affect an order to magnitude productivity improvement.

Frederick P. Brooks recently observed that "the computer scientist is a toolsmith-no more, but no less." He contrasts the scientist who is interested in discovery of facts and laws and who builds in order to study, with the engineer who studies in order to build. Brooks considers computer science as an engineering and not a scientific discipline (Brooks, 1996). The intent is to not argue Brooks' point, rather to point out the engineering aspects of software inspection and software process improvement. Software inspections constitute a significant aspect of software development and as such are an important aspect of software process improvement. In this chapter, considerable emphasis has been placed on studying inspections as a primary collaborative process with potential in a distributed contest and ultimately building tools to support inspection processes. More generally, the role of toolsmith is a valuable contribution to both software inspections and more generally to software process improvement.

Appendix 1 - Feedback Survey Format

Introduction and Purpose of Survey
I am researching code inspection processes and want to explore the impacts of process maturity and reviewer proficiency on the inspection process. The following 24-question survey is being distributed to software developers in a number of diverse organizations. Individual information gathered IS STRICTLY CONFIDENTIAL. Let me know your email address only if you are interested in obtaining the resulting research paper including survey results. Feel free to contact me directly if you have additional questions or suggestions. Thanks for you help.

Background Information:
The following information is gathered in order to understand your software development background and in how many inspections you have participated.
1. (OPTIONAL) Your Name and email address:
2. Date:
3. Company:
4. Position Title:
5. Years of software development experience:
6. Years with current employer:
7. Approximately how many inspections (formal technical reviews) have you participated in as a code author or reviewer?

	during last 12 months	during entire career
a) code inspections:	_____	_____
b) design reviews:	_____	_____
c) other formal technical reviews:	_____	_____
d)= (a+b+c):total number of inspections	_____	_____

Process Maturity Related Questions

Maturity is the condition of being fully-grown or developed. Inspection processes can be considered more mature as they become established, predictable, and ultimately managed. Process maturity does not necessarily imply formality or predictability. By formality, I mean that the process does not have to be formally defined as long as the participants understand their roles and expectations. By predictability, I suggest that a process can be mature (in the sense of being well established) and yet ineffective. For example, a mature process would be one in which the participants know exactly how many defects they are expected to find and are given opportunity to manipulate the results.

For this section, answer questions based on the last inspection in which you were a reviewer.

8. Describe the nature of the inspection {type and composition of review team}:

9. What did you expect to accomplish? (select all that apply)
_ help establish standards
_ find general defects
_ find specified defect types
_ learn the inspection practice of the company
_ others describe: _____

10. What (maturity level) best describes your inspection process? (select one)
__ student/cross-cultural (lacking development experience between reviewers)
__ ad hoc/chaotic/informal (new or infrequent use of code inspections)
__ repeatable (code inspections have been done on a somewhat regular basis)
__ defined (the process, standards and defect types are well understood)
__ managed (number of defects to be found is anticipated based on experience)
__ optimized (process is or can be tailored to find specific types of defects
      can be manipulated by the reviewers)

11. Which of the following applied to the inspection? (select all that apply)
_ student project   _ first-time experience
_ reviewers came from same project   _ reviewers came from same company
_ reviewers came from same division   _ reviewers came from same development
                                        team

12. How were reviewer roles defined? (select one)
_ informally
_ all or most reviewers were assigned the same task to find defects
_ each reviewer was assigned a different main responsibility
_ other method (please describe):

13. How formally was the inspection process defined? (select all that apply)
_ informally   _ written process
_ written standards and guidelines   _ defect codes and types
_ checklist   _ scripts
_ scenarios for specific defect types

14. Approximately how much was inspected? (indicate all that apply)
lines of code: _____   _ unknown
pages for review: _____   _ unknown
other measurement (include description):

15. What best describes the composition of the review team? (select all that apply)
__ first time to work together

___ worked together numerous times {about ____ reviews during last 12 months}
___ worked with individual members on similar reviews numerous times previously
16. For what type of defects were you looking? select one
__ unknown
__ those indicated in a checklist or defect list
__ specific pre-designated types such as:
17. How many defects did your review team anticipate and then find during the inspection?
Number of defects you originally expected to find :

total number of defects:	_____	__ unknown
major defects	_____	__ unknown
minor defects	_____	__ unknown

Number of defects you actually found:

total number of defects:	_____	__ unknown
major defects:	_____	__ unknown
minor defects	_____	__ unknown

18. What impact (if any) does process maturity have on inspections? More specifically, does the nature of the inspection change as the process matures?
19. Does process maturity vary between inspections within your organization and depend on factors such as team composition?

Reviewer Proficiency Related Questions

Proficiency refers to the ability to do something very well. Reviewer proficiency specifically refers to the ability to find defects in another person's work. My main question is whether reviewer proficiency can or should be assessed formally or informally. The thrust of the following questions is to assess acceptability and appropriateness of reviewer proficiency information.

20. In order to be a proficient reviewer, how important are the following:
(using a 7 point scale where 1 = no consideration;   3 = little consideration;
5 = moderate consideration; 7 = high consideration),

a) experience being reviewed as an author   1 2 3 4 5 6 7
    you have reviewed before
b) experience as an author being reviewed   1 2 3 4 5 6 7
    you have been reviewed before
c) programming language proficiency   1 2 3 4 5 6 7
    you understand the development language
d) development environment proficiency   1 2 3 4 5 6 7
    you understand the operating environment
e) cognitive ability to find defects: 1 2 3 4 5 6 7
    you have experience and reputation for identifying problems

21. Assuming the following information can be recorded or derived about prior individual performance, how acceptable is it to use the following information in order to select and assign inspectors to an inspection team? (using a 7 point scale where 1 = no consideration;   3 = little consideration; 5 = moderate consideration; 7 = high consideration),

experience: (number of prior inspections)   1 2 3 4 5 6 7
           (pages of lines of code inspected) 1 2 3 4 5 6 7
productivity: (number of defects per page/
           lines of code)   1 2 3 4 5 6 7
           average number of defects per quantity inspected

| | (# defects found per hour of inspection preparation) | 1 2 3 4 5 6 7 |

(# defects found per hour of inspection
preparation)   1 2 3 4 5 6 7
(#defects found per hour of
inspection meeting)   1 2 3 4 5 6 7
review rate: (lines of code reviewed per hour)   1 2 3 4 5 6 7
how quickly one reviews material {too slow or too fast is not good}
efficiency: (% of defects found per defects suggested) 1 2 3 4 5 6 7
percentage of "real" problems to perceived problems

22. Assume that inspector proficiency information is not formally recorded or available, what factors should be considered when inspectors are selected and assigned to inspections? (using a 7 point scale where 1 = no consideration; 3 = little consideration; 5 = moderate consideration; 7 = high consideration);

experience: as inspector   1 2 3 4 5 6 7
              as an author of reviewed materials   1 2 3 4 5 6 7
              with the programming language   1 2 3 4 5 6 7
              with the development environment   1 2 3 4 5 6 7
productivity: as a person who can find defects   1 2 3 4 5 6 7
review rate: as a finder of defects   1 2 3 4 5 6 7
efficiency: as a finder of defects   1 2 3 4 5 6 7
other factor(s) (please specify):

23. Should a person's past performance be considered when an inspection review team is formed? If so, how? If not, why not?

24. What concerns (if any) do you have about formally recording inspector proficiency information?

References

Austin, R. D. (1996). *Measuring and managing performance in organizations.* New York, NY: Dorset House Publishing.

Brooks, F. P. J. (1996). The computer scientist as toolsmith II. *Communications of the ACM, 39*(3), 61-68.

Brothers, L., Sembugamoorthy, & Muller. (1990). *ICICLE: Groupware for code inspection.* Paper presented at the ACM Conference on Computer Supported Cooperative Work, October.

Chillarege, R., Bhandari, I. S., Chaar, J. K., Halliday, M. J., Moebus, D. S., Ray, B. K., & Wong, M.-Y. (1992). Orthogonal defect classification-a concept for in-process measurements. *IEEE Transactions on Software Engineering, 18*(11), 943-956.

Ebenau, R. G., & Strauss, S. H. (1994). *Software inspection process.* New York: McGraw-Hill.

Fagan, M. E. (1976a). *Design and code inspections and process control in the development of programs* (Technical Report TR 00.2763). Poughkeepsie, NY: IBM Corp.

Fagan, M. E. (1976b). Design and code inspections to reduce errors in program development. *IBM Systems Journal, 15*(3), 182-211.

Fowler, P. J. (1986). In-process inspections of workproducts at AT&T. *AT&T Technical Journal, 65*(2 (Mar.-Apr.)), 102-112.

Freedman, D. P., & Weinberg, G. M. (1990). *Handbook of walkthroughs, inspections, and technical reviews.* (4th ed.). Boston: Little, Brown.

Gilb, T., & Graham, D. (1993). *Software inspections.* Reading, MA: Addison-Wesley.

Gintell, J. W., Arnold, J., Houde, M., Kruszelnicki, J., McKenney, R., & Memmi, G. (1993, September). *Scrutiny: A collaborative inspection and review system.* Paper presented at the 4th European Software Engineering Conference, Garwisch-

Partenkirchen, Germany.

Grady, R. B., & Van Slack, T. (1994). Key lessons in achieving widespread inspection use. *IEEE Software*(July), 46-57.

Harjumaa, L., & Tervonen, I. (1997). *A WWW-based tool for software inspection.* Oulu, Finland: University of Oulu.

Hollocker, C. P. (1990). *Software reviews and audit handbook.* New York, NY: John Wiley and Sons, Inc.

Humphrey, W. (1995). *A discipline for software engineering. (SEI series in software engineering* ed.). Reading, Massachusetts: Addison-Wesley Publishing Company.

Humphrey, W. S. (1989). *Managing the software process.* Reading, Mass.: Addison-Wesley.

Johnson, P. M. (1998). Reengineering Inspection. *Communications of the ACM,* 41(2), 49-52.

Johnson, P. M., Tjahjono, D., Wan, D., & Brewer, R. S. (1993, October). *Experiences with CSRS: an instrumented software review environment.* Paper presented at the Pacific Northwest Software Quality Conference, Portland, OR.

Jones, C. L. (1985). A process-integrated approach to defect prevention. *IBM Systems Journal,* 24(2), 150-166.

MacDonald, F., & Miller, J. (1996). *Automated generic support for software inspection .*

Mashayekhi, V., Drake, J. M., Tsai, W.-T., & Riedl, J. (1993). Distributed, collaborative software inspection. *IEEE Software,* 10(5 (Sep.)), 66-75.

Porter, A., Siy, H., Mockus, A., & Votta, L. (1998). Understanding the sources of variation in software inspections. *ACM Transactions on Software Engineering and Methodology,* 7(1 (January)), 41-79.

Porter, A., Siy, H., & Votta, L. (1995). *A review of software inspections* (NSF #CCR-9501354 CS-TR-3552 http://www.cs.umd.edu/TRs/authors/ Harvey_Siy.html). College Park, MD: University of Maryland.

Porter, A. A., Siy, H., Mockus, A., & Votta, L. G. (1997). *Understanding the sources of variation in software inspections* (CS-TR-3762 http://www.cs.umd.edu/ TRs/TR.html). Baltimore, Maryland: University of Maryland and Bell Laboratories.

Porter, A. A., & Votta, L. G. (1994 (May), October 1995). *An experiment to assess different defect detection methods for software requirements inspections.* Paper presented at the ICSE-16. 16th International Conference on Software Engineering (Cat. No.94CH3409-0) (1994) p103-12, Sorrento, Italy.

Putaala, M., & Tervonen, I. (1996,). Inspecting Postscript documents in an object-oriented environment. Paper presented at the *Proceedings of the 5th European Conference on Software Quality,* Dublin, Ireland.

Rodgers, T. L., Vogel, D. R., Purdin, T., & Saints, B. (1998, January). In search of theory and tools to support code inspections. Paper presented at the *Proceedings of the 31st Hawaii International Conference on Systems Science,* Big Island.

Toffler, A. (1980). *The third wave.* (First ed.): William Morrow and Company.

van Genuchten, M., Cornelissen, W., & van Dijk, C. (1997,). Supporting inspections with an electronic meeting system. Paper presented at the *Proceedings of The 30th Hawaii Information Conference on Systems and Software.*

van Genuchten, M., Vogel, D., & Nunamaker, J. (1998,). *Group support in primary processes.* Paper presented at the Proceedings of the 30th Hawaii Internation Conference of the Systems Sciences, Big Island, Hawaii.

Votta, L. G. (1993, December). *Does every inspection need a meeting?* Paper presented at the SIGSOFT Symposium on foundations of software engineering.

Chapter 11

A Technical Infrastructure for Process Support

Shirley A. Becker
Florida Institute of Technology, USA

Daniel E. Ladino
American University, USA

Data is one of an organization's key resources because it provides a wealth of information that can be used for performance, quality, time-to-market, resource, product, and process improvements. It provides a means for setting goals, tracking them, and then determining changes needed at personal, team, project, and organization levels. Thus, data needs to be managed at various levels of abstraction from granular levels of development work to higher levels of organizational strategic planning and goal setting.

Tools and techniques are needed to store and retrieve the data in a meaningful format to support process activities. Tools are needed to support front-end user capabilities ranging from daily work logs to decision-support and trend analysis. Techniques provide a structured approach for performing process activities ranging from specification and design work to strategic management.

Together, these components comprise a technical infrastructure that is necessary to support process activities throughout the organization (Zahran, 1998). Figure 1 illustrates this concept whereby data, tools, and techniques are used in an integrated fashion.

The technical infrastructure has as its foundation the organizational processes, strategies, goals, and other components necessary for achieving higher levels of maturity. Organizational maturity as defined by the Capability Maturity Model (CMM) is based on key process areas that rely on the availability of data necessary for planning, tracking, and assessing goal-specific improvements (Paulk et al., 1995).

The components of the technical infrastructure are based on the organization's requirements for data management including legacy and

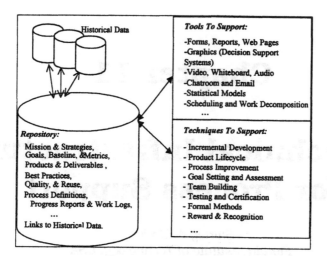

Figure 1: Components of the Technical Infrastructure

operational database systems, existing platforms, work distribution (i.e., global or local), and communication mechanisms, among others. An effective technical infrastructure encompasses all user requirements in order to promote tools and techniques that satisfy the organization's process needs.

Unfortunately, organizations may have cutting-edge database technology, tools, and techniques but they are not utilized to promote process improvement. What is needed is a means of managing data for its timely and appropriate use in process improvement and assessment activities. One of the greatest difficulties that an organization faces is that data is not readily available to support the technical infrastructure that has been put in place. This may occur when data is not stored in a consistent and standard format, its storage location is unknown or not readily accessible, or it cannot be retrieved in a timely manner (Watson, 1996).

An effective means of data management is needed to provide mechanisms for maintaining data quality, supporting levels of data abstraction for various end users, allowing global and local data access, promoting easy access to data, and ensuring high performance and reliability. Without an effective data management component, an organization may face great difficulty in implementing and monitoring a process improvement plan.

There are success stories in the development of an effective technical infrastructure. One such case is the Software Engineering Laboratory's Software Management Environment (SME) (Decker et. al., 1992). The SME environment supports project goal setting, tracking, and assessment necessary for monitoring the impact of a change and sharing best practices throughout the organization (Basili, 1989). The technical infrastructure includes a comprehensive relational database, front-end user capabilities for storing and retrieving data in a decision-support context, and support for various goal-specific improvement techniques.

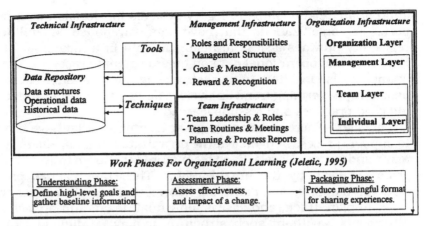

Figure 2: A Process Support Framework

This chapter describes the use of database and Web technology in the development of a technical infrastructure to support process activities. A framework for process support is described that is the basis for the discussion on database and Web technology. It is not the intention of the authors to recommend a specific data management architecture but to provide an illustration of what can be done to develop automated process support.

Process Support Framework

The technical infrastructure is one part of an overall framework for organizational learning. (Organizational learning focuses on early and continuous feedback on personal, team, and project performance.) It is important to understand the relationship of the technical infrastructure with other structural components of an organization in order to determine the data, tools, and techniques necessary to satisfy process requirements. These components comprise what is called a *Process Support Framework* as shown in Figure 2.

A management infrastructure is needed to identify roles and responsibilities in the organization (Zahran, 1998). The organization also has an infrastructure in terms of personnel and work activities that represent levels of abstraction necessary for effective information flow. These components are supported by a simple process of continuous improvement used within and across organizational layers. Each of the components of the Process Support Framework is briefly described.

◆ *Technical Infrastructure*—A data management system with tools and techniques for process support is needed because of the complexity and size of data generated. The technical infrastructure is comprised of:
  • *Data Repository*—The physical schema of the operational database needs to be able to handle existing data requirements as well as have

appropriate relationships to legacy systems for decision-making support. For organizations that have data warehouse capabilities, the repository provides access to historical data in a meaningful format. Historical and operational data on organizational processes, products, quality levels, and time-to-market provide the means for establishing baselines, performing trend analysis, calculating metrics, and identifying good practices and lessons learned.

- *Techniques*—There are many popular techniques that have been used to support process activities at the organization, management, project, team, and personal levels. Each technique is employed to accomplish the goals set forth by the organization. These approaches provide a structured approach of gathering information and performing work in order to plan, track, and assess individual, team, and project accomplishments. Without such structure, it may be difficult to identify improvements and share them for ongoing learning.

- *Tools*—There are customized and commercial tools available to support process improvement. These tools may be used in a distributed mode (client-server or Web technology) or may be used as stand alone support. Tools play an important role in gathering and disseminating information in a timely manner. Tools also provide for the manipulation of information such that quick feedback on organizational goals and performance is achieved.

◆ *Organization Infrastructure*—Each of the organizational layers; organization, management, team, and personal, require a process improvement plan, tracking mechanisms, and assessment support. A learning environment would allow for experiences and improvement practices to flow bottom-up and top-down in order to promote effective communication within and across these layers.

◆ *Management Infrastructure*—The management infrastructure must identify the roles and responsibilities of line and project managers in order to meet project goals. In addition, the relationships of management and teams and other personnel must be established in order to work collectively towards common goals.

◆ *Team Infrastructure*—The team infrastructure must provide for team roles and responsibilities. This includes establishing team routines, team leadership, communication mechanisms, progress reporting, and work activities necessary for producing its deliverables and achieving its goals (Becker, et al., 1996; Janzon et al., 1996).

◆ *Feedback Mechanism*—A process by which an organization can learn from its experiences is needed in order to continually improve and meet goals. A simple process is provided by Deming (1986) whereby an organizational component plans, works, acts, assesses, and improves. Another process has been presented by Jelectic et al. (1995) as shown in Figure 2 whereby three phases are performed iteratively. These include understanding, assessment, and packaging phases. These phases support a learning environment by promoting the dissemination of lessons learned and best practices.

The Process Improvement Framework provides a basis for identifying the data requirements necessary to support each of the components in an integrated fashion. For example, an organization may manage projects using the Experience Factory approach whereby changes are monitored for improvement opportunities (Basili, 1985). This requires a database system that supports the assessment of process, product, quality, and other goal-specific activities for improvement opportunities.

The front-end tool support may be form-based such that management may enter and retrieve data as needed for planning, tracking, and assessment support. In addition, a decision-support system may provide analysis capabilities in order to identify trends, and calculate metrics, among others.

Data Requirements

In the past, data requirements often focused on the management aspects of goal-specific improvements. With the introduction of database and Web technology, it is viable to support all of the layers in the organizational infrastructure. An automated environment that dissemi-

Technical Aspect	Data Requirements
Process	• Process definitions, guidelines, and templates for planning, working, and assessment phases. • Process data generated during planning, working, and assessment phases for personal, team, and project work. • Organization infrastructure, resources, training, technical expertise. • Reward and recognition mechanisms. • Best practices and lessons learned.
Product	• Mission statement, user requirements (high-level), constraints, risks, and assumptions. • Detailed user requirements and supporting documents. • Specification, design, inspection documents. • Conceptual and physical designs of data. • Code generation. • Markov usage modeling, stratification, and abstraction. • Statistical test generation and test results.
Quality	• Team review and inspection outcomes. • Completion and correctness conditions specified for reviewed documents. • Defect logs, corrections, and modifications.
Resources	• Personnel profile in terms of skills, education, experience, roles, and responsibilities. • Personnel location and availability.
Time	• Increment plan and scheduled due dates. • Work decomposition charts. • Time-to-market constraints.

Table 1: Technical Data Requirements

nates information within and across organizational layers should be able to support personal and team efforts.

The data requirements for each layer are briefly described from an end-user perspective. This discussion may be viewed as a basis for the conceptual design of the data repository.

*   *Technical Data*—The technical data that may be stored in the data repository is illustrated in Table I. The technical data is typically produced by individuals and teams during the planning, tracking, and assessment phases of work. The technical data includes process-related data such as process definitions, guidelines, and templates for plans, progress reports, action lists, and experience reports, among others. It also includes product-related data generated during work such as specification and design documents, user documentation, and product deliverables. Quality-related data may include testing results, error types and rates, and team review and inspection documents. Personnel-related data may include expertise, skills, experience, and education,

Project Aspect:	Data Requirements:
Process	• Process definitions, guidelines, and templates for project planning, tracking and assessment phases. • Ongoing assessment of project, team, and personal processes, productivity, and quality adherence. • Evaluation of training programs and toolsets. • Project infrastructure, roles & responsibilities, resource availability, training, & process expertise. • Reward and recognition. • Best practices and lessons learned.
Product	• Baseline, project goals, mission, user requirements (high-level), constraints, risks, and assumptions. • Incremental development plan. • Product deliverables. • Configuration management. • Conceptual and physical designs of databases.
Quality	• Testing and certification results for deliverables. • Completion and correctness conditions specified for the project. • Summary reports on defects, fixes, scaled-back functionality.
Resources	• Management profiles of experience and expertise. • Management roles and responsibilities. • Database of skills, education, experience, and expertise of project teams and support personnel.
Time	• Project plan, scheduled due dates for increments/deliverables. • Project critical path, slack, and contingency plans. • Incremental development plan.

Table 2: Project Data Requirements

Organization Aspect:	Data Requirements:
Process	• CMM goals and achievements. • Learning environment in terms of dissemination of best practices and lessons learned. • Metrics and trend analysis regarding organizational maturity.
Product	• Product functionality & reusability. • Advances and improvements in technology. • Customer satisfaction.
Quality	• Quality levels of products, increments, and deliverables. • Quality improvement plans and programs. • Quality reward and recognition programs, personnel, and accomplishments. • Trend analysis of defects, fixes, changes, complexity, and reusability.
Resources	• Productivity improvements related to training programs, process improvements, rewards and recognition mechanisms. • Resource utilization in terms of new technology and personnel expertise. • Management profiles of roles, responsibilities, and accomplishments. • Compilation of skills, education, experience, and expertise of management, teams, individuals, and support personnel.
Time	• Time-to-markets goals, achievements, and improvements. • Analysis of product completion time in terms of project complexity, learning curve, technology, training, reusability, and expertise.

Table 3: Organizational Data Requirements

among others. This detailed information is ideally linked to the team and project levels for accessibility during planning, reporting, and evaluation activities.

- *Project Data*—The project data that may be stored in the data repository is illustrated in Table 2. This data may be obtained by abstracting, aggregating or compiling data from individual, team, and project efforts during the planning, tracking, and assessment phases of work. The data should encompass all lower level data described at the technical level. It also includes goal-specific data that is necessary for decision-making at the project level. This data ideally is linked to the team and the organizational levels for bi-directional accessibility during planning, reporting, and evaluation activities.

- *Organization Data Requirements*—The organization data that may be stored in the data repository is illustrated in Table III. This data is typically abstracted or compiled data obtained from project, team, and personal levels during the planning, tracking, and assessment phases of work. The data provides the capability of continuous assessment of the organization in meeting its mission, strategies, and goals. It is important to develop data links between operational and historical data in order to establish baselines and calculate metrics.

A technical infrastructure developed to handle these data requirements provides the capability of goal setting, tracking, and evaluation within and across team and project structures.

Data Repository Objectives

The data repository of the technical infrastructure must be built to support data quality, system performance, ease-of-use, and accessibility. The overall goal of the repository is to provide maximum support for tools and techniques to meet the needs of a particular end user. This goal can be decomposed into a set of objectives that include:

◆ *Accessibility* —The timely retrieval of information is negatively impacted when data is not stored in a meaningful format. Cryptic variable names of data objects may be misleading and may "hide" its contents from the user. Data may become "lost" or difficult to locate when the contents of the data repository are not properly documented. Historical and operational data may not be integrated thus losing valuable information about long-term trends. Problem areas associated with accessibility are briefly described as:

• *Historical and operational data have different meanings.* The meaning of data may change over time impacting the end use of the data. For example, a set of quality codes has changed to reflect its current use. The operational data would reflect the use of these new codes. The historical data would contain data codes that represent the old business rules. The use of the historical and operational data in any type of data analysis would cause data integrity problems until the discrepancies between old and new codes are resolved.

• *Hidden data.* Data that is hidden within text strings or is unidentifiable because of cryptic data definitions is virtually inaccessible to the end user. Combined data (e.g., last name, first name, and middle initial are stored as one character string) may require data extraction to obtain the sought after information.

◆ *Flexibility*—Data relationships must be correctly maintained in the repository to support the capability of data aggregation, abstraction, and compilation, as well as, the decomposition into granular details. At any time, data may be requested to be displayed using different formats and at varying levels of detail. Several problem areas associated with flexibility include:

• *Multiple data definitions for the same data.* Data with the same meaning may appear in more than one table with different data definitions making it difficult if not impossible to manipulate the data correctly. For example, columns containing social security numbers may be various lengths (9 no dashes, 11 with dashes) with different data types (numeric, character, or varchar). As a result, primary and foreign key relationships are not supported.

- *Missing granularity.* There may be a level of granularity of data required by a user but that is not available due to the physical design of the data. This occurs when operational data (e.g., dates, amounts, and events) is stored in an aggregated format.

◆ *Quality*—The data that resides in the database must be correct and complete in order to meet the requirements of the system. Data correctness means that the physical design maintains consistency with the logical design of the data (the data that is retrieved is what the user expected to retrieve). Completeness means that null values are updated when data become known and data relationships are physically supported. Several problem areas associated with quality include:

- *Missing data.* There may be several reasons for missing data. Data integrity constraints may cause cascading deletions thus removing necessary historical data. Data integrity constraints (e.g., for cascading insertions and updates) may be missing thus resulting in inconsistent and incomplete data. Missing data also occurs when there are null values in the repository even though the data values are known.

- *Incorrect Design of Data Objects.* Data objects (e.g., tables, indexes, and constraints) must be designed and created correctly in order to support high-quality data. This includes referential integrity, normalization, and appropriate use of indexes and constraints.

◆ *Performance*—Data quality, search mechanisms, and query optimization all impact database performance. When operating in a real-time environment, high performance is crucial for effective decision-making capabilities. Several problem areas associated with performance include:

- *Improper Use of Search Mechanisms.* Performance is greatly enhanced when indexes are built to support large tables (and column) that are accessed often and have a high degree of variability. When indexes are used inappropriately, retrieval time may be negatively impacted. When indexes are not used to support data manipulation, search time may make the data virtually inaccessible.

- *A Lack of Query Optimization.* Response time is negatively impacted when queries are not optimized for fast data retrieval. The SQL structure of a query will determine its access paths. Tools should be used to assess a query structure in terms of the search algorithm and indexes used to ensure a high degree of optimization.

Techniques

The techniques used for ongoing improvements and their supporting processes compose a major part of the technical infrastructure. Techniques typically offer a structured approach to performing work activities. They have been developed to support organizations, projects, teams, and individuals in managing their work and accomplishing goals.

A technique is important in determining the front-end support required by a particular user. For example, if a project manager uses a project planning technique to develop a work plan, then the front-end support would allow for project decomposition, scheduled due dates, resource requirements, and the critical activities necessary to meet time-to-market goals.

Figure 3 shows a technical infrastructure that encompasses the techniques selected to support various organizational levels. In this environment, the data repository would contain the necessary information to support a particular development or improvement technique. The tools that are integrated into the environment would offer data manipulation capabilities necessary for the effective use of a structured technique.

A technique typically has a process definition that provides guidance on its use. Process-related data would be accessible in the data repository in order to plan, track, and assess the impact of introducing or modifying a technique based on improvement initiatives.

For example, the Cleanroom Software Engineering techniques as described in (Becker & Whittaker, 1996) were developed by Mills (et al., 1986) as a means for developing high-quality software. The use of these techniques have been tracked in terms of quality gains in the development of various software systems (Linger, 1994). These techniques are summarized in Table 4.

The "good use" of these techniques requires process and assessment mechanisms in order to ensure that they are used effectively and are appropriate for the successful achievement of improvement goals. Information can be gathered regarding the use of a technique in order to establish a baseline and measure its impact on goals.

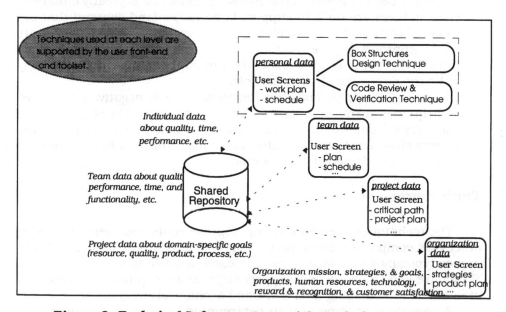

Figure 3: Technical Infrastructure with Technique and Tool Components

Technique:	Description:
Incremental Development	Intellectual control is maintained during systems development by decomposing a system into manageable increments. Each increment is a fully functional subsystem with enhanced functionality over previous increments.
Specification and Design	The formal basis for specification and design is box structure notation. Box structures are used to describe system components in three levels of increasing detail: the black box, the state box, and the clear box. Box structure specifications and designs are organized in a hierarchical structure called a Box Structure Usage Hierarchy in order to support top/down decomposition of each increment (Mills, 1988).
Correctness Verification	Correctness verification proves that a design correctly implements its specification. Team verification provides for improvements in design as completeness and consistency can be verified for each system component.
Reliability Certification	The function and usage specifications are used to build a set of random test cases. Test cases are often built for an increment during its design phase since the specifications are sufficient to define system functionality. Once the increment is designed and implemented, it is integrated with previous increments and statistical testing is performed (Whittaker, 1996).

Table 4: Cleanroom Software Engineering Techniques

Tools

The third part of the technical infrastructure is the tool component whereby tools are integrated with the data repository to support work activities. This environment is illustrated in Figure 4 where various data entry and manipulation capabilities are available to the end user.

The front-end tool support may be form-based such that the user enters and retrieves data necessary for planning, tracking, and assessing work activities. An ad-hoc query capability provides the flexibility of manipulating data "on the fly". Ideally, ad-hoc query capabilities support fast data retrieval for decision-making and analysis capabilities. Report generators execute a canned query (or queries) to produce reports for a periodic evaluation of process and work activities. A decision-support system provides multi-dimensional analysis capabilities for tracking goal-specific improvements and evaluating trends in the marketplace, among others.

It is important to identify the requirements of the toolset in order to meet the needs of various users in the organization. The type and range of

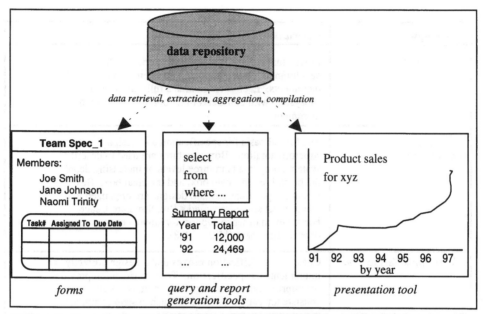

Figure 4: End User Interface

data capabilities should be considered when selecting a toolset. For example, the same data may be used by different end-users in varying formats thus requiring the flexibility of graphical or textual manipulation, data extraction, aggregation or decomposition, search and retrieval mechanisms, and dissemination capabilities, among others.

Many organizations have a wealth of data residing in archives, microfiche files, and old databases that are not utilized during trend analysis. These old file and database systems require links between historical and operational data. The cost trade-off of linking systems needs to be assessed in terms of the learning potential for process maturity, time-to-market, customer satisfaction, product quality, and resource utilization. The data that resides in these systems may provide baseline and measurement data that currently is not available. Data warehousing (e.g., data extraction and cleaning tools) and data mining tools provide opportunities for linking historical and operational data in a meaningful way (Barquin & Edelstein, 1997).

An Illustration of a Technical Infrastructure

What is needed is a technical infrastructure that supports multidirectional communication such that feedback occurs within and across the organization layers. Information flow within a layer is crucial when individuals and teams are geographically dispersed. Information flow across layers is also important in managing projects and assessing the organization's strategies and goals. Information may flow downward such that individuals and teams have read access to higher-level information including process, quality, productivity, and time-to-market goals, organizational maturity and improvements, organization chart, project plans and progress, training programs, job opportunities, best practices, and others.

The technical infrastructure that is described in this section focuses on the team aspect of process improvement. The technical infrastructure is comprised of a relational database using Web technology to access the data. The front-end component is a set of forms that manage data at the project and team levels of work. The specification of the system focuses on supporting structured teamwork as presented in the planning and tracking phases of Team Assignment Process (TAP). The Team Assignment Process (TAP) is a structured approach to teamwork whereby teams plan, track and assess their work (refer to Janzon, et. al, (1996) for a comprehensive discussion).

The technical infrastructure requires a shared environment where all the team members contribute to the database in order to improve communication and productivity. Each team member's work activities are stored in a database that may be accessed by other teams, support personnel, and management. This information is extremely useful for project management to monitor the progress of deliverables. It also provides valuable information to external teams managing interdependent work activities. From a historical perspective, it establishes baselines and builds data for trend analysis.

The application that has been built to support a technical infrastructure is based on initial work done by Becker & Gibson (1997) to develop an environment for goal-specific improvements at various organization levels. The data management system is a web-based application with a relational database that enables team members to work together and share information efficiently and easily over an Intranet. It also provides tools to support team planning and tracking of work activities.

The overall behavior of the Intranet in terms of its application support and component dependencies is shown in Figure 5. This usage diagram shows information and control flow from the project level to team assignments. It also shows information flow from a team to its work processes and activities.

Each team is assigned a component of work that is part of the project deliverables. The application will support this hierarchical decomposition where the root is a project decomposed into one or more team assignments. Each assignment is decomposed into one or more tasks that contains detailed information including the team member responsible for a task, estimated start and complete dates, actual start and completion dates and work status (e.g., completed or in-progress). As an assignment is worked on by a team, action items may be identified that must be resolved by the team. An action item would include its anticipated and actual resolution date, a description of the resolution, and the team member responsible for resolution.

The Intranet environment provides a user-interface that supports the

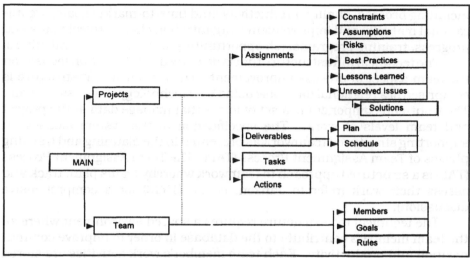

Figure 5: Usage Diagram

data requirements shown in Figure 5. The user-interface is designed to support the project by managing its team assignments, and promote team collaboration in planning and tracking the successful completion of each assignment.

Intranet Technology

Intranets appear to be the simplest collaborative environment in terms of learning curve, accessibility and security. They are very cost-effectiveness because many organizations already have Web access. Navigation tools, such as browsers, enable access to data residing on the servers from any computer within the organization. Intranets offer many advantages including:

- *Initiation of internal discussion forums.* Best practices and lessons learned can be shared via chatrooms or discussion groups in order to reach globally distributed teams and support personnel.
- *Dissemination of information in a "user-friendly" format.* Information is easily accessible via browsers and other tool support. This ease-of-use will promote the sharing and utilization of experiences throughout the organization.
- *Centralized administration of the data.* Data is centralized for security, performance, and accessibility benefits. Information is shared only with those who have access rights.
- *Platform independence.* In the past, teams and management using different platforms had difficulty sharing data especially in a global environment. The Web has virtually eliminated platform issues thus supporting a global environment.

- *Global and timely access to data.* Information is readily available regardless of differing time zones, computers in use, or geographic dispersion. When data is updated, the changes are available immediately to all users.
- *Inexpensive when compared to proprietary GroupWare.* The development of Intranets may be less costly than buying commercial software and support applications.
- *Lower cost of training, software distribution and maintenance.* An organization may reduce its costs associated with using other environments due to software licensing, maintenance and training needs. Web technology offers lower costs in terms of training because of its widespread use in industry. Software licensing agreements and maintenance requirements are minimized due to data and tool centralization.

An Intranet offers a shared environment whereby teams can plan, report progress, and assess their work activities within the context of an improvement process (e.g., Deming's (1986) iterative cycle of work). An Intranet supports team interaction that is necessary for effective teamwork including decomposition of a team assignment into tasks, scheduling resources to complete the tasks, identifying expertise and skills necessary for task assignment, as well as other activities. Team collaboration can be readily supported using the Intranet even though team members may be geographically dispersed and in varying time zones.

By identifying assumptions and risks associated with the team's assignment, the team can evaluate the feasibility of its goals during the planning phase and continue to monitor its progress during the work phase. The Intranet becomes an important tool for collaborative work activities and as such keeps everyone informed of delays, quality levels, task completion, and resource availability. The capability of working collaboratively in this interactive environment is a remarkable advantage of an Intranet.

Another major advantage of using an Intranet for technical support is the flexibility of working in a team without the physical constraints of a physical location. Team members may be more productive in a flexible environment where they are not subject to frequent calls and interruptions. Team members have the flexibility to work at home or in other locations because of the easy access of an Intranet and its supporting tools (e.g., email and calendars) (Kling, 1995).

Structured Team Work

In order to take advantage of the Intranet capabilities, a structured work environment is needed to support teams. The Team Assignment Process was used as a basis for the workflow supported by the Intranet. This structured approach to teamwork promotes team planning and progress reporting in order to determine whether team goals will be met. Typically, a team plan contains information about each team member including roles and responsibilities. The team plan also contains information regarding the team assignment including team goals and routines, a work decomposition of tasks, scheduled due dates, risks, and assumptions made by the team (Becker, 1997).

The Intranet supports interactions among team members by allowing read and update access to the shared schedule and task list. The schedule and task list, shown in Figures 6 and 7; respectively, reflect the actual and estimated data as entered by the team.

In addition, teams have the capability of recording best practices, lessons learned, and unresolved issues experienced during the development of a project. This automated feedback environment supports team members in achieving team goals. The Intranet promotes the development of a knowledge database containing learning experiences of the project teams that can be disseminated throughout the organization.

Intranet Components

A relational database was built to store the information needed to support structured teamwork within the context of a project management system. Oracle Web Server 2.1[1] was used to build the front-end application that would allow the interaction of the database and the browser over the Intranet. To enhance functionality and presentation, dynamic HTML and

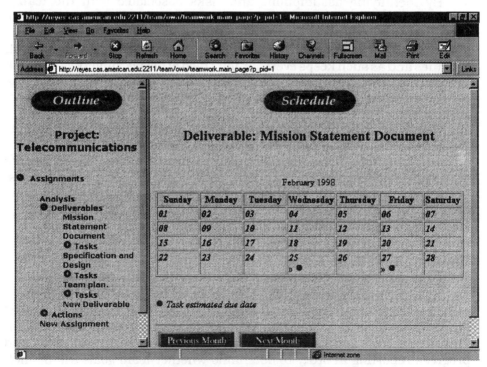

Figure 6: Team Schedule Web Page

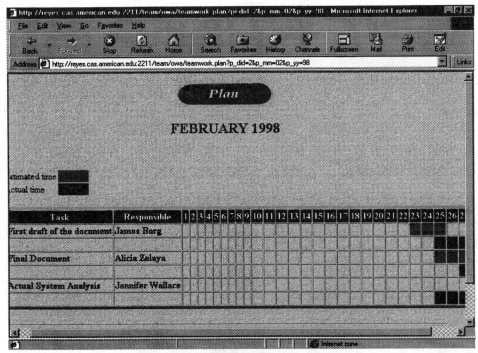

Figure 7: Task List Web Page

JavaScript were used so that the application would have a user-friendly graphic interface.

Conceptual Schema

The Entity-relationship diagram (ERD), shown in Figure 8, encompasses the data requirements resulting from the use of structured planning and reporting activities at the team level of work. The ERD includes a link to the project component that could readily be integrated into the logical design of an existing project database system. For example, the project database that has been developed by the SEL (Decker et al., 1992) for assessment and improvement capabilities could be linked to the team database.

The advantages of linking the project and team assignment databases include data abstraction and decomposition capabilities within and across projects. Project planning, progress reporting, and assessment capabilities are supported by an automated environment whereby information can be disseminated in a real-time mode. Projects and its team assignments could be monitored continuously for improvement opportunities.

A link could also be made to an existing personnel database in order to gain access to a wealth of information about the skills, training requirements, expertise, years of experience, and other data. The advantages of this link are two-fold. This information would not be redundantly stored in the Intranet's database. Secondly, valuable information residing in human resource and training databases would be accessible by the

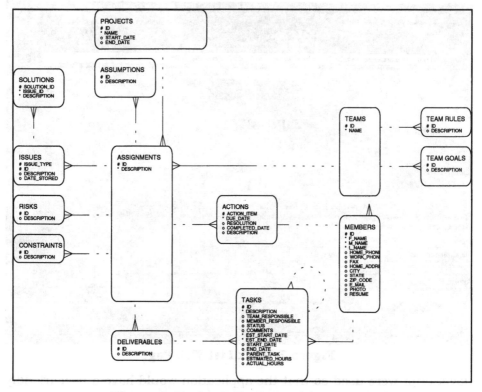

Figure 8: Entity Relationship Diagram

project, team, or individual according to appropriate security controls. Thus, historical and operational data could be used to compose teams based on skills, expertise, availability, locality, and other factors.

The conceptual design, as shown in Figure 8, is inherently complex in order to support the flexibility required for managing team assignments. The ERD shows that an ASSIGNMENTS object has many links to other objects in order to support data abstraction capabilities. The design links an assignment object directly to its deliverables, actions, risks, assumptions, constraints, team assigned to it, and its parent project. Each assignment is also indirectly linked to a set of tasks, and team members.

In the ERD, the DELIVERABLES and TASKS objects have a hierarchical relationship as a team deliverable is decomposed into many work tasks. Each task may have dependencies on other tasks for its initiation and successful completion. This parent-child relationship supports the evaluation of teamwork in terms of its critical work path and slack associated with task dependencies.

It is also interesting to note that the ERD includes ISSUES and SOLUTIONS objects that promote the sharing of lessons learned and best practices. At a more granular level, the ACTIONS object identifies actions that need to be taken in order for team's to work effectively. This object supports the use of an ACTION list whereby items that need to be resolved

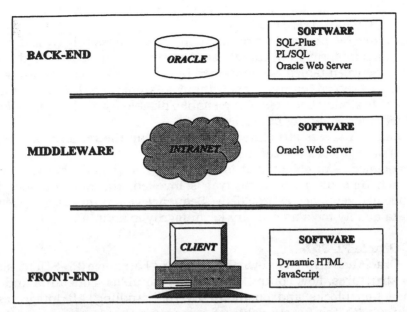

Figure 9: The Development Environment

can be tracked for closure.

Physical Design

There are three layers that comprise the physical design of the Intranet structure as shown in Figure 9. Each of these layers is briefly described in terms of its relationship in the physical design. These layers include the server side of the application, the Middleware components, and the client side with its user interface. The discussion that follows illustrates the capabilities of process support using Web and database technology.

Back-end Component. The Intranet data management component was designed using Oracle database technology because of its fast response time, reliability, performance, and security. In addition, Oracle provides a relatively sophisticated toolset including Oracle Web Server 2.1 necessary for integrating tools and techniques. The Back-end tools are briefly discussed.

SQL-Plus

SQL-Plus is an Oracle tool used to execute queries and statements in order to create and maintain database objects including tables, attributes and constraints. It was used to create the tables, indexes, and constraints necessary to support the conceptual design (as previously shown in the ERD). A set of objects has been developed as the physical representation of the conceptual schema. Each of these objects is described as follows:

• *Table*—Database object that is the physical representation of an entity or a complex relationship as shown in the Entity-relationship diagram. It stores attribute data about the entity including a unique identifier and foreign keys to related tables.

- *Constraint*—A physical representation of a business rule typically enforcing data integrity in the database. For example, a parent-child relationship between tables is maintained by a foreign key constraint whereby children records cannot exist without a parent record. Constraints offer great flexibility because of the enable/disable capability that allows for user enforcement of business rules.
- *Index*—An access structure used to speed up the retrieval of records in response to certain search conditions.
- *Sequence* —An object that is used to generate consecutive numbers. (Each time the method nextval is invoked, the next number in the specified sequence is provided). Sequence generators can be viewed as data quality tools as primary key integrity is maintained.

Oracle PL-SQL

Oracle has defined its own Programming Language (PL-SQL), including loop structures, flow control statements, variables, constants and types, transaction blocks and customized error handling. It integrates SQL features with the functionality of a programming language, so that the application can manipulate ORACLE data with a high degree of flexibility while maintaining a high level of security. Its support of structured

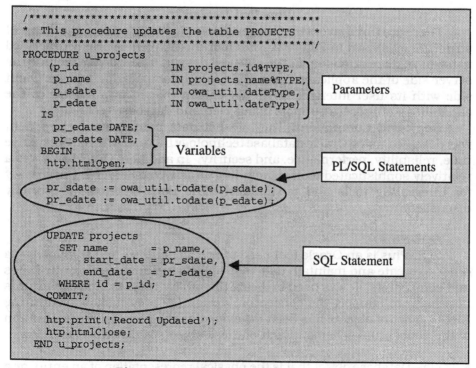

Figure 10: Oracle PL/SQL Procedure

programming constructs ensures consistency and correctness of application design and implementation. PL-SQL blocks of instructions arecompressed in procedures that are compiled by the Oracle Server (refer to Figure 10), and later executed by the application. Oracle PL-SQL has the following advantages:

- *Support for SQL*—PL-SQL encompasses the benefits of using SQL language for data manipulation while allowing for sophisticated data handling.
- *Higher productivity*—Procedures in PL-SQL can be reused in other applications including Web-based and form-based systems. A major benefit of using PL-SQL is that Oracle provides predefined packages with standard procedures already optimized.
- *Improved Performance*—Performance is significantly improved because once a procedure is compiled the Server does not check it for syntax errors. Frequently executed procedures that are used by an application are stored in memory. Thus, response time is significantly reduced.

Middleware Component. The Oracle Web Server is a product used to develop distributed applications on the web using HTTP (HyperText Transport Protocol). It combines HTML code with data retrieved from a database,

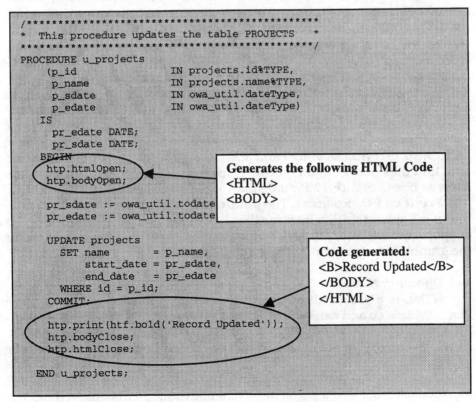

```
/**************************************************
 *  This procedure updates the table PROJECTS   *
 **************************************************/
PROCEDURE u_projects
      (p_id              IN projects.id%TYPE,
       p_name            IN projects.name%TYPE,
       p_sdate           IN owa_util.dateType,
       p_edate           IN owa_util.dateType)
   IS
     pr_edate DATE;
     pr_sdate DATE;
   BEGIN
     htp.htmlOpen;                    Generates the following HTML Code
     htp.bodyOpen;                    <HTML>
                                      <BODY>
     pr_sdate := owa_util.todate
     pr_edate := owa_util.todate

     UPDATE projects
        SET name        = p_name,     Code generated:
            start_date = pr_sdate,    <B>Record Updated</B>
            end_date   = pr_edate     </BODY>
      WHERE id = p_id;                </HTML>
     COMMIT;

     htp.print(htf.bold('Record Updated'));
     htp.bodyClose;
     htp.htmlClose;

   END u_projects;
```

Figure 11: Oracle PL/SQL Code

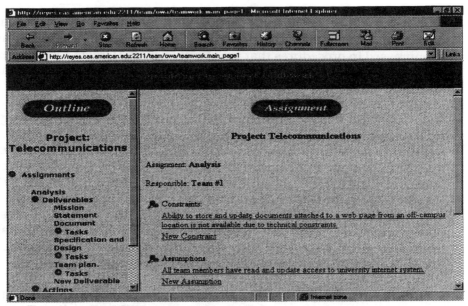

Figure 12: Dynamic HTML and Java Script

enabling developers to build powerful web applications using stored procedures written in PL/SQL. Those procedures use packages that create the HTML tags to be returned to the browser. Figure 11 shows the statements to create some of the HTML tags embedded into the PL-SQL code. For each tag in HTML there is a function or procedure written in PL-SQL to generate the proper tag with its own parameters.

When the WebServer receives a Uniform Resource Locator (URL) from a browser, it uses information from the database and from the Operating System as necessary to handle the request. The URL structure to request a page from the Oracle WebServer contains three basic components: Oracle host: http://reyes.cas.american.edu; Configuration path: 2211/team/owa, and the Package and Procedure: teamwork.main_page. (Refer to the address box in Figure 12 for a display of the configuration path.)

Front-end Component. The front-end of this Intranet structure uses Internet Explorer 4.0[2], a browser that has dynamic HTML capabilities. It supports the execution of JavaScript functions and features that enhance the graphic interface and improve functionality.

Dynamic HTML

HTML is a standardized language used to publish hypertext on the World Wide Web and can be created and processed in a wide range of tools from simple plain text editors to sophisticated WYSIWYG authoring tools. HTML uses tags like <h1> and </h1> to structure text into headings or paragraphs.

One of the disadvantages of plain HTML is that once the page is loaded into memory (client) there is no way to change the contents unless the client requests from the server another page. Another disadvantage is that

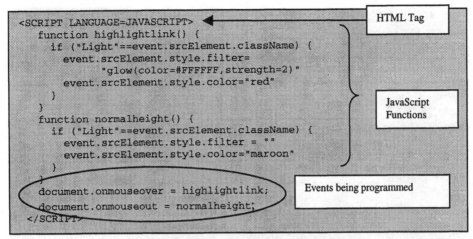

```
<SCRIPT LANGUAGE=JAVASCRIPT>                              HTML Tag
    function highlightlink() {
        if ("Light"==event.srcElement.className) {
            event.srcElement.style.filter=
                "glow(color=#FFFFFF,strength=2)"
            event.srcElement.style.color="red"
        }
    }
    function normalheight() {                          JavaScript
        if ("Light"==event.srcElement.className) {     Functions
            event.srcElement.style.filter = ""
            event.srcElement.style.color="maroon"
        }
    }
    document.onmouseover = highlightlink;      Events being programmed
    document.onmouseout = normalheight;
</SCRIPT>
```

Figure 13: Java Script Code

positioning objects on the page is static and is handled by the browser.

Dynamic HTML, however, allows a web page to change once it is loaded into the client's memory. (In other words, it does not have to make a trip back to the server for an update.) An example of this is when an image is moved on a page in response to an event, such as clicking on a button. Another advantage of dynamic HTML is that objects can be displayed or hidden at any time. In addition, there are a wide variety of properties that can be changed dynamically depending on the type of object.

During the development of this project, Dynamic HTML was used to build an outline of the project with expand and collapse capability. When users click on the plus or minus sign by an item, the browser hides or displays the sub-tree below the item. This feature, illustrated in Figure 12, was developed using a combination of Dynamic HTML and JavaScript to maximize user functionality.

A disadvantage of using Dynamic HTML is that there is no standardized version supported by Netscape and Microsoft Corporations. As a result, web pages developed for Internet Explorer are not fully compatible with Netscape Communicator3.

JavaScript
JavaScript is an interpreted programming language developed by Netscape that can be executed by a browser to manipulate the objects on a web page. The end result of this capability is the creation of interactive documents. It also provides developers the ability to program events (e.g., onclick, onmousemove, or ondoubleclick). The "miniprograms" associated with an event would be executed when the user generates the events. This feature increases the functionality of a web page thus enhancing end-user support.

Figure 13 contains an example of JavaScript code that is executed when the user moves the cursor over a link (event: mouseover). The browser would highlight it by changing the color of the text and using a filter to change its appearance. Figure 14 shows the effect achieved by using

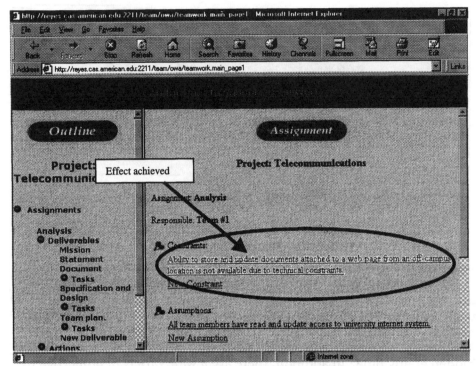

Figure 14. Effect Achieved by the Execution of a JavaScript

JavaScript.

Application Screens

The control flow of information to the end user is based on the invocation of the main page as shown in Figure 15. This screen provides important information to the user about the objective and major components of the system. The user has two paths that can be traversed based on the desired use of the system. The two paths are Project Maintenance or Team Maintenance components (as shown by the buttons on the page).

The high level Web page for the project component is shown in Figure 16. This Web page provides a means of accessing team information associated with a particular project. Each team is associated with a team assignment and thus lower level details about a team can be accessed. This page contains hyperlinks to the other components of the Intranet as previously shown in the usage diagram.

The Team Maintenance option invokes the screen shown in Figure 17. The screen is divided into two frames for visual clarity and ready access to appropriate information. On the left side, the user may select an existing team or compose the membership of a new team by clicking on the "Query" feature of the page.

On the right side of the screen, the user is presented with detailed information directly related to the item selected on the first frame. In the

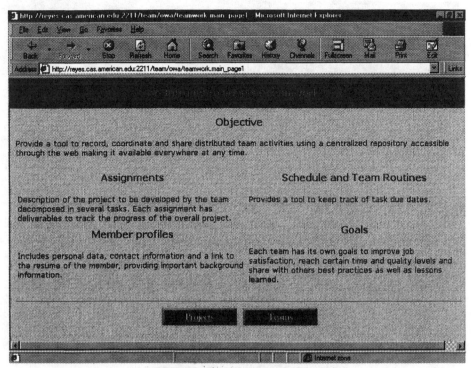

Figure 15. Main Page

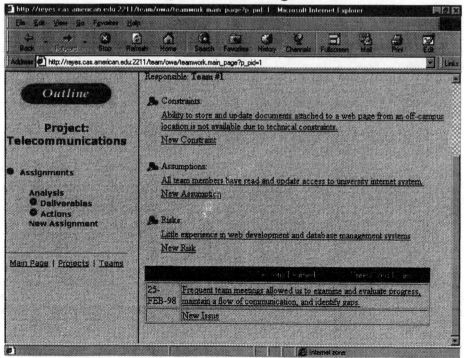

Figure 16. Project Component

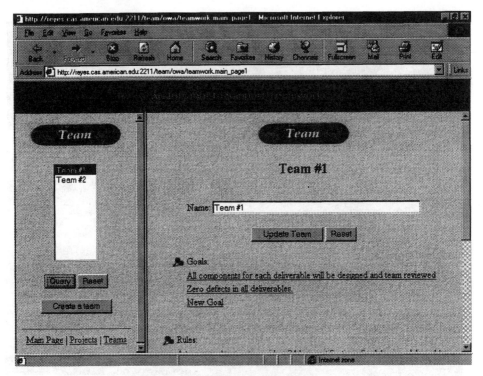

Figure 17. Team Maintenance

example provided, the user selected Team #2, and as a result, the details shown on the second frame are associated with this team. The team information that is presented in the second frame includes the Goals and Rules defined for the team.

Summary and Conclusion

It is not the intention of this chapter to show all of the components of the Intranet. Instead, it has been shown that developing an effective technical infrastructure for process improvement can be accomplished to support teams and management in daily work activities. It is important to note that the ease-of-use of this system makes it a viable candidate for effective team collaboration. At the management level, team plans and tracking mechanisms are visible in order to determine whether team goals and therefore project goals are being met.

The Intranet described in this chapter combines the attractive visual interface that browsers offer, the robustness and data-sharing capabilities Oracle tools provide, and the availability and scalability of Intranets. The integration of tools and techniques for process improvement leads to a very reliable system that can be readily adjusted according to new business rules and emerging technologies.

Endnotes

[1] Oracle Web Server is a registered trademark of Oracle Corporation.

[2] Internet Explorer is a trademark of Microsoft Corporation.

[3] Netscape Communicator is a trademark of Netscape Communications Corporation.

References

Barquin, R., and Edelstein, H. (1997). *Planning and Designing The DATA Warehouse*, Prentice Hall, Upper Saddle River, NJ.

Basili, R. (1985). Quantitative Evaluation of Software Engineering Methodology, *Proceedings of the First Pan Pacific Computer Conference*, Melbourne, Australia.

Basili, R. (1989). Software Development: A Paradigm for the Future, *Proceedings of the 13th Annual International Computer Software and Applications Conference* (COMPSAC), Keynote Address, Orlando, Florida.

Becker, S. (1998). A Proposed Learning Environment for Goal-Specific Improvements. *Proceedings of the 31st Hawaii International Conference on System Sciences*, Maui, Hawaii.

Becker, S., and Gibson, R. (1997). An Integrated Environment for Software Process Improvement, *Proceedings of the 19th Annual Pacific Northwest Software Quality Conference*, Portland, Oregon.

Becker, S., Janzon, T., and Nilsson, B. (1996). Establishing Effective Team Routines for Cleanroom Support, *Proceedings of the 1st Cleanroom Workshop*, ICSE 18, Berlin, Germany.

Becker, S. and Whittaker, J. (1996). *Cleanroom Software Engineering Practices*, Idea Group Publishing, Hershey, PA.

Decker, W., Valett, J., Hendrick, R., and Kistler, D. (1992). *Software Management Environment (SME) Concepts and Architecture*, Revision 1, SEL-89-103, National Aeronautics and Space Administration, Goddard Space Flight Center, Greenbelt, Maryland.

Deming, E. (1986). *Out of the Crisis*. MIT Center for Advanced Engineering Study, MIT Press, Cambridge, MA.

Janzon, T., Nilsson, B., and Becker, S. (1996). A Team-based Organization Structure For Support of Cleanroom Development. *Cleanroom Software Engineering Practices*, IDEA Group Publishing, PA.

Jeletic, K., Pajerski, R., and Brown, C. (1995). *Software Process Improvement Guidebook*, Software Engineering Laboratory Series, SEL-95-102.

Kling, R. (1995). *Working CSCW: Multivalent Social Relationships in Computer Supported Workplaces*. http://www.ics.uci.edu/CORPS/kling/cscwm95b.html.

Linger, R. (1994). Cleanroom Process Model. *IEEE Software*, 11(2).

Mills, H.D. (1988). Stepwise Refinement and Verification in Box-Structured Systems. *IEEE Computer*, (June).

Mills, H.D., Dyer, M., and Linger, R.C. (1987). Cleanroom Software Engineering. *IEEE Software*, 1(9).

Mills, H., Linger, R., and Hevner, A. (1986). *Principles of Information Systems Analysis and Design*, N.Y., Academic Press.

Paulk, M., Curtis, B., Weber, C., and Chrissis, M.B. (1995). *The Capability Maturity Model: Guidelines for Improving the Software Process*. Addison-Wesley, Reading, MA.

Watson, R.T. (1996). *Data Management: An Organizational Perspective*, Wiley & Sons, N.Y.

Whittaker, J. (1996). *Cleanroom Software Engineering Practices*, Idea Group Publishing, Hershey, PA.

Zahran, S. (1998). *Software Process Improvement: Practical Guidelines for Business Success*, Addison-Wesley Longman, Reading MA.

Author Bios

Conan C. Albrecht is a Research Associate at the Center for Management of Information and a Ph.D. student at the University of Arizona. He received his Masters and B.S. degrees from Brigham Young University in Accounting and Information Systems in 1996. He is currently working on his dissertation in the area of distributed document inspections. Conan extended significant efforts into the design issues and development of the CodeReview system described in this chapter.

Shirley A. Becker received her Ph.D. in information systems from the University of Maryland, College Park, Maryland. She is currently an associate professor of computer science at Florida Institute of Technology and co-director of its Software Engineering Research Center. Dr. Becker's research interests include software engineering, software process improvement, database and web technology, and team-based development. She has published numerous articles and book chapters in these areas and has co-edited a book on Cleanroom Software Engineering Practices. Dr. Becker is the editor of the Journal of Database Management and a section editor for the Journal of Informing Science. She has served on program committees for IEEE/ACM sponsored conferences and recently was the program chair for the Third International Conference on Cleanroom Software Engineering Practices.

Kirstie L. Bellman recently returned to the Aerospace Corporation after four years at DARPA to start up a new bi-coastal research and development center, called the Aerospace Integration Sciences Center (AISC). The Center serves as a research and development capability for a number of DoD and government agencies. AISC's focus is on the development of advanced system integration and analytic techniques, and evaluation techniques for understanding the impacts of new technologies. Dr. Bellman has over thirty years of academic, industrial, and consulting experience in the development of both conventional computer models and applications and artificial intelligence programs.

Peter Bennetts is a Senior Lecturer in Computing. After a successful career in programming and software design, he now lectures in software quality assurance and interpretative approaches to systems analysis. He is currently developing a thesis which takes an holistic approach to information systems quality.

Mitchell L. Bostelman received the Bachelor of Arts degree in economics from the University of Maryland, College Park in 1991, and the Master of Science in information systems from the American University, Washington, DC in 1998. Mr. Bostelman has worked in the past as a software project manager for the American Society for Engineering Education. In 1998 he joined the American Management Systems (AMS). He works within AMS' Corporate Technology Group in the area of software project management and measurement for process improvement. Mr. Bostelman is an Associate of the AMS Center for Advanced Technologies (AMSCAT) and AMS' Software Development & Information Technology (SD&IT) Knowledge Center. He provides consulting services on process improvement and measurement implementation within AMS software projects. His interests lie in software development methodology and the quantitative analysis of the software development process and product. Mr. Bostelman is a member of the Association for Computing Machinery.

Douglas L. Dean is a Research Scientist at the Center for Management of Information at the University of Arizona. He received his Master of Accountancy with an emphasis in Information Systems from Brigham Young University in 1989 and his Ph.D. in MIS from the University of Arizona in 1995. His research interests include electronic meeting system support of modeling, business process improvement, and information systems requirements collection. He also facilitates meetings in these areas. His interests also include systems analysis and design methods. His work has been published in Management Science, Journal of Management Information Systems, Group Decision and Negotiation, IEEE Transactions on Systems, Man, and Cybernetics, ACM SIG Group Bulletin, and multiple conference proceedings.

Rick Gibson has over 20 years of software engineering experience using structured, object-oriented, and cleanroom software development methodologies. He is a certified Software Engineering Institute (SEI) software capability evaluator and qualified instructor and consultant in Software Project Management and Software Engineering. Dr. Gibson has extensive experience in the conduct of SEI Capability Maturity Model evaluations and development of process maturity improvement and corrective action plans for evaluated organizations. In response to problems discovered during software capability evaluations, he collaborated with curriculum development staff on preparation of special training/mentoring programs on software process improvement, software quality assurance, and Y2K project planning. He has managed major projects in support of commercial, government, and educational organizations. He is currently an Associate Professor at American University in the Department of Computer Science and Information Systems. His responsibilities, as a full time faculty member, include teaching graduate courses in software engineering, database systems, and data communication to software engineering professionals. He has published numerous books, book chapters, and articles on software development and quality assurance.

Peter Kawalek is a Research Fellow of the Department of Computer Science, University of Manchester in England. He has a Ph.D. in Computer Science (Manchester). The focus of his work is upon the development of process systems for organizations. He has a special interest in the Viable System Model and has explored its use in software process and information systems projects. In 1998, with David Wastell and Richard Vidgen (University of Bath), Peter founded the Viable Systems Group - a group which is dedicated to exploring the utility of the Viable System Model and cybernetics in information systems research. Peter has undertaken many projects as a consultant to many industry sectors. He is a co-author of the book Warboys, B., Kawalek, P., Robertson, I., Greenwood, R.M., 'Business Information Systems: A Process Approach' (publishers: McGraw-Hill, 1999).

Daniel Enrique Ladino received his Bachelor's degree in Computer Science from Universidad Autonoma, Santafe de Bogota, Colombia, and a Master's degree in Computer Science from American University in Washington DC. Mr. Ladino was a Graduate Fellow and an Oracle Scholar at American University whereby he conducted research on web and database technology to support team processes. He also worked for four years as a Systems Analyst in Colombia. Currently, Mr. Ladino is a Senior

Consultant at Oracle Corporation. His areas of interest are databases, web technology and team-based development.

Christopher Landauer is a researcher in the Aerospace Integration Science Center of The Aerospace Corporation, working on new theories and practices in software and system integration. He has over thirty years experience in mathematical applications in computing, including (in no particular order) intelligent integration infrastructure in heterogeneous computing systems, computational reflection in autonomous software systems, computational semiotics and new theories of symbol use by computers, formal specification and verification of communication protocols, analysis and modeling of distributed computing systems, pattern detection and tracking from noisy data, statistical information retrieval from natural language text, discrete event simulation, exploratory pattern analysis and recognition systems, and knowledge-based system integration and verification.

Dave McComb is Vice President of Research and Development of Object Products. He has over 20 years experience in managing large scale software development projects, 12 of which were with Andersen Consulting, 6 with his own firm First Principles, which 2 years ago merged with Object Products. At Object Products he and a team based in Fort Collins, Colorado have built an Object Oriented Application Development Framework that enables application developers to construct enterprise-wide client server applications without writing any code, and without generating any code. Object Products has acquired 8 healthcare software companies which are now in the process of converting their existing products to a single integrated system based on this new technology. He has a BS and MBA from Portland State University.

Eugene McGuire is an Associate Professor in the Computer Science and Information Systems Department at the American University in Washington, D.C. His primary research interests are in the areas of software process improvement, software team development and organizational change. He is on the editorial board of the Journal of End User Computing and has served as guest editor for special issues of that journal as well as Journal of Global Information Management. He is also coauthor of Information Systems Innovation and Diffusion: Issues and Directions published by Idea Group Publishing.

Stella Mills is Reader in Human-Computer Interaction at the Cheltenham & Gloucester College of Higher Education. She has been involved with user-centred design projects as a means for software improvement both in industry and academia. She is a council member of the British Computer Society.

Mark Paulk is a Senior Member of the Technical Staff at the Software Engineering Institute. He has been with the SEI since 1987, initially working with the Software Capability Evaluation project. He has worked with the Capability Maturity Model project since its inception and was the project leader during the development of Version 1.1 of the CMM. He is the product manager for version 2 of the CMM and a contributor to ISO's SPICE (Software Process Improvement and Capability Determination) project, which is developing a suite of international standards for software process assessment. He is a senior member of the IEEE and a senior member of the ASQC.

Russell L. Purvis (Ph.D., Florida State University, 1994) is an Assistant Professor of Management (MIS) at The University of Central Florida. His current research interests center on organizational efforts to initiate, plan, execute, control and close-out projects. His most recent work has been on methods, techniques and structures designed to improve the quality and productivity of systems development. His publications have appeared in Information and Management, Journal of Information Technology Management, and Journal of Computer Information Systems.

Thomas L. Rodgers is a Research Associate at the Center for Management of Information and a Ph.D. Candidate at the University of Arizona. He received a Masters of Business Administration with an emphasis in Finance from Colorado State University in 1994. His research interests include software inspections, team aspects of software engineering, and knowledge management. Tom's dissertation focuses on inspection collaboration and feedback issues discussed in this chapter.

V. Sambamurthy (Ph.D., University of Minnesota, 1989) is Associate Professor of MIS at The Florida State University. His current research interests are broadly focused on the design of organizations for effective use of technologies in their business strategies and operations. His publications have appeared in the Information Systems Research, Decision Sciences, European Journal of Information Systems, and Information and Management. He is an Associate Editor for MIS Quarterly and is on the Editorial Board of the Journal of Market-focused Management.

Jose Santiago (B.S. Management Information Systems, University of Central Florida, 1996) interests lie in improving quality within the IT function.

Jill Slater is an Associate Professor of Management Information Systems at the University of Denver. She consults, conducts research, and develops teaching cases illustrating the dynamics of the interaction between organizational structure and technological innovation.

David G. Wastell is a senior lecturer in Information Systems in the Department of Computer Science at the University of Manchester. He holds a Ph.D. in Psychology from the University of Durham and began his professional research career at the Applied Psychology Unit, Cambridge. Moving to Manchester in 1980 he took up a lectureship in Medical Informatics in the Medical School, where he gained extensive practical experience in information systems development in the healthcare environment. In 1988 he moved to the Department of Computer Science. David has published widely in information systems, applied psychology and clinical psychology. His research interests are in information systems development (the effects of stress on individual and group behaviour), business process reengineering (methodology and case studies) and human factors (the design of complex human-machine systems).

Trevor Wood-Harper is a Professor of Computer Science and Information Systems. He has published numerous books as well as over one hundred and twenty research articles on a wide range of topics, including the well-known Multiview Methodology. He directs a multi-disciplinary Information Systems Research Centre, and in the UK in 1996 on a national four year evaluation, it was recognised as one of the top British IS centres. Also, he has set up one of the first Doctoral Schools in Information Systems in the country which is attracting an increasing number of international as well as national students.

Index

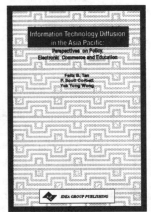

Journal of
End User Computing

Editor-in-chief Mo Adam Mahmood
University of Texas, El Paso

The *Journal of End User Computing* (JEUC) focuses on providing coverage of research findings and expert advice on the development, utilization and management of end user computing in organizations. The original articles in each issue deal with the trends, usage, failure, successes, solutions, policies, and applications of information technology resources in organizations. Along with the highly regarded peer reviewed manuscripts in each issue, is the *Industry and Practice* section featuring practical-oriented submissions, such as case studies, expert interviews and editorial/opinion pieces that are selected based on their usefulness to our readers.

ISSN 1043-6464 • Published quarterly • Annual subscription rate: • US$85 Individuals; US$175 Institutions

Journal of
Database Management

Editor-in-charge Shirley Becker
Florida Institute of Technology

The *Journal of Database Management* (JDM) is an international journal aimed at designers, developers, educators, researchers, consultants, and administrators of database management systems. The major emphasis of topics in JDM is on database issues ranging from strategic planning to issues concerning the greater utilization and management of database technology. Along with the highly regarded peer reviewed manuscripts in each issue is the Industry and Practice section, featuring practical-oriented submissions, such as case studies, expert interviews and editorial/opinion pieces that are selected based on their usefulness to our readers.

ISSN 1063-8016 • Published quarterly • Annual subscription rate: • US$85 Individuals; US$175 Institutions

Idea Group Publishing
1331 E. Chocolate Avenue
Hershey PA 17033-1117 USA
Tel: 717/533-8845 • Fax: 717/533-8661
http://www.idea-group.com